# GOOD GUYS, BAD GUYS
# BIG GUYS, LITTLE GUYS

### Upstate New York stories from the
### Syracuse Herald-Journal, Herald American

**by**

**Dick Case**

*To Larry,*
*warm regards,*
*Dick Case*
*9/97*

**A Pine Tree Press Publication**
NORTH COUNTRY BOOKS, INC.
Utica, New York

Good Guys, Bad Guys, Big Guys, Little Guys
Upstate New York Stories from
the Syracuse Herald-Journal, Herald American

*Cover Design:* Geoff Stickel
*Cover Photograph:* C. W. McKeen

ISBN 0-9629159-9-8


**Library of Congress Cataloging-in-Publication**

Case, Dick, 1935-
  Good guys, bad guys, big guys, little guys : upstate New
York stories from the Syracuse Herald-Journal, Herald
American / by Dick Case.
      p.  cm.
  "A Pine Tree Press publication."
  ISBN 0-9629159-9-8
  1. Syracuse (N.Y.)—Social life and customs. 2. Syracuse
Region (N.Y.)—Social life and customs. 3. Onondaga
County (N.Y.)—Social life and customs.  I. Title.
F129.S8C3  1994
974.7'66—dc20                                    94-38987
                                                      CIP


A PINE TREE PRESS PUBLICATION
North Country Books, Inc.
18 Irving Place
Utica, New York

*To Sandra*

# CONTENTS

## EVENTS

## BIG GUYS, LITTLE GUYS

## CITY

## PASSAGES

## GOOD GUYS, BAD GUYS

## HOMETOWN

## US

# FOREWORD

As editor and publisher of the Syracuse Newspapers, I meet more than my fair share of newcomers to our community.

I love to tell them about Central New York: its physical beauty, its cultural riches, its economic viability, its unmatched livability.

But when I am asked to describe the soul of Central New York, I simply say: "Read Dick Case."

As you read Dick's new book, "Good Guys, Bad Guys, Big Guys, Little Guys," you will discover the soul of our community, and you will be immensely entertained.

That's just as true for those of us who have lived here almost forever. Through Dick's rare gift for story telling, we will rediscover our town on a much deeper level.

This book is but a sampling of the more than 3,000 columns Dick has written for the Herald-Journal and Sunday Herald American since 1976. Dick started writing these columns just about 200 years after the first of his ancestors settled in Onondaga county. So he wouldn't be stretching a point if he claimed to come at his subject matter with a little background.

Each column is only a few pages long, so you can spend as little as five or 10 minutes with the book and come back later. Or you may find reading Dick's columns like eating peanuts: it's impossible to stop after one.

Dick and I have worked together for many years. He joined the Herald-Journal in 1959, a few years before I became a cub reporter with The Post-Standard. Each of us left Syracuse for a period only to return to our roots.

Dick's column first appeared weekly in our Sunday Stars magazine in 1976, the year before I returned home. My small claim to fame is that I coaxed him to become a full-time columnist. He began writing four columns a week in 1977, and he's been doing it ever since.

Here's a passage from one of my favorites, "Cool Cat." It'll give you a taste of Dick's easygoing style. And, in some ways, he and Cool Cat had something in common:

"Spring is here but it's not going to be the way it used to be. Cool Cat won't be back in town from L.A., New Orleans, Miami, Tucumcari or one of the other winter resorts. He didn't make it this time.

"Cool Cat's heart gave out up at Unity Acres last November.

"I don't think the streets are going to be the same without Cool Cat out there on the bricks. Some people might say he was as much of a Syracuse landmark as, say, the Columbus monument or Blackie, the one-legged pigeon."

The memorable and light-fingered Cool Cat may have been a Syracuse landmark. But if we're talking about real landmarks, then we're talking about Dick Case and his stories.

—*Stephen A. Rogers*
Editor and Publisher
The Syracuse Newspapers
1994

# INTRODUCTION

I'm from here.

I pass my grandfather's house on Teall Avenue, I see him sitting on the porch, smoking a pipe, reading a paper. The fruit peddler's cart is parked out front.

Aidan Hickey was an Irishman from Wexford, born in a place called Enniscorthy. He arrived in Syracuse with a group of pals and went to work in a bakery.

My grandmother, Margaret McLaughlin, had come from Ireland too, to live with her kin, the Fords, who worked the salt wells in Salina. The village is our North Side and it's full of reminders of what it used to be. My mother was born on Park Street; my daughter lives around the corner.

My father connected to Howlett Hill; once they called it Casetown for all the family clustered there. The cemetery on the hill behind the church is lined with Cases, and Robinsons, our cousins. Last year we took Cousin Chuck Robinson up there to join the ancestors, including Giles Case and Thomas Robinson, who were here just after a county called Onondaga was made.

Onondaga was 200 years old in 1994.

Connections.

The house where I grew up sits on the hill south of the school in Marcellus, which had been a meadow of the Reed farm when my father was a kid. His house is on Orange Street. Half a block south of that is his father's place, now the Masonic Lodge. It was built by one of our grandfathers in the 1830s.

My own home sits next to Cold Brook, a trout stream trickling down into the Onondaga Valley. Just south of us it passes the place where the council fire of the Iroquois Confederacy once burned, in a village the Onondagas called "Ka-na-ta-go-wah." Their apple trees still bear fruit.

Our relics are landmarks to the past in the present. They reassure us we've been somewhere. They're ghostly but warm to the touch. We know them. We connect.

This is what I write about, the place where I live and work, where I was born. I've been away over time, and come back. There's no letting go of the long roots that make me a hometown guy.

These are some of the stories I've been told across the last 20 years about my kin, my friends, my neighbors. It's what I do.

I tell people I have the best job in town. I believe that. I've been a reporter more than 30 years with a charter to write about the people and events I know.

I've seen their horror, their joy, their surprise, their embarrassment, their pride, their moments of hate and tenderness. It's been quite a time.

My first day on the city desk at the Herald-Journal I hit the streets. I've been on them most of the time since. Don't ask me how many words I've used to make a living.

I wrote my first column for the newspaper in 1976. It was called Upstate Notebook and appeared once a week, in the Sunday Stars Magazine. Later I moved my bunk to Sunday Empire Magazine. I stayed until the fall of 1979, when the first Dick Case columns were published four times a week on the Herald's Metro page.

I settled in.

This is my scrapbook of 18 years of columns for the Herald-Journal and Herald American. It covers a lot of time, a lot of territory, a lot of citizens and their stories.

I got out of breath wandering around through my files. There's a stack of more than 3,000 columns. I smiled, I winced, I said hello to friends I'd forgotten. Several of the columns I wish had stayed in the files.

The stories I picked for the collection jumped out at me as being right, by my measure. There's not room for as many as I thought ought to be brought back into the light for a few minutes. Maybe we'll have another rereading, one of these days.

Meanwhile, come, join us in the circle.

—*Dick Case*
1994

## Chapter 1

# EVENTS

---

## CATACLYSMIC

That ball of red and white fire brought us together again Tuesday. Before, it was gunfire that brought us together.

One minute we cheered. The next, we prayed.

It was important to be somewhere. Quickly, we got to the places it was important to be. There is comfort in arranging ourselves. And later, we would want to know where we were.

In place, we watched and listened.

I got to the restaurant at noon to have lunch with my friend. Coming in, we passed a familiar face on the TV screen next to the bar. The face was blue, but we recognized it as part of the body of the man who speaks for the president. If the voice had been assigned a color, it would have been black.

"How would you describe the president's feelings at this time?" the face was asked. "He is very concerned," was the reply.

We started to eat not knowing why the president was very concerned. Soon, we found out.

My friend's son, who is a lawyer, came in to eat. "The shuttle blew up," he said. "Did you hear?"

No.

Another time it had been, "The president was shot." Or, "Shots were fired at the presidential motorcade as it passed through Dallas today."

Outside the street was filled with cold wind. The kind that moves you along like a kick. There were fewer cars and people than there should have been. We were at our places.

In the newsroom, the shadows already had taken form. There was a large one across the page one proof on the editor's desk. "SHUTTLE EXPLODES," it read. The men we hire to arrange these shadows stood with their shirt collars pulled open, arranging.

A floor below, in the press room, the machines strained to catch up with history. They were giving us 75,000 copies an hour.

In the upper left-hand corner of the computer screens, that little green "BULLETIN" flag flashed. We had been summoned.

I started to read the editor's proof sheet. "It seemed virtually impossible that anyone could survive such a cataclysmic explosion."

Cataclysmic. I had never written the word.

Frank Sharp delivered the new edition. It sat on top of the old one, with its headline about an event that would not take place, the state of the union address of that night. How quickly the shadows had been rearranged while I chewed on a turkey sandwich.

I looked around the room. Everyone had a new edition for a face.

When the phone rang, it was a biologist who wanted to remind me we are the children of technology. Yes, she said, from the toaster to the fuel mix of the rocket injection system. Pull the plug, and we are back on all fours again.

As I drove home, I listened to the radio. First the engineers in Florida were talking, then a psychologist in New York. The engineers said they knew nothing. The psychologist said we had to be up-front with our kids about this. Tell them "no guts, no glory," he said.

I remembered the picture of the New England school teacher a few days ago in the newspaper and the night before, when the 11 o'clock news showed a clip of a technician at the space center trying to break the lock on a shuttle hatch with a busted drill bit.

One small step for man. One busted drill bit.

The TV was on at my house. My wife and kids arranged before it, eating apples. I heard Tom Brokaw apologizing for showing the explosion again and again. He showed it again. Educational, he said. To help us understand.

I saw the ball of red and white fire at the end of my living room.

In a few minutes the president was there. His face was gray. Heroes, he said of the dead astronauts.

Also, this is the way it is in a free society. Up front and in public we watch the heroes fall to earth.

One day, when he has the time, the president ought to lecture to the school teacher's students who gathered in the auditorium to watch the launch about being up front in a free society.

"Some of the debris didn't come down for 45 minutes," my daughter said.

The president had a parallel, too. He said the old English explorer of the seas, Francis Drake, had died on board his ship off Panama 390 years ago Tuesday. Yes, he too was buried at sea.

When the "Newlywed Game" came on, we turned off the TV and had supper.

I found out a man I know, Ted Kaniares, was at the first shuttle launch in April 1981. Ted is an Air Force photojournalist who is studying at Syracuse University.

He got the day off to take pictures at The Cape four years ago. It was hot and buggy that day and he made his shots with the other journalists three miles from the pad at the edge of a field. What a sight! Such great power! he said.

Ted has watched every launch since, on TV. "I feel sort of like family," he said.

Tuesday, he was in the bar at Marshall Square shooting pool when the big TV screen rolled over from MTV to CNN. The first thing Ted saw on the front of that sparkly box was open water. Why are they showing open water? Then it hit him.

Yes, he said, "it's like someone in my family died."

Mine too, I said.

$-1986$

---

# WALLIE

We buried Wallie Howard Jr. Saturday. The air was as warm as May's. The chill was in the heart.

Syracuse Police Officer Wallie Howard Jr. died in a shoot-out in a grocery store parking lot on South Salina Street. Wallie was undercover in a federal drug unit. A coke buy went bad and the officer died a hero.

Saturday we buried him from the Church of the Assumption, a Roman Catholic church on the North Side. Assumption is the congregation of the Franciscan friars. Wallie was a Baptist. The "home going services" blended the two faiths.

Wallie went home under gold and green plaster and marble columns embossed with angels. Rosebud Odum sang a gospel hymn in the choir loft. The mayor, the chief of police and the state police superintendent were on the altar with the priests and ministers.

The place had been swept for bombs before the service. Cops with guns walked the roofs of nearby buildings.

They told us we had close to 1,000 mourners in the church and several thousand more outside, in Salina Street, and on the sidewalks. A few hung out windows.

I sat down with a little boy named Sean who squatted with his toys on his front steps next to the church. What's going on? I asked him.

"Police died," Sean said.

Police die and the brotherhood gathers. "Wallie was a brave and loyal member of the brotherhood," his pal, Officer Tom Seals, told us during his words of memoriam inside the church.

Yes, the mourners in the street were of the brotherhood, hundreds of cops ranked in file and stretching six blocks north, to the funeral home. They'd parked their cars to the south, starting at Catawba Street. When the casket came out of the church, the red lights were turned on.

They flashed in silence all the way to the cemetery.

Some of the cops were crying.

Assumption was picked for the funeral because of its size, and accessibility. Sheriff's Deputy David Clark's rites were here three years ago. David was the last officer made a hero by gunfire in our town.

Before that, it had been 1929 when we last lost a city officer on the street. He was James Hannon. Jim's sendoff came under the twin spires of Assumption, too.

Accessible or not, the services had this square of the North Side well-noosed by 10 a.m., when the people standing in front of Onondaga Vacuum heard the first drum beats of the pipe band coming down Salina.

"It's like a parade," a woman said.

No one said much. The block in front of the church got quiet, in a way it's never been quiet. Those drums, moving closer.

Ratta-tap-tap.

Is there a more mournful sound?

I walked up and down the ranks in the street. Square cut haircuts here, pig-tails and flowing locks there. Undercovers who worked with Wallie.

Down the way, a retired undercover. The former deputy chief who's a federal marshall. The district attorney. The U.S. attorney. The congressman. The mayor's guys.

We stood there waiting. We looked up when the state police helicopters buzzed Salina Street. We listened as Lt. Gary Corbett, at the microphone on the church steps, called the officers to attention.

Armond Magnarelli, the state park official, is next to me in the crowd. A young woman approached and squeezed his hand. She was crying.

"I knew him at Henninger," she said.

The horses arrived. The drug-sniffing dogs. The sheriff. The FBI.

Followed by a Garland Bros. gray hearse with the mayor and the police chief in front of it. Walking.

The church music was coming out of the loudspeakers next to Pavia's Market by that time. And soon the words of the preacher. Wallie's brothers and sisters from the department walked up the steps to their pews with the words of the Old Testament psalms in their ears.

Deputy chiefs, captains, sergeants, rank and file. Clerks, dispatchers, the guy who cleans the offices.

There wasn't room inside for all of the visiting officers. They were told to have coffee at the parish center and reform in the street in 60 minutes.

The Rev. Jeremiah Dyer, Wallie's pastor, gave the eulogy. He told us the officer's life spoke for him; there was nothing to be added, or subtracted.

"God knew what he was doing," the minister said. "His friends tried to save him, but their arms were too short."

The eulogy built to a pitch; the reverend sang from his pulpit and a few of the mourners cried out. They clapped softly; tapped their feet.

"Brother Howard is just a step away," he shouted.

Thomas Constantine, state police superintendent, said "Wallie Howard didn't lose his life over narcotics; he lost his life making it possible for us to enjoy our freedom. The responsibility now passes to all of us . . . we can't be a bystander or an observer."

Rev. Dyer stood in the street praying as the pallbearers came down the stairs to the hearse. "Father, son and Holy Ghost," he prayed, overlapping with a command of "Detail, Attention!" from the p.a.

Three jets screamed by the church spires and the bagpipes started again. "Looks like everybody in town is here," the man next to me said.

I knew of one absence. Margaret Savage had told me the day before she'd miss Wallie's funeral.

Too much, she said. It brought everything back.

Sixty-one years ago Margaret was in Assumption church praying for her husband, a city police officer. Her name was Margaret Hannon then. Jim died in the hospital of blood poisoning 44 days after a burglar shot him when he surprised him breaking into a drug store.

Jim was 29 in 1929. Wallie Howard, 31, in 1990.

Margaret, remarried and widowed again, still lives on the North Side. She went to Wallie's wake and those memories of 61 years ago rushed back. They hit her hard.

"Officer Howard looked so nice," she said. "In his uniform and his hat there and all. All I could think of was Jimmy. He looked just like Jimmy laid out."                                                              —*1990*

---

# MARGARET

Margaret Savage has not spoken to David Clark's widow. Some day, maybe. If the time were right. Just now it is OK there are no words to be spoken across this strange bond between the two women.

Wendy Clark was widowed last month when her husband was killed by a man who wanted to escape from the two deputy sheriffs who had taken him to court in DeWitt. David Clark was one of the deputies.

It was said he was the first sheriff's man ever murdered in the line of duty.

Margaret's husband, Patrolman Jim Hannon, was the last Syracuse police officer killed that way. He died 58 years ago this spring after a burglar pulled a gun on him. Until last month, the event had been put aside. Most of us forgot about Jim.

Most of us but Margaret, of course. She remarried, lost a second husband and the tears still come for Jim.

That's one of the things Margaret would say to Wendy, should they meet.

"You sort of work your way out of it, but you never forget," Margaret will say. "It takes a long time, though. And you never forget. Never."

Even then, 58 years after she watched her husband die in a Syracuse hospital, Margaret had to cry, just thinking about it.

We talked one night after Margaret had dinner with Rod Carr, his wife Margaret and Jonathan, his son, at their home. We had coffee and cake in the living room and Jim's widow, who also is the widow of Lt. Thomas Savage, Syracuse Fire Department, showed us some of the leftovers she had of May 1, 1929, the day of the shooting. She left them with Rod for his police museum in the Public Safety Building. Rod is a city cop, too.

I took Jim's bravery medal and ran a finger over it. Real gold, Margaret said. Handsome thing. The widow took it posthumously for the hero from "Bud" O'Hara, publisher of the Syracuse Herald.

There was a news clip and a picture, also. The picture had Margaret in her widow's weeds next to Bud and Rollie Marvin, who was mayor then.

A snapshot of Jim in uniform after he went on the force midnight of Christmas Day 1925 dropped from the pile. The Hannons were newly married, and Jim went on even though he really wanted to be a firefighter, according to Margaret. They told him they had enough firefighters so he became a cop.

It wasn't even four years before he was dead.

Jim was a regular foot patrol in the East Genesee Street business district when he found the padlock pulled out of the cellar door at Walker's Drug, at Genesee and Irving. The cop knew something was up because the door was locked from the inside. He called Precinct 1 and "rushed back to the store."

I know these things because Margaret showed me Jim's report to Chief Martin Cadin, written in his own hand. He was shot and wounded, but he still wrote his report to the chief.

"I intended to get in behind the store and wait (for backups to arrive)," he reported. "I did not have time, for as I was crossing Irving Ave., Pickard (who was arrested as an accessory) walked boldly out of the cellar. I put the gun on him and called hands up. As I said this a gun barked and I was hit.

"I thought Pickard was alone. I took license no. of car after lock picked from door."

The shot hit Jim's elbow and shattered it. It also cut across his chest. There was a picture of him in the hospital that night in The Herald. "An intensive man-hunt" for the shooter was mentioned.

As it turned out, the hunted man, William McCarthy, 27, wasn't arrested for several months. That happened when he went back home to Buffalo. He was convicted and served a long term at Dannemora.

Margaret said she never knew what became of the man who shot her husband. She didn't really care to know, as a matter of fact.

The Herald news story also mentioned that Jim was being treated at Crouse-Irving Hospital. "He will recover," the reporter wrote.

That didn't happen. Jim died 44 days later of blood poisoning. He had never left the hospital and never stopped thinking that he would.

Margaret was up there in Jim's room every day. One morning his doctor came in and checked him over. Strong and healthy, he said to Margaret. Then a buddy of his from the force, Mike McNeary, laid down next to him and gave him a transfusion of his own blood. A while after that, according to Margaret, "he just died."

Jim was 29 years old at the time he died.

The Hannons had a little house on Butternut Street. The wake was held there. A funeral mass was sung for Jim at Assumption Church, where a mass would be sung for another cop, David Clark, 58 years later. "All the policemen stood outside at attention," Margaret said. It was quite a sight.

Yes, Jim was buried in Assumption Cemetery, too.

The widow tried to cope; it was hard. It took a long time to catch the killer and then there was a trial. Chief Cardin told Margaret not to go. She didn't go much of anywhere for a long time. She didn't work for a year after Jim died.

Later, she talked to her doctor and her priest and they advised her to study to be a maternity nurse. She tried that for a while. Margaret signed on at St. Mary's Hospital on Court Street. She worked nights and it was lonely, sometimes. Especially when she looked out the window at Assumption Cemetery and thought about Jim.

"I quit, finally," she said. "It was too hard on me. They got me in over at Borden's, and it worked out OK."

After a while she married Tom Savage, a fireman. Tom got to be a lieutenant before he retired. Tom was a good man too, according to Margaret.

Margaret told Rod Carr and me she never made a big deal out of being the widow of a hero. Jim hadn't made a big deal out of being a hero, either. Danger went with the job. However, when she read in the paper at the time David Clark died that another officer, who was murdered in 1925, was the last city cop killed on duty, she decided to "set the record straight," just that one time.

She phoned Rod and he went to see her. She offered to donate Jim's medal and the other memorabilia to the department. Later she got a letter from the Chief, and Rod invited her to dinner.

Margaret, who lives alone, said that pleased her very much. Very, very much.                                                                —*1987*

---

# THE MAN IN THE ROAD

It was one of those nights when you sat on the steps in front of the house with your shirt off. There was something cold in your fist.

When you looked around, the whole town seemed to be going out for ice cream.

Downtown, the MONY tower thermometer still said 80 and the sun was gone. It had fallen into a ragged cloud bank looking like a big, hot penny. The heat stayed behind. Someone's dirty T-shirt was thrown over a parking meter as if it were a bedpost.

Cars, trucks and bikes ran overhead on the sluice that is Interstate 81. Traffic is there all the time, light and dark, mindless of the hour. The roadway is a flight path from here to there. Pennsylvania to Canada. Tully to Cicero. Matson Avenue to Liverpool. Court Street to downtown.

You get on and follow the stream, most of the time.

Around 10 p.m., the flow was broken for a while.

There was a man in the road. Shortly, there was a man's body.

At first, drivers saw the man walking near the edge of the northbound lanes, near the Court Street exit. They were surprised. The interstate is not for walkers. The man appeared to be confused. He may have been trying to reach the other side, where 81 is bounded by a steep embankment and a wall.

This is the point highway reconstruction begins. There are temporary concrete barriers between opposing lanes. Shortly, the man was seen to jump the barriers.

The first car coming under the bridge took him.

The police commander was eating a beef sandwich at the Public Safety Building when his phone rang. A pedestrian on I-81, the caller said. Someone reported a man in the road. He may be dead. Let me know, the commander said.

He finished his lunch and the phone rang again. The man is dead, the caller said.

The police chaplain was jogging when he heard the radio call on the monitor that is with him most of the time. The cops, and their clients, are his congregation. One day, they'll want him to talk to an officer and his wife who are having problems. The next, it will be one of the men getting married. After that, a funeral. In between, a soul in flight, needing a prayer to kick it on its way.

Tonight, it was a soul.

The priest got there before the commander. Red, white and blue patrol cars lined the edge of the road with their red lights flashing. There were flares sticking into the soft tar. Construction cones cut the traffic path to one lane. There were people on the bridge, looking down to see why the sluice was clogged.

Four cones tacked down a yellow blanket up ahead in the right lane. The priest went to the blanket. A rivulet of blood ran toward the wall. There was a head sticking out.

"He's dead," a cop said.

The priest was dressed in shorts and sneakers. He said a prayer that had nothing to do with what a man is wearing. It was honest and anonymous.

"Poor man," the priest said afterward. "They don't know who he is. I hope I helped some."

The commander got there. He had on a white shirt with the tie pulled open to let in cool air. Colleagues in blue shirts came up, one by one, and told him about the accident. Another man in a blue shirt took pictures. The corner of the blanket was lifted.

FLASH. A line was made to the edge of the road. FLASH . . .

"The driver's over there," a cop was saying. "He just ran out in front of the car. He'd got some ID but two different addresses."

"Next of kin notified?" the commander asked. "Get that done."

"Yes, sir."

The priest stared at the blanket. Traffic crept by. The drivers looked too. So did the gallery on the bridge. Beyond the flashing red lights, yellow headlights kept coming and waiting. A cop bent over the road picking up things and putting them in a plastic bag.

A packet of tobacco. A ballpoint pen with the lid gone. A wristwatch. The watch still worked.

Two men in suits came across the barriers with briefcases and clipboards. "From the DA's office," someone said. In a few more minutes, the man from the morgue arrived in the van with two collapsible stretchers. He pulled up the edge of the blanket too, then went back to move the van closer. A man with a TV camera at his shoulder took his picture.

"I won't want his job," the priest said of the man from the morgue.

Shortly, this man and a cop rolled the body in plastic and lifted it onto the stretcher. The cars kept coming but most of the gallery had gone home. The van rolled away.

The priest in the sneakers and the commander in the white shirt returned to what they had been doing an hour before. Two fire trucks pulled up and washed the blood off the road. The cops stepped on the flares.

Before long, traffic was moving north again, the way it's supposed to.

*—1983*

---

# BABE

We're mourning Babe. It's tough saying goodbye. She'd been here five years.

Babe'd found a place in Syracuse, according to Chuck Doyle, her best friend among those of us with two legs. Chuck's the Burnet Park Zoo's senior elephant handler.

A place in our hearts. And in her barn. She was the herd's matriarch, according to Chuck.

The keepers made sure the other three elephants got to say goodbye to Babe last weekend, before the Niagara Mohawk flat-bed truck drove her body to the animal pathologist at Cornell.

Elephants want to caress an old, dead friend with their trunks, Chuck explained. They may do that for months, even years, after the death of an elephant in the wild. Even when the friend is a set of baked, white bones next to the water hole.

We mourn. The herd mourns.

"The other elephants knew there was a loss," Chuck continued. "We let them see her, touch her. You could see they were moved by it. They did what we expected them to do. And now they know she's gone."

So do we.

Why do we care so much about Babe?

We're sad, and we're mad. The sentiment is strong.

We're sad because Babe lost her calf and then her own life, at the end of a long and, now we know, difficult pregnancy.

One minute, she was standing there purring to her keepers. The next thing they knew, she lay down and let go. Abdominal inflammation and kidney failure, the Cornell vets said. Babe couldn't drop her calf because he breached; after that, she couldn't get the placenta out, and it killed her.

There's plenty of anger, too. Some of us think Babe is a casualty of a breeding program we don't understand, or don't want to. "Why are we trying to raise Asian elephants in Syracuse?" we ask.

Babe was a 36-year-old animal. Somehow, she seemed more than that to us.

"Tears came to my eyes as I read about a great lady like Babe lying down for her final time," one of our readers, Lee Brown, wrote.

Tears wet a lot of the mail. I read through several piles, here and at the zoo. Each writer seemed touched in a personal way by what happened.

One man shouted "murder" at the zookeepers. A woman suggested a memorial fund. Another yelled at the media to lay off the zoo. Some folks praised Joyce Goike, the county legislator and animal-rights advocate who pleaded that Babe be put down to end her suffering. Others asked Joyce to shut up.

Zoos are the last hope of threatened species. Or do we have no business fooling with nature?

This is a fire that's going to be sparking awhile.

Barbara Pickard let me look at some of the mail in her office in Burnet Park. Barbara is the executive of Friends of the Zoo, the support group with 12,000 members.

"Our mail's been unbelievable," Barbara told me. "Most of it's positive. We've had a few negatives. One zoo patron won't renew, but others have renewed membership or just sent us checks."

She showed me two sympathy cards with pictures of elephants on them.

People called the zoo asking about a memorial service, Barbara said. Those were tough calls to handle. There will be no service. "It would be inappropriate," she explained.

As far as breeding elephants is concerned, Chris Spire, the Friends' president, indicated last week the group is behind the program, with spirit and money.

I asked Barbara about our love for Babe.

Well, she explained, it's easy to love an elephant. Look at Dumbo. Look at Babar. Look at our Babe.

"There's so much interaction here with the elephants," Barbara continued. "I'd say 95 percent of the people who come to this zoo literally touched Babe. You could stand there and hear an 8,000-pound animal purring!"

Barbara said she cried. Babe's death really took hold of her when she arrived for work, early one morning last week. She saw Chuck Doyle leading the two surviving female elephants, Siri and Romani, through the grounds to the woods, for a bit of open air before things got busy.

"I don't know how many times I saw the three of them—Siri, Romani and Babe—go up there, trunk to tail. When I saw Chuck with Siri and Romani, it really hit me. Babe's not there; she's not going to be there."

I spread the question around. When I was in Jordan Friday, at the elementary school, I questioned sixth-grade pupils. Most of them shrugged. Yep, they knew about Babe but, well, shucks.

"People like elephants," one of the kids said, finally.

My friend Larry was far more cynical about our community mourning. He reminded me how intense our interest got to be in the whales trapped in the sound in Alaska last year.

Cozying with creatures gets us off the hook, Larry went on. "It allows people to empathize without getting involved."

I asked Bill Langbauer at Cornell. Bill's a research scientist who studies the low frequency calls made by elephants. Babe was part of Bill's studies, which will take him to Africa this summer. He knew her to be "a really sweet elephant."

There's something about elephants that strikes a chord of response in people, Bill said. These large, majestic animals have behaviors similar to our own.

Chuck Doyle has run our elephant program almost as long as we've had an elephant in Syracuse. We got Siri in 1972. Chuck hired on four years later.

Last week wasn't an easy one for him.

He had to deal with the loss of a friend and tend to the survivors. He told me he was comforted by the good things people said and stung by the criticism.

Odd, though, isn't it? How this big, wild animal from Bangladesh, stolen from the jungle to be a gift to an American ambassador more than 30 years ago, got to us the way she did? Anything mystical here? Two people I spoke to last week reminded me that elephants are revered in the country that gave us Babe.

Her last five years in Syracuse were her best. Chuck, her pal, swore Babe herself would say that, if purrs could be transformed into words. She'd been in a private zoo, alone, and then in a herd where she was a stranger to the other beasts. Syracuse received a very nervous elephant when Babe joined us. She'd never lay down; that was a sign of discontent.

Elephants form up in family groups dominated by the older females. Males wander off to stud when they mature. The cows cluster: a grandmother, her sisters, their daughters, their daughters. One becomes the matriarch.

Yes, Babe found her place in Syracuse. She eased up, according to Chuck. The TLC worked. She got her herd and became Our Babe.

No question, Chuck said, "she was the matriarch here."                 —*1990*

---

# THE SOCCER BALL

Frankie Heid's day of reckoning was very polite. Far more polite than the day that got him in debt to society.

No one mentioned the beating, choking, stabbing, rape, robbery and murder of Veronica Nunnally April 18 at her home in The Valley. No one mentioned the soccer ball.

Frankie came into Judge P.J. Cunningham's small courtroom in cop bracelets. He wore a sweater and a jail tan. He is 20 and grew up a neighbor of Mrs. Nunnally. She was 82.

His lawyer was asked to speak to The Court, which in this case was referred to as It. He spoke of The Court's pre-sentencing report on the lad. How clean it appeared to be. In fact, Frankie's attorney pointed out, the only thing in there is The Incident itself.

Oh, yes. The Incident.

Frankie had told the cops, in his statement about The Incident, that he got into his neighbor's house in the middle of the night by throwing a rock through a window. He found Mrs. Nunnally in bed. He jumped on top of her. Then he started punching her in the face until he saw a lot of blood.

Then he grabbed her by the neck and choked her. Then he raped her. Then he went to the kitchen, got a steak knife and stabbed her.

Frankie's lawyer told The Court his client had a drug and alcohol problem of seven years duration. His family was said to be unaware of it. He should be treated for the addictions in state prison.

The lawyer said his client's habit of putting foreign substances into his body in large quantities was the only explanation for The Event.

The Event.

Frankie could not say, when he talked to the cops after his arrest, why he picked Mrs. Nunnally's house that night. The place is kitty-corner and across the street from the home of Frankie's mother and stepfather where he lived. There were other houses closer, where women slept.

He had done marijuana, coke and beer before he beat, choked, raped and stabbed her. Was that why? Young men have done marijuana, coke and beer and not murder.

Frankie stole $7 from the neighbor's purse after he killed her. Then he shut the door and left. The knife he threw into the woods. He got into his car and went to the all-night gas station where a friend works. The friend noticed Frankie's hands were covered with blood. Frankie said he washed up, drove home, threw the bloody clothes into a hamper and went to bed.

The judge couldn't understand how This Act had happened, either. After all, P.J.'s wife is a volunteer at the very hospital where Frankie used to work as a janitor. And to do This Act in the "worst manner in the world," well, the "piper must be paid."

He gave Frankie 19 years to natural life. "You're 20 years old at this point," the judge explained to him.

It was a busy morning in court. Tight schedules were to be kept. Frankie was hardly through the brown door behind the judge's platform before another account was in front of The Court to be settled.

No mention was made of Veronica Nunnally. No mention of the soccer ball.

•    •    •

When the police investigators sat down to talk with Frankie about

The Event, they had great curiosity about the young man they had arrested. Why, they wondered, had he committed this terrible crime? And why Mrs. Nunnally?

Frankie was not providing a motive. He said he didn't know of one. He was able to give up very explicit details about what he had done in his neighbor's house that night. But not why he did those terrible things.

Isn't there anything you can think of? the cops asked. Did you have a grudge against the woman?

No, Frankie replied. She was a nice, old lady.

The only problem he ever had with her was about the soccer ball.

The soccer ball?

Yes. When Frankie was about 5 or 6, he had this soccer ball and he kicked it into Mrs. Nunnally's yard. When he went to get it back, Frankie remembered he said something nasty to the nice, old lady.

Then she wouldn't give him the ball. No, not until he went home, got his mother, and came back to apologize to her.

Frankie went home but he didn't come back with his mother. He didn't apologize.

Mrs. Nunnally never gave back the ball Frankie kicked into her yard. She kept it forever, you might say. When the cops searched her house for clues to help them understand why she was murdered, they found it. That was after Frankie mentioned it to them in his statement.

The old ball, kicked up pretty good, had been put away in her basement by the woman Frankie murdered.

Last week, Frankie looked at that ball for the first time in years. He started to sweat. His heart rate speeded up.

The ball was taken as evidence. Lt. Dick Walsh of the Criminal Investigation Division brought it downtown to the Public Safety Building, hoping he had a clue to Mrs. Nunnally's murder. But when Frankie spoke about it during his first interview, he said it was no big deal. Dick had a piece of evidence, but not a clue.

Last week was different. Frankie had been brought back to the division to discuss a few loose ends in the case with investigators before he was sentenced to state prison. While he was there, Dick Walsh showed him the soccer ball.

"It seemed to stun him," Dick said. "Took his breath away. He was sweating. He said his heart was beating a mile a minute."

What's going on here?

"There's some kind of connection," Dick said. "When he saw the ball, he remembered right away. And it affected him. She kept it all those years. It had significance to her too. Who knows?"

Maybe Frankie knows. Dick told him he would keep in touch. Maybe in a year or so, the cop will look up Frankie in a state correctional facility and ask him again.

Hey, Frankie. Tell us about the soccer ball.                    *—1986*

---

# THE SEER

The man had been traveling a long time when he got to the modest house where the old woman lived. He had hired a car to make the trip. He paid for the gas. He thought it was worth it. He knew the old woman would have a lot to say.

He had been there before.

The house is in Canada. On the Six Nations Reserve on the river west of Buffalo. The traveler was from Onondaga, south of Syracuse. In his way, he was the wise king of nations. He looked like a retired farmer. He didn't tell people he was a chief, unless they asked.

Yes, Leon Shenandoah, chief of chiefs of the Iroquois Six Nations. An Onondaga, by birth. By endowed title, entangled one. Hair swarming with snakes.

The old woman spoke with the dead. Gifted, was the way the chief put it.

Leon Shenandoah had some powers but nothing like the old woman's. She had refined what the Native Americans feel they were born with. All over the turtle's back, and then some, the people knew about her. Came to her for help.

The chief carried a package to Canada. The clothes of a 6-year-old child who used to live in Syracuse.

He wanted her to read the pieces of stitched fabric that had touched the little boy.

James Allen then was two weeks missing from his house on the city's Southwest End. He was discovered missing when police broke into his mother's apartment and found her stabbed to death. His father was in jail on a parole violation.

We looked everywhere for James; he was nowhere to be found. As it turned out, we hadn't looked in the right place.

Once before, in the early 1970s, the chief had gone across the Niagara Frontier from Onondaga with another package. That time the goods belonged to Karen Levy, a missing Syracuse University student. The old woman read the clothes and told the chief where the woman's body was. She was correct, but Leon made a bad guess of direction and a true fix wasn't obtained.

It took some detective work by a state trooper to get at the truth. Her killer was arrested and showed the cops the grave.

This time, the investigators were equally frustrated. Where was James?

The chief rode a horse around his own territory at Onondaga with the policemen because the dead mother had been taken there and beaten once by her old man. When they found nothing to help them understand what had become of James, he offered to go to Canada and get a reading from the Iroquois wise woman. It might help. Sure, the cops said.

In the room at police headquarters where murder investigations are coordinated, two shovels stood against the wall. Just in case.

The chief gave James Allen's clothes to the old woman when he got to her house. She felt of them and asked if he could come back in a while. She would dream on them. Sometimes she used cards, too. But it is better, if you have the time, to dream on them. The chief wanted to start back before darkness so he went away and let the old woman's thoughts sink into the lad's clothes. When he felt she had dreamed on them long enough, he came back.

He was put away, the old woman said to the chief.

She told him James was dead. His body floated in water.

He will rise in time, she said.

The boy had been abused before he died, she felt. Went through a lot. He was bright, smart, but in six years, a lifetime was created.

The old woman said he was killed at night and put into the water. There was a good reason for this, she said. A reason why he was put out of this life.

The chief understood. The reason was that James had witnessed the murder of his mother.

The body was under a bridge, a foot snagged in a tree branch. This was a bridge of three lanes near the city line, but outside the city. Near a business district.

When the water rises, the body will loosen and flow with the current of Onondaga Creek.

Wait, the old woman said. Wait and the water will do its work.

The chief was driven back to the place where the Iroquois council fire burns. He had James's things and a souvenir of the infant found in the hallway of a Syracuse apartment house last January. When the baby was discovered, and placed in a foster home, she was described as Native American. The chief wanted to know if that was so.

No, the old woman said. Not Native American. And the mother remains in Syracuse.

When he was home, the chief called the police and told them what the old woman said about James Allen. Where he was. How she said to wait and the body would rise.

The cops looked under the bridge closest to the Barge Canal terminal, anyway. The water had been dredged two weeks before. They probed again. Nothing.

That was Friday. Saturday, the old woman in Canada had her way. James's body was found in the reeds at the south end of Onondaga Lake.                                                                 *—1985*

----

# THE WORM TRIAL

The worm trial is winding down. Thursday we got to hear from the worm-maker

We are not in Judge Howard Munson's federal district courtroom in Syracuse to learn about any of the many slender, soft-bodied animals, some segmented, that live by burrowing underground.

No, no. This is a worm of the New Age. A creature of electrical energy made by a man to insinuate itself into another man's business.

A computer worm. A most magnificent cluster of positive and negative charges, for sure.

I sat and listened, close to fascination.

Now, here we have a worm, for instance, that talks to other worms. This is done in 5,000 places around the country, practically at the same time. The worm's powers of insinuation are so strong it is able to breach gates and unscramble passwords designed to keep it out.

And once inside a system, it masquerades as other worms. Flattens itself against a filing cabinet when the night watchman flashes his beam down the corridor.

It survives, to insinuate another day. Even if the electricity is shut off, it does not die.

But wait! There's more, according to what I heard Thursday. The worm's gifts are such it is able to talk other worms into killing themselves. In a matter of seconds!

All this, and super-users, well-connected machines, time bombs, trap doors and Trojan horses. Not to forget computers with names, such as "Ernie."

I sat on one of the judge's hard benches staring at the great seal of U.S. justice, which hangs directly over Howard Munson's head. The worm-maker was a distance in front of us, to the judge's right, in a chair next to a microphone.

Who is this guy, anyway?

His name is Robert Morris. His age is 24. He said he works as a programmer of computer software. He is suspended as a doctoral student at Cornell University.

Robert is the chap the feds decided to prosecute for writing the program that got into more than 5,000 computers in November 1988. He claims the program was an intellectual exercise to show the vulnerability of the system. The government says it was a federal crime.

That's because the worm Robert made wouldn't stop. He tried to kill it, and it wouldn't die.

The worm-maker is a slight man with reddish-brown hair who wears eyeglasses with dark rims. My kids might say he's a nerd. People say he's very smart. His parents, who sat with us in the gallery, are said to be very smart too. Dad is a computer genius for the federal government.

Robert's speaking manner from the witness box Thursday was calm and informed, like a teacher's. He had to be asked to speak up.

He balanced one leg on his knee and swiveled in the swivel chair. He turned toward the jury and opened his fingers to punctuate his answers. He got to the point almost every time.

Which was?

Hey, I'm sorry. My experiment failed. Let me tidy up, if I can.

Robert was questioned by his own lawyer, then ours. Both times the message was clear: The worm-maker knew what he was doing.

Yes, he told the prosecutor, he was a hacker who broke into other people's computers. Why, he had done that when he was 15 or 16.

Broke into the Bell Laboratories system, in fact.

Bell wasn't pleased, according to Robert.

When had he thought of this worm business? The month before he did it. And why, exactly? Well, Robert didn't remember, except that worm-making was part of his discipline— that was what he called it, discipline—of computer security. He told us he had to learn how to worm in to discover how to keep the rest of us out.

How did he do this, exactly? By sitting in his office at Cornell and unscrambling the codes of computers on the network he wanted into. One vital aspect of Robert's mind game was to feed all of the words of a dictionary into his files, then run each of the passwords through the book, word-by-word, until a key was found.

Yes, his worm had to be hard to detect and hard to kill. When he found ways to do those things, Robert told us he was very excited.

He got scared, he said, when he saw the mess his worm made. He called two friends for help. Then he screwed up his courage and called his father. Robert said Dad was not amused when he told him what happened.

His father told Robert to go to his room and go to bed. Shortly we'll know if the jury of his peers says the same thing.          —*1990*

---

# DELBERT

Leland Fanning said he'd take me to see the most famous man in the Stockbridge Valley of Madison County. Wednesday we drove out to Johnson Road and met Delbert Ward.

Leland took Delbert out to lunch at a restaurant next to Burton's Livestock Sales in Vernon. Delbert had a roast beef sandwich and a big slice of cherry pie with whipped cream on top. We talked about cattle, bankrupt farms and how it's taking longer for silage corn to ripen this year.

We also talked about second-degree murder.

Delbert's the farmer accused of fratricide. A county grand jury indicted him Aug. 3 in the death in June of his brother, William. They found Bill dead in the bed where the two of them slept.

The four bachelor Ward brothers lived on the 90-acre hillside dairy farm at the time.

The district attorney claims Delbert suffocated Bill. Delbert swears Bill "died natural."

Most of the neighbors who've spoken up agree with Delbert, Leland Fanning among them. Leland, who lives over the hill from the Wards in Siloam, put in with eight other of Delbert's friends to get him out of the jail at Wampsville on bail.

Several thousand dollars also were collected at two benefits. At one jamboree in Munnsville, folks paid a dollar to dance with him. That fund will pay the legal expenses to defend Delbert against the murder charge when it goes to trial.

Delbert's lawyer, Ralph Cognetti of Syracuse, said he's just as sure the prosecutor will try the case as he is Delbert is not a murderer.

"To know the Wards is to know a murder couldn't be committed," the lawyer said. "The DA wants to send Delbert to state prison."

"They live a very simple lifestyle," Leland explained when he told me about putting up Delbert's bail. "They don't even have a car. Truth is, Delbert never went anywhere. He's been in jail up there all his life."

The brothers live in their grandfather's old house; the home across from them is long-empty. Both have seen better days.

Delbert stalked down to us at the driveway. Leland greeted his friend by calling him a celebrity. Delbert smiled and tugged his green Burtons' cap so it pinned one of his ears to his head.

Delbert's in his 60th year and is the baby of the brothers.

The Wards milk about 30 cows. They tank 600 pounds of milk a day. Delbert, who quit school at Munnsville at the start of the seventh grade, keeps track of the milk money and some of the cooking. "The boys," as the neighbors call the Wards, share the chores.

We leaned against Leland's car and talked next to the dairy barn. Four cats—one of them had but three legs—played in the yard. After a while, Delbert's brothers came out of the house and waved to us. Roscoe sat in a lawn chair under a tree. Lyman squatted on the house stoop next to the old school bus where their cousin, Ike, lives.

How'd this mess get started? Delbert shook his head.

"Bill'd been hollering all the while," he said. "He was cut chain-saw-ing and got blood poisoning. Oh, he'd been hollering awful."

Real sick? Delbert nodded.

The brothers found Bill dead around 6 a.m. By night, just after chores, according to Delbert, the troopers and others in authority were at the farm to take him into custody. "They broke in and took our guns and the cow clippers, too," he said.

Delbert was questioned by troopers and the DA's staff. This produced a four-page statement in which he said he'd discussed with Lyman putting Bill out of his misery. After they went to bed, the statement quoted Delbert as saying he held his hand over his brother's mouth for about five minutes.

His lawyer said the statement is fiction and he will move to suppress it from the trial at a hearing next month.

"Here's a man who can't read or write, and he gives a statement that sounds like a Harvard dissertation," Ralph commented.

Delbert surely doesn't talk as a Harvard man would talk. The words come out of his mouth slowly, with the ring of Upstate back country to them.

He drives his tractor to town, Munnsville or Stockbridge, if he needs to. When he worked at Burton's in Vernon, he made the trip on the tractor, too. The farthest from the farm he's been in 50 years is Oneonta, about 50 miles.

"I went down there once and helped a guy pick up some furniture," Delbert said.

The Ward farm catches the colors from the trees this time of year. Leland pointed to a brilliant row of maples across the valley on East Hill. Lyman yelled at us to check out the geese on the horizon.

"Seen any turkeys this year?" Leland asked. "Plenty of 'em," Delbert said.

This man accused of murder can't find the best words for how he feels about his neighbors. "Real good" will do for now. He was in jail "pretty near 20 days." He's glad to be up home again.

"I didn't care for it," Delbert said to me and Leland. "There's no place to move. The food was no good. The coffee tasted like they washed dishes in it."

Leland asked him if they were going to dig up Bill. Delbert said he didn't know.

The first death certificate, signed by Dr. Humphrey Germaniuk, deputy Onondaga County medical examiner, listed the cause of death as "pending." He amended it to read "homicide by suffocation" after visiting the farm and speaking to state police.

Later, the DA asked an outside pathologist to review the medical examiner's procedure in the Ward autopsy. He found them satisfactory.

Since then, publicity about the case reached other pathologists. They offered help. Delbert said he'd been told "one of them did the autopsy on Martin Luther King."

His lawyer said the experts will look at the autopsy findings and may ask that Bill's body be exhumed.

I asked Delbert how he thought this would end for him.

"I don't know yet," he said. We could hear the geese calling from 500 feet overhead. "They say it'll work out all right. I hope so."     —*1990*

---

# THE BULLET

I had seen Hercio Possamai one time before Tuesday. I saw him Saturday night, right after the strangers robbed his store at North Townsend and East Division Streets and tried to kill Hercio and his wife, Teresa.

Teresa was hit. There's a slug next to her spine. Maybe she'll never move the lower part of her body again. Saturday, Hercio kneeled on the floor next to the counter at his North Side Market. He had his wife's head cupped in his palm. She'd fallen on her back; blood curled onto the tile.

Hercio's eyes met mine.

How do you describe the face of fear on a man? The terror, the sorrow, the hate?

"They're coming," someone said. We caught a faint cry of a siren moving closer.

Hercio glanced up at the man next to him. He said something to him about a gun, about these men who'd come into the store. Two of them.

They'd fired twice. One shot went through the window. The other went into Teresa.

And after that, the strangers got into a car and drove through a red light on Salina Street. They didn't even turn the headlights on.

Hercio, 48, and Teresa, 36, opened the place two months ago. It was a pizza joint before that. He quit his job at Syracuse China. His wife kept working her two, one cleaning, the other sewing at Learbury's.

The door to North Side Market was open practically all the time, 7 to 11, seven days a week. Teresa came in weekends, to help, to be with Hercio.

The Possamais live on Marcellus Street. They're from Brazil, and still speak better Portuguese than English. Jose, their friend, who's been in Syracuse from Brazil 23 years, tells me the Possamais worked very hard for what they had, which was a one-room Mom and Pop in an old North Side building, 318 E. Division St., across from the Cornerstone Christian Church.

"Very hard," Jose was saying. He's tight with Hercio, like a brother. "They try to make something for their dream and something awful happens. It's tough, real tough."

North Side Market was dark Sunday. Monday Hercio reopened. Tuesday morning he stood there behind the cash register, right where he'd been Saturday when the strangers ducked in, pretending to want to buy candy.

He pointed to the scar in the panel over the window. I saw a hole large enough to pass a bullet into your heart.

Hercio explained, Jose helping, that the two men got in front of him and his wife and one of them—he remembered the jerk's hand shook —fired a round directly at them and missed.

Then they grabbed at the bills under the change tray and Teresa ran around the end of the counter saying she'd call the police. That was when the jerk fired again, true to his mark that time.

How's she doing? I asked Hercio.

He shrugged. OK, up here. He pointed to his heart. Down there, no good. She was in fair condition today at University Hospital.

Would he stay? Oh, yes. Sure. They all shook their heads: Hercio, Jose, his other pal, Mike, and his son, Oberti, who'd just come in to relieve his dad for a few hours.

Aren't you afraid? No, Hercio said. No.

He left us to talk about violence in our lives. Jose? Well, he'd wish us a better society, a gentler way of life than the one that showed its two ugly faces at North Side Market Saturday.

Oberti, who studies political science at SUNY Albany, doesn't understand the craziness that took down his mother. In Brazil, he said to us, the economy's much worse and crimes of violence fewer.

Hercio Possamai didn't have a gun in the store Saturday. He will next Saturday.                                    —*1991*

# THE COP AND THE MINISTER

Two men were thinking about God in Marcellus the other day. One of them has to; he's a minister. The other had a shotgun shoved into his nose.

Keith Shinaman is the Presbyterian minister in Marcellus. Has been for 25 years. He's also the fire department chaplain. When the volunteers move, so does he, to offer comfort and keep people out of the way. The ministry is a very special one because Keith knows that, for many of the men and women of Marcellus, the fire department is its own church.

Dick Clark is a sergeant in the Onondaga Sheriff's Department. He's put in 15 years and has a gold badge and two medals for valor. Tragedy and death ride with him when he goes on patrol. All in a day's work, he says.

The minister was in his study Monday with the fire monitor going, as it is, day and night, waiting for the signal. Marcellus is a quiet place and even when the alarm does let go, it is more likely to be an aged widow who fell out of bed, or a chimney that won't stop smoking.

Monday, when the call came, it was a man with a gun in the house with the fake brick siding next to the creek where Main Street turns into East Hill.

The man, they told Keith, was shooting. There was "Pep" Pepperman parked in front of the post office with a hole the size of a crab apple in the side of his car.

Dick Clark was following his regular road patrol. He was on Route 81, northbound near the Liverpool exit, when the radio told him to go to Marcellus because there might be a sniper. Marcellus is a long way from the Liverpool exit, but Dick turned his black and white into a Lear jet.

When he got to East Hill, they told him Frank Ventre, a Marcellus officer, was in the house. They heard a shot and Frank didn't come out.

Dick went around to the side, expecting to find his colleague. Instead, he saw the glint of a gun barrel through the window. Then he heard three clicks. Later he found those clicks had his name on them. He also found out they were the wrong size shells for the chamber.

Frank, it turned out, hadn't been shot. He was hunkered down behind the house. Dick sized up the situation and joined him. He would be there more than three hours, talking and sweating and looking into the round hole at the end of the muzzle.

The minister, meanwhile, was standing in front of the Arco station, a long block away, waiting to do things that needed to be done. He was thinking, too, preparing himself as he usually does when he turns into the fire chaplain.

What might happen on this lovely fall afternoon here in my quiet town? How will I serve? When will they need me? Will I be comforting a widow? Staying up all night in the hospital with the family?

Looking out at Main Street, Keith thought how unreal it looked. All the people flattened against the edges of the street, out of a possible line of fire. The yellow police line strung across Orange Street. The harvest dinner sign in front of the old mansion the Masons use for a temple. The tall man in a hunting shirt with a rifle as he crouched behind a tree in the temple's front yard. The undersheriff in his business suit, leaning another rifle across the hood of the station wagon behind Arco. The Big M, all quiet and empty. The villagers standing on the steps of the liquor store looking down at the Ernie Dodrill house and wondering what the hell was going on inside.

A man with a gun was yelling at Dick Clark from Ernie's. The man was shouting he'd kill anyone who came near him. He said he had a gun.

"I just started talking," Dick said. "Talked about any damn thing I could think of, just to get him to put down that gun. I'd get him to put it down, and then something would happen and he'd pick it up again. I said I wanted a drink of water. I said my boss was with me and he'd fire me if he picked up the gun again. Gradually, I got his confidence. We started calling each other by our first names. But I was never sure what was going to happen."

Keith tried to keep busy while Marcellus held its breath. He went down to the school and got a bus brought up and parked on Orange Street so the kids from school who would have walked up East Hill on their way home could be moved around the flash point. Mel Corp was worried about his mother, who lived near Ernie's house, so the minister drove up to Limerick Street in the chief's car and made sure she was OK.

Goes with the job, Keith thought, and it's better than just standing around with your hands in your fire department jacket.

Dick was still talking. He and his boss, Capt. Mike Goudy. They had taken off their gun belts so the man in the house would get the idea they wanted a peaceable settlement. They were talking through a back window and finally Dick got the man to unlock the door and let him into the kitchen for a drink of water.

"He still had the gun and when I went for the water, he had it in my nose. I kept saying we had to trust each other and he kept yelling they were going to kill him. He was scared. So was I. Especially when he heard something outside and pulled the trigger again. The next round turned out to be a good one. But we had a drink of water together and finally I got him to lay the gun down. I told him I wouldn't let anyone hurt him, and you know, after three hours, I wouldn't have let anyone touch him. I meant it."

Keith and most of the rest of us didn't see how it came about that Marcellus got to be a quiet village again. The cop in the sweaty uniform and the man who used to have a gun, his pot belly poking out of a sweat shirt, hugging each other. Captor and captive coming out of Ernie's house in an embrace.

"I know there's a God," Dick thought. The man said he was sorry.

Keith went back to his study and the kids walked up East Hill, home from school. Dick was so tired when he got home he couldn't even watch the football game. Actually, just how close it had been didn't hit him until the next morning, when he was taking a shower.

Then he went to work and he had tended to two dead bodies before 9 a.m. "All in a day's work," he said.                                    *—1980*

---

# "A REGULAR JOE"

We killed time in City Court Friday making bets what Bill St. Germain looked like. The young Syracusan would be charged pretty soon with murdering a 3-year-old girl by smashing her body, choking her, slitting her throat and throwing her into a bathtub of water.

After that, Bill sat down and watched TV.

After that, he called for the Secret Service, saying he planned to hitchhike to Washington if they didn't come for him. When he got to D.C., Bill said, he would kill President Reagan and Vice President George Bush.

He does brag that way, especially when he's got some champagne and Yukon Jack whiskey in him.

Syracuse police said Bill both killed and bragged early Friday before the sun came up. That brought us to Judge Lanston McKinney's courtroom later in the afternoon.

The press watch in the front row of the room sat staring at the white ceiling fan over the judge's chair as it spun. We also observed the words "In God We Trust" on the wall behind the chair. The court calendar dragged on without the man we wanted to see because a bit of a challenge came up about getting a free attorney for him.

One Syracuse lawyer noted for defending the entangled and powerless, told the court he didn't do persons charged with murdering children.

We waited and chewed gum. We had different opinions about Bill.

One of us thought he would be dark and squat. Another thought tall and blond, as well as gaunt, with a face whose sides did not match. Moustache and glasses another said.

It's not hard to reach into a goodly store of stereotypes and pick one for the next citizen you see who is accused of murdering and maybe raping a little kid. Bill fooled us Friday afternoon. This has happened before.

When he was brought in, cuffed to the waist and chained by the ankles, in his white jail slippers and tan JAIL blouse, he looked the Regular Joe a cop who knows Bill told me he was.

Bill is a nice-looking young guy. If it weren't for all that damn metal jangling on him Friday, and the tense sheriff's deputies at his elbows, I could have taken him for the pleasant chap who runs the dishwasher at Hotel Syracuse.

"He is able to exist in society because he can be a Regular Joe," the cop had explained. "He relates well. But if you look at his record, you'll see there are times when he can't cope, when he strikes out. I think there's a deep psychological problem there."

The record is a dark, dank document, for sure. It is a list of sex crimes and assaults. The targets were female. Some of them prostitutes. If Bill's rap sheet is to be believed, there were times when the man simply exploded in the presence of a female.

His brother told the cops Bill was mean when he had been drinking. The people assigned to watch him when he was on probation said he abused alcohol and wouldn't do anything about getting on the wagon.

Bill was born in Syracuse. The family lived on the West End at the time. His last permanent address was a girlfriend's home on Shonnard

Street. His mother, who is remarried, lives in Oswego County.

There were no warning signals on his school record, except where it reveals he moved through seven different schools, city and county, between kindergarten and the fifth grade. In the fifth, he moved to Bridgeport. In the ninth, he quit and didn't come back.

Bill listed his occupation as laborer. He has a quarter moon tattooed on his left hand, a cross on his wrist and a star at the bottom of a thumb.

The night Kara Schoff was murdered he was wearing an orange and blue SU scarf. Her mother, Lisa, had found him standing at her door with a bottle of Yukon Jack in his hand. He asked Lisa if she felt like drinking. She said she didn't, but she would.

Lisa told the police later she didn't even know Bill's last name. She met him a year ago, when he was living at the Rescue Mission.

They drank, watched TV and talked. Then Lisa started to have cramps and Bill got her a cab for the hospital. He told her not to worry, he'd watch the kids.

That probably was a very poor choice of babysitters, this Regular Joe with the small explosive device imbedded in his brain. But should we be too harsh on Lisa?

After all, Child Protective has taken her only other child, the older brother who went in and saw his sister "all dead" in the bathtub. Just when a mother needed someone to hug.

And after all, as my friend the wise cop pointed out, how was Lisa to know? "We don't send out flyers," he said. "He's not tattooed inside his mouth."

I'm guessing that Lisa didn't know about Petrina Peterson, either. Petrina was 17 in 1982 when she came to Syracuse from Albany with her pimp, a man known as "Shampoo." Petrina was a good kid gone wrong. Once, when a social worker was trying to help her, she wrote a poem about how death was near and "grudges me my 17th year."

Petrina picked up a john in Hanover Square. The next day she was found in a lot on Burnet Avenue with the four-inch knife she carried for protection still in her throat, where the killer put it.

A few days later police picked up Bill after he tried to strangle another prostitute. When officers started to interview him, Petrina's killing was mentioned. Yes, they said Bill said; I killed her.

He then gave up a number of significant details of the crime which persuaded his questioners Bill knew what he was talking about.

After about 90 minutes, the cops showed Bill a picture of Petrina dead. The interview turned 180 degrees at that point. A shrink later told the cops that was a mistake.

Wait a minute, the suspect said, I didn't kill THAT prostitute!

Shortly, a lawyer informed the officers their interview had no legal merit under the Rogers Rule, which was the extension of the Donovan Rule, out of the opinions of the judges of the New York State Court of Appeals.

I.e., a defendant who is represented by an attorney on one charge cannot be questioned by police about any unrelated criminal activity without the lawyer being present to give permission.

Bill had a lawyer to help him deal with an unrelated charge. The lawyer hadn't been there when he casually started talking about the other prostitute. The statement he gave could not be used.

Bill walked.

Investigators tried but they couldn't find anything but his words to link Bill to the murder. The district attorney even took Crouse Irving Memorial to court to try to get doctors to release medical records to show that Bill had been treated in the emergency room for knife wounds the night of the murder.

The D.A. lost, too.

Bringing us to Bill's remark to the sheriff's deputies who arrested him the other night after he said he was going to Washington to kill Reagan and Bush:

"I got away with it once and I will get away with it again."     —*1988*

---

# RED, WHITE AND BLUE

Len Markert didn't ask me to stand for applause in the Imperial Ballroom even though I made the Supreme Sacrifice, just as everyone else in the room had.

At least Len said they did.

He said he wanted to thank the men and women who bought the $250 lunches to help George Wortley run for Congress again for "making the Supreme Sacrifice." I took that Supreme Sacrifice to be the two and a-half, but I could be wrong.

My Supreme Sacrifice was watching a ballroom of Republicans eat filet mignon for lunch. The press at these affairs is kept behind ropes, away from the main courses and the main attraction. Most of us have abominable table manners and can't keep from asking ridiculous questions.

The main attraction in the Imperial Ballroom Thursday was George Bush, our vice president. He flew in from Washington to help George win this fall and remind us who he is when his time comes, perhaps in a couple of years.

Len Markert, described from the lectern by George Wortley as a "premier fund-raiser," was the emcee. Len described George as "the little publisher out East," a reference to the congressman's side bet, Manlius Publishing Co.

It turned out our man in Washington was right. Len knows where the money lies and how to make it fly into George's war chest. Before the program was too far along, the emcee held up a very large blow-up of a check made out to the "People for Wortley." Although the press was stored at the rear of the room, I believe the figure on the check was $182,250 and some change.

Len explained the 182 big ones were gross proceeds of the luncheon. Part of this came from those very devoted fans of George's who contributed $1,000 to be admitted to a reception in the Persian Terrace before the food course. Here they got to shake hands with the vice president.

In the ballroom, they sat at tables decorated with American flags set in small bases. The white linen napkins were tied with red ribbons. There was a single red tulip and thick celery stalk stuck into each goblet of tomato juice. After the party, many of the guests stuck those little flags into their pockets.

The vice president wore his.

"I'm proud to be an American," he said after he started talking. "God bless you and God bless this great country."

This was after the ice cream was passed.

Before that, warming up before the prepared text, he did the Bob Hope Part. That's when you relate to the audience so they don't ask for the $250 back.

You mention a few locals and local places. Mention how good it is to be back in . . . Syracuse.

The vice president made a joke of it. After reading a list of the states and countries he's been in lately, he added, "I'm delighted to be here in Montana."

We laughed because we knew our distinguished visitor knew very well he was in . . . Syracuse.

Really. I mean, he's been here before. Knows John Mulroy and Tim Green by name.

During that last visit, much was made of the fact the vice president—at that point he was campaigning to be vice president one more time—had been captain of the Yale baseball team. There were some baseball jokes and the visitor was presented with a bat with "George Bush" carved into it by Tom Mattimore of North Syracuse.

This time the guest of honor—Our George—made several references to the fact The Other George was a veteran of military service.

One is wise to establish such associations in a ballroom filled with American flags. In fact, the visitor was a torpedo bomber pilot in World War II.

"And he's still making torpedo runs," Our George said.

I'll say.

Now, in October 1984, the vice president did a public forum at Syracuse Stage. He used up some of his time dealing with the notion he will go for the Big One in 1988.

Rosemary Pooler he called "that woman." He suggested the congressman flash the big Len Markert check at her and she might fall by the wayside. Buck-shot, you might say.

He also suggested that the governor of New York ought to be convinced not to run, as well. He didn't say not run for what, however.

I have to say that for 250 bucks, the guests did not applaud as loudly, or as often, as the citizens of Syracuse who pay 2 bucks to listen to hillbilly music on Sunday afternoon in a bar in the West End. Perhaps that's an unfair comparison but then I was starving by the time the vice president got to the end of his speech where he waved the flag he was wearing.

I kept track. There was applause when he talked about ending the budget deficit, when he talked about rights for crime victims and when he said he wanted to make the CIA the "best intelligence service in the world." The speaker made a fist when he spoke of the deficit and smiled and looked up at the diners when he mentioned his wife, Barbara, which he did a few times.

"I'm proud that America once more stands up for what it believes around the world," he said.

• • •

Later I had soup at Zak's, across from the Federal Building. At a table nearby sat half a dozen men and women who had stood up for what they believe in. They are the Griffiss anti-nuke protesters. Their table was decorated by a red carnation in a paper cup. A federal judge had just sentenced five of them to a week in jail.

You tell me, which is worse? A week in jail or an hour or so watching a ballroom of Republicans eat filet mignon?                              *—1986*

---

# FLIGHT 103

We cried.

It was a rough time Wednesday night in Hendricks Chapel of Syracuse University. We sat there in the pews and tried to deal with Pan American Flight 103. A prayer vigil had been called in the middle of exam week four nights before Christmas.

Wait and watch, the Protestant chaplain, Paul Kowalewski, said to us. That's all there is to be done just now.

We hugged each other, held hands and prayed. We tried to make some sense out of an airplane falling out of the sky on a village in Scotland 3,000 miles away.

There was no sense to be made of it. So we hugged each other, held hands and prayed.

A lot of the time, for an hour, the sorrow in that big house of prayer was overwhelming.

Monsignor Charles Borgognoni, SU's Catholic chaplain, was right on, as Father Charles usually is.

"I've been on this campus for 26 years," he said. "Never have I seen an outpouring of grief and pain as I have seen today."

Only the day Jack Kennedy was murdered came close, according to this grim priest.

No, the old school never had a night as bad as this. Thirty-six students dead and the counting not over yet.

I came up Crouse Hill with the basketball crowd. I was on my way to church and so were my walkmates. Two Domes beckoned. Both were ringed by yellow lights. Hendricks and Carrier.

One held up by air, the other by a substance without weight.

The walkers diverged. Twenty thousand of us went to watch basketball. Several hundred others went to wait and watch.

The mourners among us walked those many steps into Hendricks alone, in pairs, hands touching, and in long lines. The place quickly filled. In one long line of students, each of the women carried a lighted candle. One guy was in a wheelchair.

We arrived and sat in silence. We sniffled and rubbed each others' coat sleeves. We embraced and stared at the squares of the dome's underside above our heads.

The sextons with cameras and microphones had been placed in lines along the sides. The journalists were asked to not ask questions until they got outside or downstairs, in the chaplain's offices. No one could silence the shutters clicking.

I sat there and wondered about the history of this grand, old meeting hall of SU's. Surely, it had been much more than a church over the years. I had seen Martin Luther King at that dais; Ayn Rand; Bobby Kennedy and a troop of students performing a Christmas show. Weddings, concerts, political speeches, memorial services, and sermons.

Now this.

We were not prepared for a tragedy this deep, the Protestant chaplain said when he started speaking. That was correct.

One minute we were studying for two exams on Thursday, the next we sat in front of a TV set as the names of our friends —last name, first initial only—rolled before us like a memorial tablet.

A lot of aging was done in an afternoon's time.

Each of the men spoke, as best he could. Each mentioned the remarkable lack of power words have at such a time. Each read a prayer and asked that we pray in silence. The organist played Bach, and we prayed some more.

Rabbi Charles Sherman said it was a sense of community which brought us toegether.

"We in Syracuse, we are a community in pain," he said. Then the rabbi motioned over his shoulder to the other hall with a dome.

" A few steps from here, 20,000 people are watching a basketball game. We know what is really important. It's not basketball, it's prayer."

He read from the Wisdom Literature:

Don't restrain your mourning but don't continue your sorrow, either.

Father Charles prayed, "The Lord lead them safely home." He meant to heaven. Also, "life has changed, not ended."

He asked us to grab hold of our neighbors' hands and say the Lord's Prayer with him. His voice trailed off, and so did ours. All of the red was gone from the chaplain's ruddy face.

We were finished praying about the time they finished playing basketball next door. Some of the students were still crying and hugging each other on the way out of the church. Two young women went up to the front and asked the chaplains for candles from the altar stand. They walked out with them, still lit. They just couldn't stop crying.

I saw my friend Bill, the teacher, leaning on a pew at the back. We shook hands and shrugged. "Bad day," I heard him say. "They could have canceled that basketball game."

Bill said he had seen the list of names on TV and he still wasn't sure if any of his students were on that plane. He knew one thing, though; he didn't need to ask any of the people in that room where their sorrow was coming from.

The two students with the candles walked by us. We looked at the floor.

"Right now, what these kids need most is their parents," Bill said after a while. "But this did them a lot of good. It was an important thing to do."

Later, I ran into a sports reporter. I asked him how it was under the other dome. There had been a moment of silence at the suggestion of the Lutheran chaplain, he said.

And then? "Once the ball went up, it was business as usual." *—1988*

---

# GENNIE

Lloyd was puttering around the yard when I came up to him and asked if he was Lloyd. He was.

Yes, it is a beautiful day. Wonder how long this good weather will hold?

And yes, he remembered March 3, 1966. That was the day the little girl went into the creek.

Lloyd's yard is small and neat. He put his own touches into it. The flowers, the windmills, and pots for the plants and rosebushes. The street is a close neighbor, the houses small and old, snug behind the former factory buildings and not far from the place Onondaga Creek cuts through the city.

Lloyd leaned on his wire fence. I stood in the street.

Sure, he said. The little Griswald girl. She lived over there on Gifford. Probably in one of those houses they tore down. He pointed to the empty lot.

Lloyd is retired many years. Had a bout with the Big C and won. He stays home and spends a lot of time outside. When the weather is good, he is out front, sitting watch on the neighborhood. Yep, he was out that day.

"I remember the little girl came over and asked my daughter to come out and play," he said. "What was her name?"

Gennie, I said.

She was 7. Went to Seymour School.

"They went off to play. I guess they got down to the creek. I heard later she dropped her doll in the water. That's what people said. Pretty soon there was a ruckus down at the bridge. A boy came running up here and said the little girl was floating in the water."

Who was the boy? Lloyd can't remember. That was 18 years ago. Many faces have gone by Lloyd's yard in that time. The little girl's brother was down there too. Lloyd recalled that.

In March, Onondaga has its spring flow. The water is as deep as it gets. There is mud, on the banks and in the mainstream. The flow is rapid. That was the time of year when Onondaga got its nickname, "Killer Creek."

It killed that day.

"I went down to the Bargain Center (Easy Bargain discount store, where the Rescue Mission sits) and her mother came in," Lloyd continued. "Oh, she was a crazy woman. She knew me, as a neighbor. She grabbed hold of me and wouldn't let go. Oh, it was a terrible thing."

Gennie was gone by then. The cops and the firemen got there and all they had was the word of two little boys. The child was missing, but where? This was a challenge the adults had faced before. Somebody who kept track told reporters it was the 23rd time in 35 years a child vanished in that moist, brown tunnel to the cemetery.

Eight skin divers went into the water. They followed the creek all the way from Gifford to Kirkpatrick Street, where Onondaga empties into the Barge Canal harbor. Most of the time the divers couldn't even stand because of the current. In some places, the water was five feet deep.

They found nothing.

That night, playing hunches, the cops spread out in the neighborhood. Maybe Gennie had been snatched. Maybe she wandered away and was in an abandoned house or factory. They looked all night. They didn't find her, either.

The two boys were talked to again. So were their parents. The little boy whose name Lloyd couldn't remember had told his mother the kids were on the railroad tracks above the creek when they saw an object in the water. It looked like a doll. The boys and the girl went to the water's edge. Gennie tried to reach the object. She slipped and fell into the creek. He saw the whole thing.

The little girl's brother had a different story. He told the cops the other boy pushed his sister into the creek. He saw the whole thing.

An officer took the boy to the place where this happened. Under the bridge, in the mud. OK, the cop said to the kid, what happened?

The boy said Gennie called him a bad name. She reached out to hit him and as she did, she slipped and fell.

The boy said he broke off a tree branch and tried to reach Gennie. Once, she had hold of it but let go. The water took her downstream. He ran to a house for help.

Another officer talked to the boy's mother. He told her what the brother said. He told her her son's two stories. The mother was very upset. No, she said. The other boy doesn't know what he's talking about.

A month later a city worker found Gennie's body under another bridge. The one at Kirkpatrick Street. The medical examiner ruled she had drowned. He said it was an accident.

The years passed and Lloyd, faithful watchman of the West End, lost track of Gennie's family and the little boy.

Lloyd keeps track in other ways. He likes to watch TV. Lately, he has been keeping up with the accounts of the murder trial over in the courthouse. Where the young man with the moustache and the shadows around his eyes faced a jury because The People said he murdered a young woman in Onondaga Park last May. She was 16.

Lloyd saw the man come into the courtroom each day in handcuffs, with two tall sheriff's deputies hugging him. He saw the prosecutor wheel in a cart of evidence, including a tree branch wrapped in plastic. The prosecutor claimed the killer stuck the branch into his victim. The man claimed three strangers did it.

Lloyd was watching when the man walked out of the courtroom after the jurors convicted him of murder.

He didn't know that Robin Murray, when he was 6, was a West End neighbor of his. He didn't know he was the little boy who was playing with Gennie Griswald under the bridge the day she went in to the creek.                                                                —*1984*

# Chapter 2

# BIG GUYS, LITTLE GUYS

---

## THE MILLIONAIRE

Sgt. Andy Mrozienski and Investigator Denny DuVal had never arrested a millionaire, so they didn't know quite how to react the other day when Stephen started telling them about his assets.

Stephen is a slight man of 31 who lives in St. Paul, Minn. He wears an oversized and tattered Army greatcoat of many pockets and says he is heir to a $6 million trust fund.

On Monday afternoon, on Syracuse's South Side, Denny and his partner, Dick Culeton, arrested Stephen for stealing door knobs.

No wonder the cops were puzzled. Denny and Dick work on the sergeant's CAT (for Criminal Activity Tracking) squad. Usually they cruise the streets on watch for people who want to rip off each other and the city. These people often have criminal records longer than the arms they are using to reach into other peoples' broken windows.

Stephen doesn't. He prowls the continent in a 1960 Cadillac limo he bought for $70 looking for old things. He is not a criminal. He likes old things.

He also is, authorities believe, a millionaire six times over.

This is what happened, according to police records.

Denny and Dick were passing the 1700 block of South Salina when they noticed a head and hand reaching out the front door of a vacant house. The head wore a black fur cap and the hand held a screwdriver. It appeared to be trying to take off the door knob, so the officers got out of their car to investigate. Before they knew it, head and hand were running out the back door and through backyards.

The CATs chased him, and along the way, he dropped a screwdriver, four door plates, a door knob and an assortment of screws. One of the items got under Dick's foot and he fell, hurting his wrist.

Denny caught up with the suspect, and he was taken to the Public Safety Building for questioning. When the boss, Andy Mrozienski, searched him, he found in the Captain Kangaroo pockets of the Army coat $670 in American cash and about $50 in Canadian.

This struck the investigators as odd because the assets didn't match Stephen's appearance. Another puzzling thing was that the bills were all 100s and still were in $1,000 stack wrappers.

How come? they asked Stephen.

Well, he said, his great-grandfather, a chap named Moses Zimmerman, had been one of the pioneer settlers in the Twin Cities. He sold horses, farming them into St. Paul from a couple of ranches he owned in the West. He was rather tight, and when cars started coming in, he invested his profits from selling the Army cavalry horses into real estate. The nest grew comfortably, and when he died, it was divided among family members, including Stephen's father, who is a physician in St. Paul. Stephen's share is in a trust fund, and he draws on it as the need arises.

Stephen went on to explain that while his family is prominent for its wealth in the community, he picked a slightly different lifestyle. He dropped out of high school and turned his natural curiosity about "old things" into a profession. He used some of his inheritance to buy a 35-room rundown mansion in a St. Paul neighborhood and although his cousins are lawyers and business executives, who look down on him for the way he lives, he is the only one who regularly turns a profit on his investments, including the house.

One reason for this, Stephen explained, was that, over the years, in his travels around the United States in a series of large, worked-over vehicles, including a hearse, he developed a good knack for scavenging, buying and trading architectural ornaments. He barters stained glass windows, molding, door panels, lighting fixtures, as well as old coins, books, papers and other antiques.

Andy and Denny knew about some of this because they impounded the old limo and found lots of interesting things inside, including Oriental rugs, door knobs and rats' nests. There seemed to be receipts for everything except the rats' nests.

But what about the way you look? the investigators asked, sniffing the air around Stephen.

I dress this way so I won't get mugged, he said.

The officers still were curious, so they telephoned St. Paul police and got confirmation of Stephen's connections. He hadn't been arrested, but they knew of him.

After I talked with Stephen, I called Gary Hebert, who writes a column for the St. Paul Dispatch. He had profiled the young man a few years ago and knew his father. "His father is as square as the Rotary Club," Gary told me, "but Stephen is different. Avant-garde, I guess."

Gary said he ran into Stephen's father not long ago and inquired after the son. "Oh, he's still collecting," the parent explained.

Stephen said he had been doing just that over the last few months. He came to Syracuse, he explained, because it was one of the cities he wanted to visit and never had the opportunity. He had some old postcards of our landmarks, and he wanted to look them up and make notes about how they had been preserved. He likes to make architectural sketches; he was written about once by the National Trust magazine.

Just then he was sitting having a cola with his captors, Denny and Andy. He was out on bail, waiting to go to court next week to face the burglary charge, which the cops think may not end up being a burglary charge.

Now, in talking with Stephen, a new light flowed over the case; he thought he was scavenging a house ready to be demolished, as he had many times, one step ahead of the wreckers, in Minneapolis and St. Paul. After all, it was only a door knob.

"I never thought I'd feel sorry for a millionaire," Andy had said to me. "You've got to," said Denny.

Stephen was showing us an 1876 quarter he'd pried out of an old lock. "One of my little secrets," he said. "I go through old houses and get hunches. I've found stuff behind old baseboards. Once I tore apart a furnace and found a lot of old coins that had been dropped down the register in the store."

He said he'd had some close calls, collecting antiques the way he does. Hassled by the cops in North Minneapolis when he was wallboarding with a flashlight. Had to dive through a window when he stumbled on a group of muggers in an old ruin.

"You've got to be careful," Andy said. "We don't want to see you hurt."

"Yeah," Stephen said in his soft Middle West twang. "Sometimes it's a frightening way of life."

"When we get this cleared up here," Andy said, "I think you better head home."

Stephen nodded. Andy offered him a smoke.

"No thanks," he said. "The only bad habit I have is taking door knobs."

*Footnote:* After this article appeared, Stephen went into City Court and pled guilty to a reduced charge of criminal trespass. Judge James Fahey gave him a conditional discharge. One of the conditions was that he stay out of trouble; the other was that he leave town. He did, heading back toward Minneapolis-St. Paul in the limo with the built-in attic. Before he left, I took him on a tour of some of our local architectural gems. One of his favorites was Crouse College, at SU. Stephen said he'd never seen such interesting door knobs.     —*1980*

---

# THE MONSIGNOR

If you asked me for a list of the most interesting people in town, Adolph A. Kantor would be on it.

Adolph A. Kantor is the 73-year-old Roman Catholic priest who has been pastor of Sacred Heart parish on Syracuse's West Side 18 years and a priest 45. Everyone knows him by his clerical title, "The Monsignor."

Three years ago, The Monsignor got involved in healing the sick. This added a new layer of interest to the man.

Now, once a month, healing masses are held at the large, handsome church at the end of Park Avenue, across from the funeral parlor and the fish fry. There are usually about 500 people in the pews as The Monsignor raises his arm in blessing again and again during the three to four hours it may take to complete a healing ministry.

He prays over the ill and the ill-at-ease all around Central New York. If you should come to the door of the Sacred Heart rectory, The Monsignor will find the time to see you, if he is at home.

He may take you into his den, where his canary sings what its keeper says are hymns from the liturgy and his dog, Penny, snores on the floor next to the TV set and VCR. "I must find the time," says the man whose parishioners call a "jetsetter for Christ."

Many of those who come to receive The Monsignor's blessing fall to the soft carpeting of the Sacred Heart sanctuary. This swoon is referred to among the faithful as "resting in the spirit." The slang for it is to be "slammed by the spirit."

The Monsignor isn't sure what's going on here beyond the expression of the energy of Christ flowing into those willing to receive it. He is, he says, a mere instrument of his savior.

The priest raises his arm and the people fall, sometimes like pins on a bowling alley.

When they leave the swoon, and stand without the help of an usher called a "catcher," some of these same faithful swear The Monsignor cured them. They swear they are parties to a miracle.

The man himself smiles and shrugs. God's will, he sighs; God's will.

I first talked to The Monsignor about his healing ministry a few months ago when I stopped by the rectory for his help on a story I was working on. He explained what he was up to. He even demonstrated on me how he worked the blessing.

He put a hand on the top of my head and raised the other, the way you do for a full-arm salute. He said sometimes people dropped to the floor when this was done. I didn't.

I said I'd like to find out more about healing. Stop by one of the masses next door, The Monsignor suggested. We have them one night toward the end of the month. Everyone is welcome. Believers and skeptics.

Two weeks ago my wife and I went to a service. It was a standard mass, with orations for the sick. The Monsignor prayed to Jesus to lay hands upon those with ailments, including cancer, gout, digestive disorders, headaches, liver and kidney problems "and every other ailment of mind and body."

The church was about half filled. Many of the people seemed to be older than 50. There were a few children and younger men and women. More women than men. A few walked with canes. A few wore bandages and slings. Catchers stood by and testimonies were given.

One woman came to the front of the church and said The Monsignor prayed over her husband for a growth in his throat; he felt better almost immediately. When he finally went to the hospital for surgery—The Monsignor told me later he never counsels anyone to give up traditional medicine—the problem had almost disappeared and the man required no radiation.

"We believe this is a miracle, and we publicly thank God for giving us The Monsignor!" the woman said. This was followed by a round of applause.

A second witness also testified to the miraculous disappearance of a growth in her father's throat. A third said she was a disbelieving Protestant until another priest, Father Matthew Dillon, prayed over her son's Hodgkins Disease 13 years ago and it disappeared. The woman quoted her doctor as saying he was open to the possibility of divine assistance in the cure.

At the end of the mass, The Monsignor told his audience not to be afraid to come forward. Many did approach the altar rail and kneel, as they would to receive communion. The Monsignor moved up and down the line; the catchers moved opposite him, behind the petitioners. They took the blessed under the arms and eased them to the floor, where they were allowed to rest in the spirit a minute or so.

Now and again, people fell without being touched. Some fell not at all. It was strange and quiet. No one shouted. No one praised the Lord in a loud voice.

The Monsignor explained when we talked a few days later that most of those who fell stayed down but a moment, while a few linger and have to be brought out of the swoon. One man was on the floor 20 minutes.

What's it feel like?

Like radiation traveling through the body. Like a lead ball, sinking through the head and down to the feet. Like floating. A marvelous tingling sensation. Warmth; you feel warm all over.

The Monsignor himself rested in the spirit after he was blessed by a fellow priest a few years ago. He went down and floated away.

"It was a wonderful feeling," he explained. "The heavens opened."

The Monsignor stretched out in a comfortable chair in his den. Penny snoozed next to her master's black, clerical loafers. There is a needlepoint "Jesus" sign on top of the TV set and a statue of the Pope.

The Holy Father from Poland is a special presence in this parish of Polish immigrants and second- and third-generation Polish Catholics. The Monsignor tends a flock of more than 2,000 families and a small vegetable garden behind the garage. The church yard blazes with the pastor's flowers. There is a good stock of kielbasa from a shop in New York Mills in the freezer.

The Monsignor's parents were Polish immigrants who settled at New

York Mills, where he was born, the fifth of 10 Kantors. His father wanted him to be a doctor; he wanted to be a priest. Early on in his priesthood sick calls developed a special meaning for him.

"I would spend more time than other priests, I guess, going to hospitals and seeing the sick. Sick calls didn't bother me. Even when I had to go out at night. Even when someone died. Prayer is such a great balm."

The Monsignor is well-read in his faith. He is aware that Jesus healed the sick and his apostles were given that power. He also knows miracles are taken into account for sainthood in the church, while, at the same time, healing is not a strong presence in modern Catholicism.

He told me he balanced this knowledge against the small miracles which seem to be happening in his own life.

Once some time ago, he ended a hospital visit with a man who had a tumor by touching him on the arm and saying, "God bless you." Later he was told the man's tumor disappeared and his family claimed The Monsignor was responsible.

"I just let it go then," he said. "It scared me. I knew it could happen, but I was reluctant to be an instrument. Then about three years ago a priest came to Sacred Heart and did a healing mission. I prayed with him and when he left after a week, he said, 'You do it now.'

"You know, I had a buzzing in my head as I prayed and asked myself what I ought to do. Maybe God was telling me to go into healing, I thought. I said, 'Lord, if you want me to heal, I will.' The buzzing stopped.

"Then, one night after confessions, a man came up to me for a blessing. He was ill. I touched him, and he went down. That was the beginning. I had my stamp of approval."

The Monsignor is, by nature, an exuberant man. A man fired by enthusiasm. When he showed me around his church, he started singing, the better to display the acoustics. "How Great Thou Art," he sang.

Still, he said he wanted to carry out his healing mission in a low key, without show. No crutches thrown on the altar. No screams as the spirit moves. No, he said firmly, I'm not a charismatic.

"I feel compelled to continue these healing masses," he explained. "These are the people of Jesus Christ. I can't neglect them. All I'm doing is praying that Jesus Christ activate the energy within these people. It's beautiful, seeing them touched by the spirit! In my case, I think this is a reward from God for my work among the sick."

The Monsignor does not tabulate testimonies. He doesn't know about all of the claims of success, nor of the failures. Yes, he gets letters and phone calls from people who want him to know of the miracles. The skeptics are silent, for the most part. He is aware they are there.

"No prophet is accepted in his own land," The Monsignor said, with a very large smile.

The church watches in silence, too. "The church neither pushes the concept strongly, nor do we say there's nothing to it," Ronald Smith, spokesman for the Syracuse Diocese, said.

"If the Lord chooses to manifest a particular grace, it is to be celebrated," Father David Barry, a chancellor of the diocese, explained.

I asked a Syracuse neurosurgeon and a psychiatrist for their private opinions of faith healing. Both were skeptical, especially about "resting in the spirit." Mass hysteria, hypnosis, they said.

The surgeon mentioned hysterical paralysis, which might be relieved by a peaceable feeling, and the cases of cancer where remissions appear to be spontaneous. Bottom line, he said, is the combination of the condition, the healer and the person wanting to be healed.

"The overwhelming power of suggestion," the psychiatrist said.

Sure, the Monsignor said. "Not all are cured," he said. "but there is a wonderful feeling left with people. They feel good that God loves them."

The church will retire him as pastor of Sacred Heart in the fall of 1989, when he is 75. He will continue the healing mission in retirement.

One more testimony to The Monsignor. Unsolicited. From Harry DiOrio, the Herald-Journal photographer who took a picture for this column.

This young man is not a particularly spiritual creature. He is not into faith healing. He went to Sacred Heart the other day to take pictures of a priest. He had a bad headache; out drinking with friends the night before.

When the pictures were done, The Monsignor told Harry he would give him a blessing. Not to be afraid. Just walk up to the altar, and I'll put my hand on you.

The Monsignor did. He started to pray. He motioned me to get behind Harry. In a second or two, Harry went down like a sack of onions.

Wow!

Harry looked at peace. The Monsignor said he was. "Let him rest, he's fine," he said to me. Harry breathed deeply. His eyes fluttered. Tiny streams of sweat started down his face. His arms were crossed on his chest.

OK, The Monsignor said. He snapped his fingers at Harry's ear. Harry's eyelids crinkled and opened.

"How ya doin', pal?" The Monsignor said.

Harry was doin' fine. The headache was gone and he was sweating pretty good. He said he'd heard us talking yet he was at rest. For sure. Yes, at peace. Resting his spirit on the soft rug of Sacred Heart.

"Strange," Harry said.

You bet.                                                                                        —1987

---

# JOE

There is a large snake just outside of Joe Gianforte's front door in the town of Sullivan. It's very large, and coiled. The tongue is out. A flagstone tongue going at the flagstone walls of Joe's house and at his sidewalk, which is flagstone, too.

The snake is one of Joe's. "One of my buddies," he said. Buddies of the heart, buddies of stone. They count into the hundreds, these friends. Birds, frogs, creatures of the field, snakes. Joe loves snakes and he loves to cut into native stones —and here and there a slab of Vermont marble—looking for them.

He's lost track of how many stones he's carved since he started 23 years ago. He came home from his mother's funeral and picked up a cold chisel and a hammer and searched out a boulder.

"I wanted to pound something," he said. "I pounded the heck out of that stone. After a while, I had a bird-feeder."

The feeder sits on Joe's patio. That's just the beginning of the art gallery of carved stones the artist made for his yard since 1963. The big snake is but one of Joe's buddies he has found inside stones, only to put them back into the environment.

The house, designed by his wife, Addie, is in a hillside that slopes toward Chittenango. Once the land was farmed, but now the woods are returning. Deer come and Joe feeds them in the winter. Not to mention skiesful of birds. The coons make it hard to keep a vegetable garden. The weasels living in the old stone wall are white. Joe claims to have seen a coyote or two.

The dining room, and its porch, look into the north, at Oneida Lake.

That's why the telescope is there, next to the table. Around the corner, built into the wall, is one of Joe's masterworks, a flight of geese in marble relief.

"That's been there since 1967, when we built the house," Joe explained. "I'm proud of that. It was in a national exhibit of sculpture in New York."

Joe didn't start out to be a sculptor in stone. It evolved from a diversion into a hobby. He taught himself to do it because he was working, chipping away, at stones anyway.

Joe started out to be a landscape gardener in Rochester.

He went to college for two years, then joined the Army Air Corps. He was a pilot in World War II in the South Pacific. After the war, Joe and his wife, who is a landscape architect, came to Syracuse to set up a branch of Chase Pitkin, landscapers. Later they bought the business from Pitkins and ran a garden store and landscaping business in DeWitt for years.

A couple years ago the Gianfortes closed that shop and opened another, the Canal Barn, on the DeWitt widewaters. Joe works at the store but wants Chase Pitkin Pots and Plants to be known as "Addie's baby." The canal barn itself used to sit next to the Gianforte's house in northwest Madison County.

In a way, Joe's art goes back to the earth that gave him the working material. His birdbaths, fountains, feeders and figures rest easy inside or outside of a building but outside is best. Joe has harvested stones from stream beds, lakes, fields and quarries. He is familiar with geology and fossils. He knows, for instance, that there is a seam of flagstone that runs from Potsdam to Binghamton. He knows our local limestone, and where it hides.

Just as he saved shards of his own working materials when he was putting down walks and patios for clients before he retired, he now collects shards from quarrymen and other professionals. He went to Vermont to get the chisels with carbide tips the marble cutters prefer. Sometimes visitors bring him stones, hoping Joe will find a creature among the layers time baked for him.

Joe works outside, mostly. Or in his shop, in a big chair next to the wood stove that used to be in a railroad caboose. It is best to meet a boulder or slab head-on, standing up. This man circles his working material the way a fighter circles another fighter. The muscles in his arms, at 67, are hard and full. He knows just where to put that carbide tip to get what he wants.

Then the chips fly. The rock of ages goes up in little puffs. Hey, look out! Stand back, you weasels and coyotes!

This is hard work, according to Joe. I don't doubt that. Just a few whacks at a piece of marble he's changing into a birdbath the other day, and he had his coat off. Time and patience are called for. A sculptor of stone never gets out of a creation what he puts into it, by way of financial rewards.

Even though customers who come to Chase Pitkins, or Joe's house, to shop may leave him with $200 or $300 for a Gianforte lawn ornament.

"It may take me two months to do one," he explained. "but I have two to three going at the same time. Sometimes I get so involved, I can't stop. I'd go five hours a day. Then I'm really pooped. Sleep like a baby."

Joe told me the key to his creative output—he is, after all, self-taught at this— is knowing the subject. In this case, Joe knows his wildlife, his creatures, his buddies.

"I know animals," he continued. "Sometimes I can look at a stone and know what's in there. Like the rabbit in the yard. That boulder looks like a rabbit. All I had to do was work a little here, a little there, and I've got the face and ears. A good picture helps you out. I get a picture I like and I stare and stare at it. Like a little kid. Get it fixed in my head."

Joe said he will take a whack at anything that grew in the field. The harder, the better. Soapstone? That's for whittling with a kitchen knife at the movies. Joe likes the stones to put up a fight.

"If I can't see it in the stone, I get angry and frustrated. So I leave it. 'Hey, I don't want to work with you, you're so miserable.' But I love it. I love to do this."

Most of Joe's customers are women. He has sold to many different clients, housewives to businessmen. One of his stones is on the Conrad Hilton estate in the Hudson Valley.

"I get into things and I can't stop," he said. "For a while it was rabbits, rabbits, rabbits. For a year I've been doing birdbaths. I'm going crazy with birdbaths now."

Joe sees himself as a gardener with a "little hobby of stone-carving." He will admit to a sense of design but when something really beautiful happens under his chisel he will say he was "just lucky, I guess."

He carves a little wood, too. The shop is lined with spoons and ladles he whittled from applewood. These curious sticks, which Joe cures with vegetable oil, look down on what may be Joe's masterwork of masterworks. This is a hinged stone case. When you lift the cover, one of Joe's snake buddies is coiled forever inside.

Joe is a happy man as long as he can pound the heck out of a piece of stone. The only thing that might make him a little happier would be an exhibit of his work.

Yes! A room full of Joe's birdbaths. One birdbath after another, with all those goofy-looking frogs of his. And the snakes. Wouldn't that knock your eye out?                    —*1986*

---

# THE SWAN LADY

Emma Ernstsons, the Swan Lady, met me at the door of the yellow house on Sabine Street. I followed her and her striped stockings up the stairway, past the stained glass window and into her four-room widow's flat.

Here, tucked away in the modesty of the aging two-families of the Near West Side of Syracuse, was the author of the book, "Summer of the Swans."

She is small and modest herself, a woman you might see on a Dudley bus under a hair net, with a Rite-Aid shopping bag filled with groceries and second-hand Redbooks from a cousin in Schopfer Court.

"I wish I had more notice," she said as I sat down on her sofa. "I would have made apple pie. You like molasses cookies? I have some cookies and ginger ale."

The voice is filled with old-country Latvian. Mrs. Ernstsons goes off into the kitchen for cookies, leaving me with a copy of her book, which is blue and carries a picture, by her husband Fricis, of a swan rising to flight.

"As the World Turns" is burned into the small TV set in front of us, next to the table of greeting cards stood on end, a vase of plastic rosebuds and a candle.

When she comes back, with cookies and soda, I am looking at a picture in the book of a cob and his mate, with a nest of eggs. The author smiles, sits down and smooths her pink dress over her legs.

"Ah," she says, "there is no book in the world like this."

Small conceit, this. Emma Ernstsons has earned a little pride.

Since her husband, a photographer, died eight years ago, her consuming interest was the book, "the dream we had together." Now it is finished, printed and in the bookstores and the Lady of the Swans can savor its sweetness there on Sabine Street, smoothing back the pages and remembering the "Summer of the Swans."

Emma and Fricis Ernstsons were Latvians, he a photographer with his own studio, she a school teacher when they met more than 40 years ago.

Later the war came, then the Russians and Communist government, and the couple decided to take the opportunity to flee. "When Latvia is free, we said we will go back," she explained. "But that never comes."

They were displaced persons in Germany, and then England, before coming to the United States, and Syracuse, in 1958.

The summer of the book's title was spent photographing what became Fricis' favorite subject near Lincoln, England, in 1957. The Ernstsons were waiting out an immigration quota and he worked making enlargements and repairing cameras. During their free time, the couple wandered along twin rivers near Lincoln, photographing and taking notes as a pair of swans courted and raised a family.

And, as cygnets matured to adults, the idea of a picture story evolved.

"We started thinking about a book," Mrs. Ernstsons recalled. "We had the negatives and the notes but then we came to this country and went to work. But always we planned it. My husband always said we would buy a house outside the city and write a book."

The book waited as Emma and Fricis worked as domestics for rich families, in Syracuse.

Then Fricis died suddenly of a heart attack. Emma was devastated. She pulled herself back out of loneliness and sorrow with the thought she had a mission: the book.

"It was my big present to him," she said. "A monument to him."

Taking time, she pulled it all together: Fricis' pictures, the notes, the touching pieces of biography, the prose, the memories, the bits of poetry contributed by friends. And when it was ready, she borrowed from the money the couple had saved for a house, and paid for the book's publication.

She is pleased. As we sat on the sofa talking she recalled some of the people who had bought the book from her and their delight with what she prefers to think of as a work of art, rather than another book about swans.

Why, there was one man who bought a copy for each member of his family. Six books.

"Summer of the Swans" carries some of the awe the author herself has for the creatures she used to watch slide silently over ponds of the castles of Latvia when she was a child. That grace played mystical chords that echo still in that little second floor walk-up.

The Swan Lady's eyes glistened.

"I never saw anything so beautiful. And I've always liked beautiful things. They slip forward, forward, and nothing moves. They glide and it's so quiet. Swans have always seemed to me like creatures from another world."                                        *—1976*

---

## STEEL MAN

Joe Duda sat with his wife, Mary, at the kitchen table of their bungalow. They were eating kielbasa sandwiches and fresh tomatoes and cucumbers from the garden.

Joe threw down a shot and chased it with a gulp from a can of beer. "Aw, it's a good life for a man with an 11th grade education," he said.

An hour before, Joe was sweating under heavy coveralls and hard hat in the North Foundry at Crucible Steel. Joe is a hammerman at the plant. When he is gone, there won't be many more who have come the way he has.

It's hot and noisy in that big room—football field size, high beamed, doors and windows open, huge fans whirling, furnaces burning at 2,000 degrees. Joe and two other skilled forgers with several hundred pounds of glowing steel billets that look like great tongue depressors, burning pink.

I watched Joe and his eyes never left the billet. His face was set in determination. So were his helpers'. A wrong move might put you in a canvas bag.

Joe has been a steel man 36 years. When he started it was Crucible with about 3,000 hands. Now it's the Crucible Specialty Metals Division of Colt Industries.

In the 40's, when Joe was a kid breaking in on the floor, you worked those hot billets by hand, at the other end of a pair of tongs. Now Joe sits in the seat of a manipulator and rams the piece into the hammer like a scientist in a uranium lab.

The men in North Foundry wear ear protectors; they don't seem to help much. The crash of the 8,000-pound steam hammer onto the 47-ton anvil sounded to me like a safe hitting the sidewalk from the top of the State Tower Building.

Hearing loss is an occupational hazard. "You ought to listen in to two old-timers shouting at each other," Mary Duda said later.

The manipulator looks like a bulldozer with accessories. Joe works five levers to keep the billet in the hammer while another man punches the steam and a third adjusts a peg at the anvil for size.

After five or six minutes of hammering, the piece cooled and Joe spun the machine around and stuffed the billet back into the furnace. He left it to warm up and climbed down for a minute.

"We make better than 50 different kinds of steel in here, depending on the order," he said. "It's tough on the machines and workers. That hammer breaks down just as violent things do. Rods break, men break."

He wiped a palm of grime from his face. "We've had the manipulator about 10 years. It takes three men now to do what six men used to but it's a wonderful machine. No more black and blues."

He climbed back and Tom Donato, Joe's foreman, walked in. I asked him about the skill involved in the job and he said there is a lot.

"Joe's a good finisher," he shouted over the hammer. "He does things pretty close to size. The hammerman's in charge of the operation. He's the only one who can see the bends in the billet and know how to straighten them. Nobody can teach you that."

I followed Joe home to East Syracuse. He'd showered, changed clothes and looked refreshed as he showed me the 150-pound tongs painted green, like the house, planted with marigolds in the neat yard.

"When we changed over from the tongs, I took home a pair and planted them in the lawn," he said. "Some people come by and want to know if they're fence post diggers. They ought to try to pick them up. Don't think I'm kidding you; we lifted them with chains. When I was younger, working the four to 12 shift in August—oh, no one knows how hot it was in there. When you finished the shift, every bone in your body ached and the water—the sweat—squirted out of your shoes."

Joe smiled. The work drained you, maybe maimed or killed you, but there was something grand about the tradition. But you could only see it in Joe's eyes when he talked.

I forked over a roll of the sausage and waited for Joe. "We're not unique. Most steel workers are short, stout, round-bellied men but they're harder than a rock. And they usually retire at 62."

I looked at Joe's barrel chest, permanently autographed with the forge's white scale burns; his round upper arms, embossed with tattoos; the ruddy burn of his face.

"It's just like any other job," he said.                                    *—1976*

---

# MARIO

I went to Forest Hill Drive in Eastwood Friday to see Mario Di-Renzo's little joy.

Mario's little joy is a cluster of four flower beds in Forest Hill Drive, the city park of .932 acre that runs from James Street to Sunnycrest. In four years, the plantings have become landmarks in Eastwood.

"I'm a real amateur," Mario said. "But I love to see things grow. The flowers are so bright and beautiful. It's a lot of work but I don't mind. It's a little joy for me."

Mario started growing flowers in the strip of park in front of his house four years ago when he retired. In a way, the beds were an extension of the flowers he and his wife Millie have in their own yard. A citizen's campaign to perk up the neighborhood.

"When we moved here 30 years ago, that park was a lot different," Mario explained as we stood looking at his geraniums and petunias. "There was a big evergreen at the end of the park. They had lights on it at Christmas time. They took that out. Then they took out the hedges. The grass doesn't look so good either. The snowplows cut it up pretty good."

He started with a single mound of flowers, opposite the end of his driveway. The mound had only one kind of flowers. Gradually, Mario improvised, experimented and expanded.

"I added geraniums," he said, pointing to the pink and red blooms. "Then I came in with mums. Then petunias. Then yellow marigolds. Oh, they really dress things up. After that I added more mounds. It got bigger. I put in rocks from the yard to make a little crib out of it."

Mario's passion for his hobby comes on strong. His arms circled and his fingers imitated the stalks as he talked. He bent over and snipped up two or three dandelions with his clippers. He apologized. The blossoms were wet and saggy, after the long rain.

"Oh, when the sunshine hits them just right—they're so beautiful. So bright. Like a light shining underneath."

Mario's improvement project for Forest Hill Drive Park hasn't been easy. After he got his first bed planted, he was working on it one day when a man in a city car drove up and stopped. He asked Mario if he had permission. Mario said no; was there a problem? The man said no and drove away.

The biggest challenge has been the way the plow cuts into the grass edges. Each spring Mario, and his neighbor across the way, Tom Kenah, have to try to reconstruct the sod and get grass to grow. This year, the Department of Parks and Recreation helped with some fill but Mario had to buy five 80-pound bags of top soil. He's not happy with the results.

"It needs to be scratched up and seeded," the gardener of Forest Hill Drive Park said.

I said it looked pretty good.

"I'm out here every day," Mario continued. "I'll fertilize, I'll weed, I'll keep things looking good. People come by and compliment me. They stop and take pictures too. It's caught on up the street. When I started, there weren't any flowers in the park at all. Now, I counted about 20 the other day. I hear people on some of the other streets are interested too."

We went around the back of the house and Mario showed me his other garden. This one has been going about 20 years and is remarkable, considering the tiny plot next to the garage. He opened the gate and started counting the bounty.

"Tomatoes, beans, radishes, onions, parsley, carrots, cucumbers . . . those are melons over there . . . spinach, cauliflower . . . even garlic . . . I got all the neighbors started on gardens. You wouldn't believe how much stuff we get out of here. I end up giving it away."

Mario said he probably inherited his mother's green thumb. People used to stop at her house on Shonnard Street and take pictures too. "Roses," Mario said. "Roses all over the place."

When he thinks about all the time he devotes to making the lights shine from the flower beds in Eastwood, Mario said he sometimes says he will hang it up and let someone else grow flowers in Forest Hill

Drive Park. But then he talks to one of his neighbors, or a stranger whose eyes get stuck in the geraniums, and he starts planning how to add new colors to the bouquet at next planting.

"What can I say?" he asked. "They all tell me they don't want to hear that." —*1984*

---

# ROSETTA

Tradition. That's what it's all about, says Rosetta Green.

That was why she wanted us to take her picture, in the handsome buckskins she sewed for herself, with her great grandson, standing in front of the old cabin turned into a farm house at Onondaga Reservation, where the symbolic council fire of the Iroquois Confederacy burns. And to get them next to that gnarled tree, eerie ghost of itself, which carries in it a mysterious message of the universe. The tree, according to Mrs. Green, started dying at the top.

Yet life grows, in its own tradition, and the young man, whose name is Larry, gets bigger and stronger while his ancestor goes the way of trees. She is a clan mother of the Onondaga Indian Nation, widow of the Iroquois chief of chiefs, and the past is very much with her these days. She struggles to hang on to it.

The picture is full of symbols. She wanted it that way. The tree, the ancestor, the new generation, the house, the buckskin, the arms clasped.

The old clan mother whose tribal memory goes back to Hiawatha and the young man with a trophy in his hand. He won it skate-boarding in California.

Later, Mrs. Green wanted to talk, so I went to her apartment in a Syracuse public housing project where the former first lady of the confederacy lives alone in neat, cheery rooms filled with family pictures and her needlework. She was 77 in June and is small and brown, sitting in her wheelchair next to the window where she can talk to the pigeons.

It is not the Onondaga Reservation, where she lived most of her life, but the phone is handy and "they call me if they need me," she says.

It is not the woodland, either, this hot city with steam coming up from the pavements, but remembering is easy.

"I sit here alone and remember what we did, me and my husband, and it makes me feel good. He and I studied a lot about nature—about the trees and the shrubs and the birds and what we called them in our own language. That's important, knowing what the creator gave us. My ancestor, when she asked me to be clan mother, told me to study nature. You memorize it; if you believe it, you don't need to write it down."

Her husband, who died in 1964, was Levi Green, for more than 20 years Ta-do-da-ho, head chief of the Iroquois. He was a farmer and his father had been an Onondaga chief and so was one of his sons. In those days, according to Mrs. Green, traditions were more traditional.

"A wonderful man, he was," she told me. "Now, it's so different. He was picked because he was an honest man. That's what I call tradition. I'll never see another chief like him. He did everything he should do."

The clan mother doesn't talk much about today's governors of the confederacy, who are picked by the mothers of their clans. The only comment she makes is that, if they are wrong, they will see it someday.

Her's is the eel clan, "people of the rushes," family totem with the turtle, wolf, bear, beaver, snipe, deer and hawk at Onondaga. She is head mother of the eels, "Water Scarce," the name given to her 35 years ago by an old Onondaga woman Mrs. Green calls "my ancestor." She keeps it until she dies.

"She came to me and said, 'I want you to take care of this name,' and I've tried to do that for 35 years. I hold two principal chiefs, one of them I picked last April. I looked around to find him because what we need is a chief who can speak his own language at the council house, not mix with English."

In Iroquoia, women hold rank and influence. Some treaties bear their names. Children follow the mothers' clan and speeches are made in council for them. Peace or war, or matters of general welfare, rest on their decision. In the old days, for a woman's life, atonement was double that of a man.

The Onondaga call the mothers the faith-keepers, so no wonder Mrs. Green wants her chief to speak in his own tongue, as she always has, when he is at home.

"It's not right to lose your own tongue. Some day, you'll need it. It's hard, but it's important. There's no harm getting a good education—most of my grandchildren have—but hold onto your own traditions. We can live in the white man's world but the most important part for me is to keep your own language."

That's why, when she still lived on the reservation, she used to gather the children, her own and others, into the little house at night to teach

Indian words and songs to them. The young people were eager; they learned quickly. Even now, "if they want something to know from way back, they pick me up and take me home. In fact, I'm going down this weekend to my grandson's and I'll give them more of the old words."

Mrs. Green took a sip of milk from her cup and looked out the window, where a large black pigeon was looking at her through the leaves of her coleus plants. Her thoughts must have been in the woods, when she and her husband were out looking for sassafras roots for tea.

"Our tradition—we call them the Great Law—are really something. If you keep what it says, you can't go wrong. When you're alone, things come back to you. I remember old chiefs. They spoke all in their own tongue. They were the real believers."                    *—1980*

---

# CHARLIE

When he died at the age of 75, as far as anyone knew, Charlie Mac-Donald was the only person in town who lived in a theater.

For the last year or so, he had a room in the basement of the Landmark Theater, on Salina Street. Before that, he bunked behind the screen at the Franklin, on South Avenue.

Charlie was theater folk, but in a special way. For more than 60 years, he was at the edge of that big circle of artificial light that, in its way, seduces us all. He was one of the shadow figures, just out of sight at the side of the stage, making the bouncing balls bounce. We may never have seen him.

If we had, we might not have been impressed.

He was a slight man, stooped in seniority, who always seemed to need a shave and a bath. He usually wore a floppy hat with earmuffs and an old jacket with "RKO" monogrammed over the pocket. There were pliers and a screw driver in one back pocket, just in case. In the other, his traveling companion, a CB radio.

Peter Baum, one of the Landmark directors, remembers the first time he saw Charlie, the day in the summer of 1977 when the theater, once Loew's State, was opened for Saturday tours.

"I looked out through the lobby door and saw this very skinny man dressed in shabby clothes. He appeared to be a derelict. I thought we were getting off to a bad start. But he tagged onto the end of the first tour, and then followed the next one. From that time on, he became a permanent fixture at the Landmark. We found out he knew more about the theater than any of us did. He had been working in and around movie houses and theaters in Syracuse since 1916."

The theater had been closed for months at that time, threatened with demolition. At reopening, and the start of the restoration project, Charlie was coming home, in a very literal sense. When he started hanging around, every city neighborhood had a movie house and a warm projection booth. Now, they have fled to the shopping centers and skinny old men who seem slightly odd are not welcome in the garish lobbies of Cinemas I, II and III.

But at the Landmark, Charlie, who was slightly retarded, sensed he was among friends. At first, he worked as a watchman at the Franklin and spent his days downtown. Later, he became a full-time volunteer and live-in handyman for the Landmark.

Whenever anything was going on, party to play, Charlie was there, usually at the circle's edge.

Once when a theater company did "Grand Hotel" in the lobbies, he joined the cast as an extra, prancing up and down the opulent stairways.

When the house was dark, he was around, bouncing his flashlight beam around the inner caverns, playing with his CB in one of the balconies or sleeping next to the boilers. (He knew how to fix the boilers and proved it when they went off during a performance.)

"Charlie was a homeless man but he had a home here," said Rose Bernthal, the Landmark manager. "How many people do you know who live in a theater? We looked after him; built him a room down in the basement, got a bed and dresser and bought him clothes, when he needed them. He got Social Security but he was a simple man and his needs weren't that great. What little he spent, he spent on food, and that wasn't very much. But he loved it here. One day, when I asked him why, he said it was because it was so much fun."

No one knew much about Charlie's past. He didn't talk much, and when he did, it wasn't about himself. The story was he had been on his own since his mother died years ago and left him an orphan. Friends thought he had lived on Cannon Street. Or was it South Avenue?

But older members of the Syracuse stage hands union, Local 9, and the film operators, knew him only as "Charlie," someone who seemed always to be around.

They used him as the coffee and sandwich deliveryman, a menial task

Charlie apparently accepted with delight because it made him one of the group. As far as anyone knows, he never actually worked back stage or in the booth, but he had been around long enough to take over if one of the regulars wanted to duck out for a smoke. When they got a new projector at Franklin, no one knew how to start the thing until Charlie showed up. Same with putting together the old special effects machine at the Landmark, which the restorers found in pieces all over the old building.

There was some cruelty, too, like sending him out for a bucket of wind, but Charlie, Rose Bernthal remembers, "loved to laugh," and always went along with a good tease, even if it was on him.

Although he might have struck some as backward, Mrs. Bernthal felt her friend "knew everything he needed to know." After all, hadn't he gotten by, alone, all those years?

Jim Foley, the theater historian who helps to run the War Memorial, knew Charlie as the "real, sweet old character" who almost seemed part of the plaster at the old Civic, Paramount, Strand, Eckel, Keith's and some of the other vanished houses. He'd come to the Memorial, too—Charlie was familiar enough to guards, stage hands and operators not to need a ticket—and usually blended in with work crews; he acted as if he belonged, and he probably did.

"Yeah, he knew a lot about the business, despite his appearance," Jim recalled. "You'd see him backstage before a performance but he knew enough to get out of the way when the time came. Then he'd be down in the engine room chewing the fat with someone."

After he died, his friends at the Landmark cleaned out his room and found some of the souvenirs he tucked away over the years. A metal plate from a Cinerama camera, a stack of postcards from his CB acquaintances, some theater programs and a picture of Charlie at the War Memorial during the filming of the Paul Newman movie a few years ago.

Charlie had been sick with cancer, off and on, during the last year. About three weeks ago, he left the Landmark for the hospital and never came back. He had a funeral last Saturday, in the great hall of the Cathedral of the Immaculate Conception. Five people saw him off: Rose Bernthal and Mike Spitz from the Landmark; a cousin he hadn't seen in years and her husband, and a friend from the Franklin. There was no obituary. —1979

# SAM FIUMARA'S

In some small towns, the barbershop is the community center. Syracuse's West Side is a small town and one of the places it comes to sit down and have a lot of fun at doing not much of anything is Sam Fiumara's at Marcellus and Tioga.

Sam has been cutting people's hair more than 50 years. Saturdays, if you go to the shop, you not only get your ears lowered, you get music.

Music for Sam is like a big glass of wine sitting next to the hand of a beautiful woman; a big tip; a bald man who was in for a hair cut two weeks ago. It means a lot to him. It enriches the soul.

"Where else could you come and get a hair cut and hear music?" Sam asks, standing next to a customer's right ear as he tends to some pesky neck hairs.

"Do any other barber shops do this? They should. There should be more of getting people together. We don't have much business, but I have a hell of a good time."

This is what it's all about. Sam has been on the block 14 years, in the spot where Andy Sturick used to run a pool room. He's lived on the West Side almost all of his 70 years and when the wrecking ball comes, cutting another piece out of the hide of his old neighborhood, Sam feels it like a piece of his own.

Just then, as we sat there listening to Paul Firenza pull the music out of Sam's accordion and Hank Zacharek's harmonica, a crew was finishing off two buildings across the street. One used to be a grocery store, the other a house. A while ago someone set fire to them

Before I leave, it's almost a vacant lot.

"I'm going to raise corn over there," Sam said.

"I used to live there," Paul said, finishing up "There's No Tomorrow." "I've got a lot of memories. Listen, I was here before you were born. I sure like the old days better. Now? Pewwwww."

Sam came to the West Side from downtown, where he had shops 40 years. One of them was on East Washington, near City Hall, and the politicians came in to get Wildroot slapped onto the places where the razor worked. Some of the customers followed Sam's trail; they're still coming in. Paul is one of them, so is Hank.

"I've had the same barber since I was 10 years old," Hank told me. "Hey, remember those special days you used to have? Haircuts for a nickel."

"Sure, hair cuts were 25 cents then. A dime for a shave. You made your money on the shampoos and massages. I've been a member of the union since I was 22 but I get into trouble with them because I won't charge their prices. I do a regular hair cut and that's it. Two bucks."

He looked at Paul. "Hey, how about 'Danny Boy?' "

The music started again and Paul closed his eyes. He's played just about everything in his time, from a squeeze box to a banjo, but he gave it up for a while until he came into the shop one day and saw Sam's old Accordiana, which the barber had given up on, too.

He picked it up and gave the shop a floor show.

A mother with a big kid who was 12 but looked 16 stuck her head in the door. "How many waiting?"

"You're next," Sam said. She came in, smiling right away when she saw Paul and Hank. Paul was standing in a pile of hair with his cap and rubbers on and Hank was on a stool next to Sam's Number Two chair nursing a cup of tea with the bag still it it.

"Somebody ought to take a picture of this," the mother said to me. "No one would believe it."

One of the things people might not believe is the way Sam has his shop decorated. It's his attic, with memories all over the place. Somebody should take a picture.

The front window is cracked, but that's the neighborhood changing, not Sam. The crack is next to an inflatable barber pole. One of the clocks over the big mirror is a Coke model and there are plenty of calendars around, including some of Sam's own brand.

Along the shelf, over the Osage rub and the Lilly Toilet Water, Sam has pictures of neighborhood kids stuck into the Antiseptic Sterilize cabinets. Most of them, Sam said, are grown up now.

There are some big dollar bills pasted up, next to an old radio, a brass fan, a bowling ball, plastic angels, a TV set, kewpie dolls, plastic flowers, newspaper clips and pictures of the Syracuse Chiefs and the pope.

There are some old coat hangers next to the door with neckties on them. The sign says "$1.00 each."

Across the room, in an old chair, is Sam's record player, which is running when Paul and Hank aren't.

"I like music," Sam said. "Always have. I used to play myself, but I retired. I just listen. I bring a bunch of records from home every day. I like everything. Except rock. I hate rock. I've got polkas, Mario Lanza, Caruso, John McCormick, Nashville Gold . . . Hey, got to get out the

Irish records."

The big kid had gotten into the chair and Sam told him to sit up straight or he'd give him a box to sit on. Auggie Sansone was there, standing next to the strop, with his hands in his pockets, listening to the music.

"Oh, sometimes, I come in on Saturday and stay all day," Auggie said. "Just listening to the music."

"Yeah," Paul said. "Keeps you off the streets."

Then Paul and Hank swapped instruments and tried "Ave Maria."

The piece sputtered; Paul needed the music, he said. Hank took a sip of tea and Sam went after the big kid's cowlick.

"I should have gone into politics," Paul said. "You know what this city needs? Alexander ought to put in more restaurants and shows downtown. When I was courting my wife, we'd go downtown and window shop and got to a show or out to eat. What'ya got now? It stinks."

"The city's going to the country and the country's going to the city," Sam said.

"If they keep tearing down houses, where will the taxes be?"

"Don't worry. The mayor's in trouble. The women put him in before. You guys know 'Spanish Eyes?' or maybe 'Paper Roses?' "

The big kid got down and Bob, who is a grave digger, moved in for a hair cut. He's been coming in for years, too. Sam was still smiling, wrapping a fresh towel around Bob's neck, and Hank had the Echo Harp up against his lips like it was part of his face. His fingers fluttered and Paul leaned back with his keyboard, like he never wanted to stop playing.

Sam put a comb to the grave digger's hair and just because it makes him feel good he said again, to no one in particular, "Where else can you get a hair cut and hear music?"                    —1981

---

# THE DENNISES

Juliette and Maurice Dennis are thinking about moving. The house in Old Forge they took over 40 years ago—the house with the white owl carving over the garage a short spit from Route 28 and a long one to Enchanted Forest—has a "for sale" sign in front. The present is more raucous than the past.

"Old Forge is too busy," Maurice said to me when I stopped to say hello. "It's not like it used to be. If we sell the house, maybe we'll get a little place in the woods. A little farther, but not too far."

Used to be is a far piece for the Dennises. At least for Maurice. He has been in the Town of Webb, off and on, since 1917. He and Juliette may be the last Abenaki Indians left in the Adirondacks. They came into New York from their hometown of Odanak, Quebec, in the early years of the century when many of their tribesmen were Adirondack guides and woodsmen.

The last time I saw the Dennises, six or seven years ago, he was on the front porch sitting on a stool and carving a totem pole. The other day he told me the darned thing finally was finished. It fairly gleamed out there in the fall sunlight, under a second coat of strong colors painted on by Juliette.

"Wow," I said, because the Dennises' totem poles are quite marvelous creations.

Maurice asked me if I believed this pole, which is small as poles by the Dennis family go, had been 20 years in the making. Sure, I said.

"A doctor came to me with a picture of one he'd seen in Alaska," Maurice explained. "He wanted me to do one like it. I said OK. But I never got it the way he wanted. I kept it going on my own. Finally, it's finished. Most of the totem poles, I do on my own. My own style."

The Abenaki do not have a pole-carving tradition. Maurice learned it from an old man in his native village. The tribesman was "a genius with a hatchet." Later my friend worked on his own and read some books. He did his first carving when he was 15. It was a beaver's paw crooked knife handle, which he still has.

"That got me interested," he said. "I thought about making poles when I was in the Army. When I got out, I started. I've been at it ever since."

I asked Maurice how many he'd done over the years. He figured 75. Juliette, who paints the white pine or cedar shafts when the carving is done, figured more. Seventy-five is how old he is.

"They're all over," Maurice continued. "All over the world, I guess. My friend Bart Cummings—he works for Proctor and Gamble in New York—he picked up one the other day he said was going to London, England. He's bought a lot of them. One he put in the University of Illinois football stadium. Dick Cohen (owner of Old Forge Hardware) has a bunch of them at his home on Fourth Lake. And at the store. He's got 'em for sale there."

"They're in Canada, Massachusetts, Virginia, Michigan, Minnesota, the Virgin Islands," Juliette said.

"People got 'em in their backyards, their camps. One lawyer bought one for his office."

Visitors to Old Forge may see some of the Dennis poles at Enchanted Forest, where Maurice and Juliette worked as craft demonstrators for many years. Another beaut stands in front of the Town of Webb Historical Association building on Crosby Boulevard. The family donated that one to their adopted village.

Most of the poles work up to one of Maurice's white owls, with wings spread. On the way, there may be bears, beavers, fish or the face of a sorcerer. All of these images draw on Abenaki tradition. The 20-year-old pole on the porch has a turtle (Juliette is of the turtle clan) and a carving of the four Indian seasons. When Maurice is asked, he sometimes has been persuaded to work a human face into a pole. One he remembers fondly is the famous hobo clown face of Emmett Kelly, which friends of the clown got him to do as a surprise for Emmett.

Maurice, in his time, has done everything from being a lifeguard in Florida to guiding hunters through the woods. He told me he keeps a hand in many things but has slowed down a bit in respect for his age. Sometimes, he explained, he and Juliette just sit in their living room and chuckle over life, the way we were doing just then. Juliette has a good hearty laugh.

She is credited by her husband as being the "basket maker in the family." She used to weave more than she does now, because ash splints are so hard to come by. Maurice's father, Julius Paul, an Abenaki chief who died in 1953, also made baskets. He is best known for his Adirondack Pack baskets, a tradition he claimed originated with his tribe in Canada. Julius Paul said the Abenaki designed the famous splint carrier to replace the old Canadian tumpline pack, on which the strap passes across the forehead.

Maurice has made a basket or two but he prefers carving. "I like to make totem poles," he said. "Oh, I've made baskets, canoes, snowshoes, things like that. If I don't like it, I don't make it."

A man could do worse things with his life then making trees beautiful again after they fall.                                                                  *—1980*

---

# MILLIE

Mildred Przewlocki is one of those people who make the world go 'round by pushing hard at the corners.

Mildred is Millie, the Sandwich Lady. Aunt Millie. The woman at the main vehicle gate of the State Fair who has the socks, toothpaste and Pepto-Bismol. She claims to have been Fair-going for nearly 50 years.

I heard about Millie from an excited visitor to the Syracuse Newspapers booth while I was on display. My informant said there was "this wonderful woman down by the dairy cattle building who gives away tuna fish sandwiches to people. She's been there for years. Everybody down there knows about her. They think she's a saint."

I took a break and walked down Tonawanda Street to Hiawatha Avenue. There was Millie, camped out in the parking lot next to a concrete planter full of zinnias. A small crowd gathered around her. I introduced myself and the first thing she said to me was this:

"You've got to have one of my tuna fish sandwiches. They are the greatest tuna fish sandwiches in the world."

With that, she popped the trunk of her gray Mazda and Millie's Deli was revealed.

I gasped. The trunk was filled with boxes and plastic bags. The boxes and plastic bags contained sandwiches wrapped neatly in other plastic bags and foil. The tunas sat next to ham. Next to those, peanut butter and jelly. In a while, Millie explained, one of her helpers was going to deliver the peanut butter and jellies to some of the carnies who work kid rides on the midway. Next to the sandwiches, a big stash of soda.

"Help yourself to a soda," Millie said.

I had a soda and a tuna on white. When I finished, I told Millie the sandwich was one of the best I had eaten in North America. Then she showed me the back seat of the car. There Millie stores her snacks and medicines, plus more soda.

The Fair is a thirsty place. Dust rises and settles in the throat. The stomach always seems to be rumbling for more. Every turn you take, an Italian sausage is reaching for your wallet. Or someone is trying to slip a wad of pizza dough with cinnamon sugar into your shirt front.

Millie, after 49 years, understands this. That's why she drops between $600 and $700 into Millie's Deli every Fair week.

"It's for the kids," she explained, after providing Nick, a young security worker, with a bottle of antiseptic for a nasty cut on his arm. "I get

15 kids jobs in the parking lot every year. At night, they sleep in my living room. They work hard. It's so hot and dusty up there. They need the money for school. Why should they have to pay for food?"

I pointed out to Millie she had enough provender in the Mazda to feed the SU football team for a week.

"Well, there are lots of people out here who need help. I can't turn down anybody if they need it. Those carnival workers, they deserve a break. They're so good with the kids on the rides. I feed the troopers, the security people. I also take care of some people I know who want to bring their families to the Fair but can't afford to buy food. This woman from K-mart. She's got seven kids. How can she get out here and feed them? We took care of them."

Just then a young trooper dropped by for his rations. He was one of the unlucky ones who drew the traffic detail on State Fair Boulevard. A daughter of one of Millie's friends drew him a cold cola and he walked back to work with a tuna in one fist and a ham in the other.

"You get mustard?" Millie yelled after him.

Shortly, Millie was required to dip into her medicine bag again. This time the patient was a Fair patron looking for aspirin. The bag held plenty, of several varieties. Also concoctions to soothe the stomach and adhesive bandages for Fair blisters. The chap looked as if he held a winning lottery ticket. He wanted to pay Millie. No, she said. No way. "It's my donation," she told the man.

Yes, she said. Everything we have here is free.

"I go to Price Chopper every night," she said. "Usually spend 50, 60 dollars. Every morning I open 25 cans of tuna and six loaves of bread. My friends help me. They bring things too. When they find out what I'm doing, they want to help."

She introduced me to two of the friends, Tina and Joan, who were helping that day. Sometimes, her grandchildren pitch in. Also regular Fair workers.

Millie said she started coming to the Fair as a youngster with her father, Walter Balamut. The family lived on Burnet Avenue, and it was her dad's habit to gather a gang of neighbor children and treat them to a day at the Fair. Millie caught the spirit and embellished it. Her husband, the late Dick Przewlocki, got so involved that he was in line to be Fair director before his death, according to Millie.

When Millie isn't at Tonawanda and Hiawatha, she works as a county auditor. She was the first woman to hold one of those jobs.

I asked her how her heart got so big.

"It's the joy of seeing people's eyes light up when you give them something," she said. "I do it because of the way people appreciate it. Also, I think it's teaching others about the joys of giving."

Millie told me she once nearly died of cancer. The doctors, she said, gave her 30 days. She walked over the prediction and is looking good again. "I had a mission," she explained. "I had to be here."

She showed me a letter she got last week. It was addressed to "Aunt Millie, The Sandwitch Lady" from a fan in Liverpool. The woman told her she was blessed by God for what she did.

"See," Millie said, "that's what makes this worthwhile."

Before I left, Millie supplied me with a phony $100 bill with a picture of Frank Sinatra on it, six packets of sugar-free gum, three chewy fruit treats and a ham and a tuna sandwich for my colleagues back in the booth. She asked me if I needed the Pepto-Bismol.

I noticed socks and toothpaste in a bag on the front seat of the Mazda. For the carnies, she explained. Some of those people, well, they work such long hours and some of them don't even have socks on. They should be able to brush their teeth just like any other decent human being.

"We get clothes for them, too," she said.

And then, "You sure you don't want another tuna fish?"

*—1984*

---

# DEL

Summers, when the days are long, Del Logan is out in the Crafts Wagon in city parks and streets. During winter months, you are apt to find her at North Recreation Center or in a school outfitting an Indian pageant or teaching people to make things with their hands.

Del is an Onondaga Indian. Formally, she runs the crafts program for the Syracuse Department of Parks and Recreation. Informally, she is a carrier of traditions, a busy woman who has taken upon herself the task of keeping a few of the flickering candles of the "old ways" alive until they can be relit, by someone else.

Those ways were part of living when Del was a child at Onondaga, more than half a century ago.

Threads of tradition still intact, running to the time before white settlement, and the unraveling of things that are uniquely Indian.

When Del was young, a lot of the old ways were gone, pulled apart by the new, but others persisted in the log houses of the reservation.

"When I started, I learned from the old people," Del recalled the other day at her desk at North.

"They were not teaching lore; they lived that way. We would go to old people and they would invite us in to whatever they were doing."

This time of year, corn was being brought in from patches around the cabins. "They used to use everything. Make bread and soup from the hulls. Braid the stalks into shoes and mats. Even the cob was used to carry live coals. Corn was basic to the lifestyle of all Indian people."

So Del watched and joined as Aunt Marthie Brown, or one of the other grandmothers, worked behind a windbreaker of corn stalks outside the house.

"That's the way we picked things up," Del said, her voice roaming backwards over the years. "We never tore off the husks; you braided them together and then used the husks for mats and dolls."

There still were basketmakers at Onondaga then and Del absorbed that as well. Last year, when the Smithsonian needed someone to demonstrate the way Iroquois wove husks into food and water containers, she was called on to participate in the "Festival of American Folklife."

Del's parents, Lillie and Moses Logan, were basketmakers. Moses brought logs down to the house from the top of the swamp and then tapped them with a mallet to loosen the bark, so it peeled off wet in long splint strips. These were kept wet in kegs until Lillie was ready to weave, in the fall.

"They always worked as a team," Del continued. "both men and women. My father used to make handles for the baskets from hickory, using a long-handled knife."

The Logans basketed to sell, for the most part. Older baskets were saved for personal, traditional uses, such as removing hulls from corn or berrying. Her mother used to make pack baskets for Able Supply Co., in downtown Syracuse.

"They came to her because they needed someone who knew how to make them. That was about 1920 or 25. I think those were some of the first commercial baskets made on the reservation. They were custom-made, fitted to the contours of the back."

And once a year, after the fall crops were harvested, Mrs. Logan started working on baskets.

"She worked until just before Christmas. When she was ready, she'd lay out a muslin sheet—some of the treaty cloth we got— and fill it with as many baskets as she could. Then she'd ride the wagon into Syracuse and take the trolley to Cortland and Auburn, places like that, and peddle baskets door-to-door. They were always welcomed because the people expected Indian people to come. I think they got 50 cents apiece."

Learning and knowing stuck with Del as she grew, first a young Indian girl who had never spoken anything but the Onondaga tongue, then a young woman in the white schools of Syracuse. She graduated from old North, the very building she now occupies as the city's chief crafter.

"I did my higher education piecemeal, over 12 years," Del said softly. "Then during the Depression I trained people in Indian lore. I did counselor training. And I've been doing it ever since, because it's something I love to do."

Del is sensitive to the importance of Indian ways to America's cultural experience. Although she hasn't gone as far as some Native Americans, and actively boycotted our Bicentennial, she feels the role of her people has been slighted by white historians and pageant-makers as they go about celebrating the superimposing of another country atop the Indian nations.

"The Indian helped the whites survive to build that country they're talking about," she said. Then she paused and smiled. "Of course, the Indian learned from the white man, too."

Del goes about her work eager to teach, eager to share some of the things heritage has given her. She loves young people, she says, and is refreshingly frank that age does not necessarily yield total wisdom.

"Sure," she told me. "I can learn something from them, too."

• • •

Del wore out and died and they brought her to a white man's house in the city, put her in a box in her blouse and skirt, and said prayers over her because she had been baptized a Christian at the Good Shepherd mission on the reservation.

Sometimes the death rituals go the way of life. Del's did. She was in both worlds, trying to be comfortable.

So in a room with recorded music and Oriental rugs, the basketmakers' daughter, brown as the forest, was led away with words out of a white man's prayer book read by a minister who had been a friend. There were no drums.

He might have said: "The sun gives us light. The moon gives us light. She is our grandmother. The sun is our brother. All these are performing that for which they were created. So let this lift up your minds."

But he mentioned Jesus Christ and the resurrection.

A friend with dark, braided hair, beads and a feather, a chief, stood by waiting to carry Del to the ground. The People passed the box and touched her forehead and her hands.

Some of them said Del died. Some said she was tasting strawberries.

*—1978*

# COOL CAT

Spring is here but it's not going to be the way it used to be. Cool Cat won't be back in town from L.A., New Orleans, Miami, Tucumcari or one of the other winter resorts. He didn't make it this time.

Cool Cat's heart gave out up at Unity Acres last November.

I don't think the streets are going to be the same without Cool Cat out there on the bricks. Some people might even say he was as much of a Syracuse landmark as, say, the Columbus monument or Blackie, the one-legged pigeon. Off and on, he'd been around along time. He was 59 when he died.

Of course, I know other people might say we're better off with Cool Cat in the ground. They think we ought to live in houses with front and back doors and regular mail deliveries and with a color TV in the front room.

Cool Cat was the name he wore, like one of those scraggy coats of his, but he was called Carleton when he was born in Syracuse. His biography—a lot of it tucked away in old police records—has him getting in trouble for burglary, a thing Cool Cat liked to do, when he was 16, the first time.

After that, the file goes on for many pages: petty larcenies, robberies, AWOLs from the Army, shoplifting, larceny, car theft, vagrancy, forgery, transporting stolen goods over state lines, using phony names (Romaine was one of his favorites), trespassing and public intoxication. There are plenty of those old PI arrests, because one of the things Cool

Cat was, to the end, was a drunk.

He also, the cops say, was one of the best boosters they ever knew. A booster is what the cops call someone who steals things.

Cool Cat, as he honed his craft, got so he'd steal just about anything that wasn't nailed down. Downtown merchants would become nervous and watchful when they saw him around, kind of hulking through the store or restaurant checking out the goods and the customers.

He looked a little like one of those characters in "Oliver Twist," and things were always vanishing into his pockets.

One of Cool Cat's favorite boosts was to go into a restaurant, with one coat, and walk out with several. Just trying to keep warm, he'd say.

A cop I know said he arrested Cool Cat with his friend Kenny once after they hired a cab to take them on a job. The meter ticked away while they broke the front window of a TV shop on North Salina and left with a couple of floor samples.

Kenny's craft was paper hanging. He was so good at forgery that he used to draw his own checks with marking pens and fool bank and store clerks with them

He and Cool Cat got to be drinking and boosting buddies and cop cars used to turn around and follow them when they were seen together. Before long, Cool Cat was being arrested for forgery, too.

I guess one thing you could call him was an opportunist, seizing the market where he saw it. Recently, according to the police, he was into pills. Not using them, although his friends were, but taking them from stores and drug-delivery trucks and selling them on the street.

All of this did not go unnoticed, although one of the people I talked to about Cool Cat said he got away with much more than he ever got caught for.

He figured Cool Cat spent about half of the last 40 years of his life in jail, just about all over North America, because Cool Cat liked to travel.

He wintered in the warmer climates, and while he was in his home town, he lived at places like the Rescue Mission, Unity Kitchen and Unity Acres, where men without homes find a bed and few questions are asked.

Cool Cat told people he had once been a salesman, a damn good one, but he admitted it was easier to steal, so he did that. Cool Cat was like that, very up-front about things.

A while ago, when he was doing 30 days in Oswego for disorderly conduct, he wrote to a friend of his that he "no doubt deserved" the bust, because "I've been acting pretty wild lately."

Then he hit the guy up for bus fare back to Syracuse.

He also was honest, in a way you wouldn't expect, about his drinking. His friend, Bob, is a recovered alcoholic and he often tried to get Cool Cat into a program. Cool Cat always politely refused, saying to Bob he knew what he was and that was the way he was going to be.

"He never tried to use his drinking to get sympathy," Bob said.

Cool Cat, with his itch to travel and make a buck any way he could, must have had an interesting life, even though, in Bob's accounting, it was a wasted one. In fact, one of his most interesting experiences came just before he died.

It seems that cool Cat's body finally was catching up with the amount of booze he'd poured into it for years. He was in bad shape and one night, when he was having trouble walking, he was picked up and taken to a public hospital in town.

Imagine his surprise, when he looked over and saw the man he was sharing a room with. Cool Cat thought the chap looked familiar; he was. It was a local magistrate Cool Cat often had looked up at from the floor of a court room.

Cool Cat's friends said, sick as he was, he got a boot out of the irony of the situation. So did the magistrate, probably.

The booster and the magistrate were roomies for about three weeks, until somebody found out Cool Cat wasn't supposed to be in a public hospital and he was released. Cool Cat's friends claim the two old men got along just fine.

There was only one small problem, I'm told, because Cool Cat, to the end, remained Cool Cat.

After the booster had left the hospital, the magistrate discovered some of his money was missing.                    *—1982*

---

# SIMON

A small, bright light went out in Syracuse last month when Simon Klippenstein died. He was 67.

Simon lived on the East Side of the city. He carved animals and birds from wood for nearly 50 years.

Some people thought some of my friend's works were masterpieces.

I sure did.

Simon didn't say what he thought, except to seem very proud of what he was able to create with his hands, and few tools.

He'd work just about any workable material. Including used doors and utility poles. I have two hunks of pole in my driveway I meant to give to him.

When Simon died, the obits didn't mention that avocation of his. They said he was employed at Thermo-Patch for several years until his retirement in 1982.

True enough, but not the whole story, by half.

I met Simon about 15 years ago through the late Paul O'Connell, who ran Drake Art Gallery in Fayetteville. Paul encouraged Simon and showed his work. Part of the encouragement was to give the artist—Paul was one himself—a few ideas.

Ellie O'Connell and I talked a little about Simon last week. Ellie is Paul's widow, and a painter, as well. She said her husband suggested Simon should try early American carvings, such as eagles.

"He was doing small animals and things like Mickey Mouse," Ellie recalled. "Paul sort of guided him. Encouraged him to upgrade his work. Simon had a good primitive approach."

I remembered Paul telling me he was annoyed at Simon for using electric tools in the early stages of carving. He wanted his friend to carve and whittle in the old way.

Simon accepted the ideas but did them on his own terms. He went on being Simon.

"If they like what I do, it really doesn't matter what you call it," he once said to me. "I'd sooner be called a primitive than a modern."

Simon taught himself to carve, with the help of a few family examples.

He was a Canadian. Never did become an American citizen, even though he'd lived in Syracuse since right after World War II. Simon met his future wife, Eleanor, in front of the Gridley Building when he was on leave from the Canadian Army. He looked really spiffy, wearing a beret and carrying a swagger stick.

Simon came from a family of six. All of the others stayed in Canada.

He told me about watching his grandfather, Henry Klippenstein, "a Dutchman," carve scoops and shovels out of blocks of wood. His father, John, was a carpenter.

He'd always been handy, Simon said. The carving started after he and

Eleanor became house parents to a cottage of 22 girls at the Elmcrest Center. He whittled small animals as an amusement for himself and the girls. The first item he could remember carving was a Klippenstein version of an Oriental sudan chair.

Later he did toys for his own little girl, Jackie, who grew up with the foster sisters at Elmcrest.

Simon kept whittling and the carving accumulated around the cottage.

"When I first started," he said, "I couldn't give them away. They just piled up at Elmcrest."

When the Klippensteins bought their own house, he set up a workshop in the garage. Sometimes he'd sit in the living room, in his big lounger at the hearth, and cut away at a hunk of sugar pine while he watched TV. Soon a pile of wood shaving formed at his feet.

"That way," Simon explained, "I can work as fast or slow as I want. When you're doing something you like, it doesn't matter. Sometimes, out in the garage, I don't even stop to eat. In good weather, I work out in the yard."

Simon usually began a commission with a sketch. He kept the patterns he liked for second and third impressions. The outlines were transferred to the wood, then Simon rough-cut the piece with a jig saw. Small details were cut with knife or chisel.

Recognition came to Simon after he met Paul O'Connell. His work stopped cluttering the house. People bought it. Now and again, he would do commissions worth several hundred dollars to him.

He sold well at Galleries; museums put his carvings into shows. The Everson included several Klippensteins in its "Animal Kingdom in American Art" exhibit in 1978. He was the only living artist included in the "Wood Sculpture in New York" bicentennial show at the Museum of American Folk Art in New York City.

People were after Simon to carve for them. Once he said he wished he could work faster, to keep up with accommodating folks he wanted to accommodate. But he kept his own pace. He wasn't a rich man. He had to earn a living, support a family. He worked at several jobs, all of them involving hard labor.

He carved from illustrations sent to him through the mail from commissioners living in places such as California. He did a paddle for a Syracuse University fraternity, a dog in the likeness of a beloved family pet that died.

Also crucifixes, wooden bowls, trade signs, cats (he loved to do cats), birds, elephants, penguins, owls (another favorite of his), angels, woodpeckers, squirrels, kangaroos, driftwood lamps, bears, wolves . . . Well, you get the idea.

Lots of them. Hundreds, really.

Every once in a while I come upon one of Simon's carvings, I saw a pair of cats in a millionaire's home in Cazenovia recently. A wealthy businessman has a Klippenstein eagle in his Liverpool office. One of his two "cigar store Indian" figures used to stand in the doorway of a shop on Fayette Street, in the center of downtown Syracuse.

There's no way to count the inventory. Simon's daughter, Jackie Alpeter, isn't sure, beyond my wildest guess of hundreds. One night last week we sat at her kitchen table with Simon's scrapbook in front of us. He and Eleanor kept a sheaf of snapshots of some of his work.

We had fun looking at all of the interesting creations of Simon's. Jackie recognized many of them. None of the pictures had dates, or names of the new owners.

Jackie's own favorite among her dad's carving rested next to us on the table. It's a pair of doves Simon carved as a wedding present for Jackie and her husband in 1987.

Those two love birds probably were among Simon's last work. Eleanor was in bed the last year of her life and Simon took care of her. When she died five months before he did, he didn't seem to want to do much of anything.

"He talked about going back to carving but he never did," Jackie said. "The cancer stopped him."                    —*1990*

---

## THE GRADUATE

Frank Manchester graduated with the Class of 1989 of Sandy Creek Central School a week ago.

Fourteen months before that, to the day, his car hit a pole down the road from his house. He was in a coma at State University Hospital in Syracuse 22 days.

A lot of people, including his doctor, didn't think Frank would survive the car crash that put him there.

At that point, maybe it was only Frank who knew the stuff of life still moved inside of him. The doctors and lots of people couldn't have guessed a year and little more later we would see him bound across the lawn at the school in sneakers and a shiny, blue gown and claim his high school diploma.

Maybe that's why all of us there in front of the high school cheered and clapped when Frank took his certificate.

We had been told not to applaud until all 85 of his classmates were announced. We did it anyway.

It was that kind of day, for Frank and Sandy Creek. Not one of us noticed his limp for the wetness in our eyes.

I met Frank in January when I went to the school to talk with his mother, Peg, and one of his teachers, Paul Sornborger, who is called "Quincy" in Sandy Creek.

I was there because of the letter Frank and his mom wrote about Quincy. They wanted all of us to know how this devoted science teacher pitched in to help Frank and his family after the accident.

In January, the miracle already had taken place. Frank had returned to school and was in the middle of trying to catch up. He'd even played a few minutes in a basketball game.

"He's a very determined young man," Peg said of her son.

Frank still has trouble finding all of the words he needs to make a sentence. He didn't hesitate for a second in January when I asked him if he planned to graduate with his class in June.

"Definitely!" he said. Underline definitely!

So I couldn't help myself. I had to go to Sandy Creek a week ago Saturday for commencement. I had to see Frank grab hold of that crispy sheet of paper in the leather folder in front of the doorway over which was cut into the stone, years and years before the movie "Dead Poets Society" was even thought of: *CARPE DIEM*—Latin for "Seize the Day!"

Which, if you want to know the truth about Frank, was what he started doing when he woke up from that coma.

It was warm and sunny in front of the school for commencement. The seniors had painted the sidewalk from the street blue and silver, their class colors. It was a tradition. They'd also signed their names and drawn cartoons. One section of the walk was painted in memory of Spencer Bower, a classmate who was killed in a car crash during the Christmas vacation.

Sandy Creek has another commencement tradition that goes back beyond the memory of some of the grandmothers in the audience. They graduated from this school too. Each senior goes up the walk with a flower bearer. The child is 5 or younger and carries a spring bouquet. Their baskets are grouped on the platform before the ceremony starts.

The flower children went up laughing and crying. One rode a senior's shoulders. Another was carried in a graduate's arms.

Frank came in with Katherine Carnes, a neighbor. He had a big smile. People took his picture, snapshots and video.

We stood under the trees for shade and fanned ourselves with the programs, which had a drawing of Donald Duck on the front waving a banner "We made IT!" Some people sat in folding chairs. Some brought their own.

There was a big American flag hung over the front door of the school. The band played "Pomp and Circumstance." The valedictorian tossed lollipops and bubble gum to his mates and wore several funny hats when he gave his valedictory address.

The emcees read a short biography, past and future, for each senior. Some were very short. "Enjoys fishing and plans to enter the work force," was one graduate's vita.

When they got to Frank, his big involvement in sports was mentioned. The day before the accident he'd pitched in an exhibition game at Doubleday Field in Cooperstown, for example. He was given the Clark Memorial Award for "perseverance."

Frank surprised his good friend in the class, Jamie Cheney, with an award for him from Frank. It was a friendship citation. Jamie was one of Frank's buddies from school who spent half of his time driving to Syracuse to be with Frank in the hospital.

Jamie and Heidi and Chanda and Quincy and Frank's mom and dad spent hours talking to Frank and squeezing his hand during the time he just lay there in his bed with tubes coming out of him. They weren't sure if he was listening, but they knew it was important for him that they talk anyway.

The Manchesters' friend, Barbara Joslin, was next to me during commencement. She told me that Frank already received the class award for leadership. It was named for Bill Seweryneuk, a Sandy Creek student who was killed in a car crash.

He also got the Babe Ruth sportsmanship award and a ball from the Hall of Fame game autographed by the SU football team.

Barbara said the ball was sent to Frank by Coach Dick MacPherson.

She said the coach heard about Frank through his secretary, Karen Ponzo.

He was moved by the way Frank "fought back from nowhere" and wrote him a couple of letters of encouragement. Dick told Frank sometimes we have battles in life that are a lot tougher than football games.

When I told the coach how much his letter meant to Frank, he was delighted. "Hearing that is just like another win," Dick said.

After the ceremony, the Manchesters invited me to Frank's graduation party, which was at the Mad River Club in Boylston. Peg and her kin spent the day before cooking and decorating the hall. There were balloons and signs and tubs of ice. The grandparents took pictures. Later, a DJ would appear.

Frank came in after a while; we grabbed some ham and beans and talked. He had his Sandy Creek baseball cap turned with the peak at the back of his neck; he looked like an 18-year-old kid who just graduated from high school.

Yes, Frank said, he would go to college. He had already received his class assignments for Jefferson Community College in September. He would study accounting for two years and then, well, we'll see.

"I'm going to take it easy for a while," he said. I said he'd earned a rest.

Frank left Syracuse for Children's Hospital and Rehabilitation Center in Utica. Now he goes to Watertown once a week for therapy. Some left-side physical impairment remains. He will have to take medication for seizures for at least four more months. He drives a car and works a computer.

Quincy tended to his pupil's intellectual rehabilitation. This started last summer, in slow, painful steps, every day at the Manchesters' kitchen table.

In the fall, when Frank returned to school, Quincy tutored him in his own subject, chemistry, so he could finish his last junior year requirement.

When we talked in January, his teacher said helping Frank had been one of the great experiences of his life. He's been teaching at Sandy Creek 22 years.

I saw Quincy Saturday after commencement. He was on his way to some parties. His smile was the only one in town bigger than Frank's.

—*1989*

# HAPPY HAROLD

The thing that struck me about Harold Stahl's world was how small it was. Standing in front of the old house on Seymour Street where he had a room, I could have aimed a small pebble at most of the parts.

Across the way, the Top Hat Tavern, where he often sat in the back booth nursing a beer for hours. Where he made like he was playing piano at the bar. Where he danced. Where he kept his plants in the front window.

Just a block away, Unity Kitchen, where he usually had a free supper at 5 in the afternoon. Where they called him "Happy Harold." Where almost all of the good old boys loved him.

And behind me, the small, dirty room where he started to freeze to death two weeks ago.

Up Seymour, the other way, is the Medical Examiner's office. That's where they brought Harold after he died March 3 at State University Hospital. They may have put him on the same table his twin brother,, Harvey, had 13 years ago when he was hit by a car and killed walking near his home on South Bay Road.

"Happy Harold" was 63. Some people think he shouldn't be dead.

One of them is Wainetta, who tends bar at the Top Hat. She was part of the family the streets gave Harold in Syracuse. Even now, when she talks about him, her eyes cloud up.

"Harold? Well, Harold was Harold. Everybody liked him. When he died, most of us couldn't believe it.

"See those flowers up there in the window? Harold brought those over. Anybody he liked, he gave them a plant. He used to work summers for Hafner's and he'd start plants over in the apartment house and bring them over. Vegetables, flowers, everything. Gardens were everything to him."

Bill sat at the bar listening and then he spoke up. "Hey, that guy was something else. Man, was he. Good people. People just liked him. Harold was himself."

Maybe that's why they didn't end up putting Harold in the potter's field at Loomis Hill. No next of kin could be found after his death, so the other family took over.

This is a tough part of town to pass the hat in. But over at the Kitchen, they got up $20 for flowers. Another 50 bucks came from one of the churches Harold went to, Plymouth Congregational. Wainetta's boss, Jim Pierce, turned over a day's proceeds and with what Harold's friends have put in, the fund stands at about $400 "and more is still coming in."

Wainetta went behind the bar and brought me a voucher. Already, they had bought Harold a lot in Walnut Grove Cemetery with money left over for a headstone.

"We gave him a nice funeral and calling hours," Wainetta said. His friends at Plymouth, the Rev. Fred Lowry and Larry Kinner, arranged for a funeral. Henry, Big John, Charlie and some of the men from the Kitchen were pallbearers and afterwards, they passed out flowers to the mourners, just like Harold used to do at services, sometimes, on Sunday morning.

"Harold liked to make people happy," Larry said. "He drank a little but he never bummed around. He never talked much about himself or his background, but he sure had a lot of energy."

That was one reason his friends are puzzled about the way Harold went.

Henry came into the Top Hat and told me about what happened to his friend. Henry rooms down the hall from No. 10 at 122 Seymour, the green house with the cupola across Onondaga from the Top Hat.

Sunday night, Harold was in the tavern having his few beers. He'd usually sit there and nurse four or five for an evening. Maybe he'd be talking about his flowers, maybe about how he played softball with the Cyclones, the senior citizen's team, or how he used to visit his brothers down in Hornell. Or he might do a little dance and tell someone he used to be a dance instructor. But if a visitor tried to close in on Harold's life, he'd head for the back booth and clam up.

Harold helped Wainetta close that night. It wasn't late. She watched him, as she usually did, walk to the old house.

Sunday morning, around noon, Henry came out of his room and found Harold sitting at the head of the stairs. Other times, he had found him sleeping at the other end of the hall in the bathroom, where the landlord used to keep a heater. Too cold in the room, he said.

"He didn't have any register in his room, no heat," Henry told me. "He couldn't even keep his plants in there; too cold. I think it bothered him but he never complained to the landlord that I knew. Paid $15 a week for the room, just like me. Funny thing about Harold, he never complained or asked for anything."

Henry didn't see Harold again until about 5 the next afternoon. During the night, the official Syracuse temperature got down to 13 below zero.

The friends usually went to the Kitchen together for supper. When Henry knocked on Harold's door, he didn't answer, but he knew he was in there. Henry's a nurse and he knows a death rattle when he hears one. He pushed open the door and found his friend cold, clammy and distressed, half-clothed, in the old iron bed.

Henry got the people downstairs to call the police for an ambulance. On the way out, the only thing Harold said was "thanks." He went to the hospital, into intensive care, and Henry went over to the Top Hat.

Later that night someone called and said Harold was dead. The policeman who came with the ambulance thought it might have been a heart attack. The hospital said something different, that long word that makes street people shudder just hearing it: Hypothermia. "Abnormal lowering of the body temperature."

One way of saying it was that "Happy Harold" froze to death.

Not all of the returns are in. An official verdict on the cause of death awaits study of microscopic sections taken during the autopsy. Dr. Martin Hilfinger Jr., the medical examiner, said at week's end that the death undoubtedly was related to hypothermia.

Meanwhile, the Health Department and Division of Buildings and Property have been asked to look at 122 Seymour Street. Before Harold died no complaints had been filed. Afterwards, there were a few and last week several men with official badges were looking at 122 in ways they hadn't before March 3.

Bill and Wainetta, from the bar, can see them coming and going. All Bill can think about is the time, a year ago, when he went over and found Harold sick and shivering in the room.

"I tried to get him to go home with me to warm up, but he said no. He said he was OK. Just stubborn, I guess."

The barmaid looks at Harold's plants in the window, under the red Genesee sign. Across the street, there are a few more, still sitting in the hall windows where Harold left them, out of the cold.

After I finished writing about Harold, I got a call from a friend of Henry's, the man down the hall. It seemed the landlord of 122 Seymour St. had just evicted him. He told Henry, according to the friend, he didn't want him to get cold. *—1980*

———————

## Chapter 3

# CITY

---

## 213 GIFFORD

The old house at 213 Gifford St. had some genes dancing in it the other afternoon when I stopped for another look. I had been there before.

The rose bush blooms at the back stoop, the way it has for years. There is grass needing to be cut and stray bricks needing to be put back into walls. The windows are gone; even the plywood that replaced the windows is gone. So are the people. By the looks, no one has lived at 213 a year, or more.

Still, the roses are out. They are red. Apple-red.

I wrote about 213 a year ago. How lonely it is, a survivor of a neighborhood without many neighbors any more, there in the West End, near the arterial.

Vacant lots to the left and right. Cornices hanging. Foundations crumbling. Yards messy as a sleepy head. Taxes in arrears.

A shell of house and not much more.

I went looking for a history to the place. I didn't find much.

The house probably was built in the 1880s. John G. Glazier, a conductor on the New York Central, lived there. Later, 213 was a rooming house for many years.

I said I wished I knew more. In time, three people put some genes into the shell for me.

One was Hurlbut H. Smith of Syracuse. H.H. was one of the Smiths who made typewriters. His great uncle, he said, was Hurlbut W. Smith, who was president of Smith-Corona when he died in 1951.

He wanted me to know he had a wedding invitation for 213. That was Oct. 15, 1889, when his great uncle, who later became one of the community's greatest industrialists and civic leaders, married Mina Glazier.

Mina was the daughter of John and Theresa Glazier, who may have been the first owners of 213.

I looked through a crack in a sheet of plywood the other day and tried to imagine the wedding ceremony in the front parlor. Followed by a reception in the yard, next to the rose bush.

I had a hard time doing that. H.H. Smith was going to get back to me with some more information on his kin and 213, but he died a few weeks ago.

Elizabeth Barnett of Liverpool got in touch with me, too. Elizabeth is retired as a decorator at Syracuse China. Her husband, John, is retired from Crucible.

Fifty-four years ago, Elizabeth and John moved into a furnished apartment at 213 on their wedding day.

Elizabeth wrote: "Nov. 22, 1934, we got married in the St. John the Evangelist Church and that day we moved into 213 Gifford St. It was a furnished apartment. The building had furnished apartments.

"We had a little kitchen and bed and living room combined and paid $4.50 a week. A Mrs. Richards was the landlord.

"We lived in the upstairs front apartment and upstairs it had one bathroom for three apartments. Next door it had a building with three outside steps. It looked like Brooklyn, N.Y.

"On the corner of West and Gifford was Rothchild's drug store; on Granger and Gifford was the lithographer; down the street was Remington typewriter. At West and Gifford was Nojaim's. Where the apartments are now was the A&P store.

"It was a nice, clean building. We had fun in those days. Work was scarce. My husband worked one or two days a week (for the city) and I worked three or four days (at Syracuse China). It was tough living.

"Some weeks we had $1.50 to live on. We walked up and down Salina Street. The people were more friendly then."

Elizabeth and John lived about a year and a half at 213. They have a lot of good memories of the place, Elizabeth told me when I called her to talk about the letter she sent me. The neighborhood was beautiful then, she said; so were the neighbors.

One thing she wanted to tell me about that little apartment was the secondhand radio the Barnetts bought in 1934. John had to run a wire out the window to get it to work so they could bring in Eddie Cantor and Lowell Thomas.

I asked Elizabeth if she'd seen 213 recently. She had. "We went down and took pictures of it. To remember it," she said.

Another piece of the history of the house was provided by Nancy Pizzuti of Syracuse. Nancy said she was born at 213.

"It was my grandmother's house," Nancy explained. "She owned it for five or six years in the 1940s and rented rooms and apartments to people. Her name was Alexina Duhamel. She lived in a downstairs apartment and my mother and father lived upstairs. I think there were two other couples up there. It was all families that lived there.

"There was a smaller brick house next door in those days. I remember the lady had a Boston terrier. And I remember sitting on the porch of my grandmother's house and watching my mother walk up the street to Rothchild's."

When I got back to the office, I found out 213 and the lot next door, which holds an old brick carriage house, have a new owner. He plans to rehabilitate both buildings. There will be apartments again at 213.

(Two years later the house burned.)                    —*1988*

---

## SO BIG

Two things Ted Frey is soft about—dogs and flowers.

That's why you see this hand-lettered sign, inside a picture frame, nailed to a piece of pine among the zinnias is Ted's front yard in the 1600 block of Lodi Street.

"This garden was planted in loving memory of So Big. To every one who has lost a pet."

"So Big" was a liver-colored beagle who had lived with Ted in the old brick house for 10½ years. He was this man's best friend and when he died last November, Ted felt he had to do something nice for his pal. Naturally, he thought of flowers because "Biggie," Ted's pet name for his pet, liked them too.

"He spent a lot of time up in that window, looking out at the garden and the street," Ted said, pointing to the second floor north. "When I was working on the flowers, he was always out here with me or he'd sit on the sidewalk and look up the street."

The memorial garden—actually two small plots on either side of the walk into the house—was a good idea, as well, because Ted has had his green thumb going at the yard for about as long as he had "So Big." He told me he decided to brighten up the neighborhood just for the love of flowers.

"I really like flowers," Ted said while he was weeding. "It's my hobby, a way of relaxing. I enjoy other people enjoying them."

Most of Ted's neighbors seem to feel Lodi's bright blossoms are better seen where they are, than in someone's fist or flower vase. Ted doesn't have too much trouble with pickers, although he did have to politely turn down one merchant neighbor who wanted to know if he could pick one of the flowers each day.

"Actually," Ted said, "the only trouble I've had was with the statue."

This spring, when the seeds went in, Ted also bought himself a life-sized concrete beagle as part of the memorial. He set it out in the garden and the next thing he knew someone ripped it off.

"I advertised in the paper and a woman called me and said two kids on bicycles had dropped it in her yard It weighs 50 pounds; I wonder how they did it. Anyway, I got it back, but I keep it inside now."

Ted, as an urban gardener, started his flower patches by adding a little top soil to the turf of the North Side but that's all he gave to the plots, beyond plenty of TLC. "I don't use any sprays or fertilizers, don't believe in them. But everything comes along nice. You should have been here when the roses were in bloom."

He got to talking about dogs and it didn't take long to see how Ted felt about his. He went into the house and brought out the photo album he kept about "So Big" to show me. It was the kind some people might use for baby pictures. Lots of snaps of "So Big"—sitting in his favorite chair, wrapped up in his blanket, at the table—along with newspaper and magazine articles and poems about dogs Ted saved.

Ted's finger reached out and touched one of the pictures.

"That's the last picture I have of him," he said. "Taken last August."

We talked some more and it turned out that "So Big" was a sort of neighborhood celebrity, up there around the Roma Bakery. People especially liked the way he was always in the window; maybe it made them fell secure to know that while a lot of things were changing around them, a few pieces of the landscape stood still, wagging their tails. That's why some of the neighbors come by and pause in front of Ted's house these days, looking at the flowers instead of "So Big."

"He was a different dog, that's for sure," Ted was saying. "Everybody knew him. All the kids. They were always stopping by and asking about him."

Ted knows he'll probably never get to own a hound as good as "So Big" but he is thinking about buying a pup, the way he bought "Biggie," one of these days. Meanwhile, he has "Tammy," a female beagle, waiting for him when he comes home from work as a private mail deliverer.

"Tammy" was sitting there on the sidewalk, in "Biggie's" favorite spot, while we talked. She looked a little like a beagle Buddha, but she seemed to be smiling, looking up at us.

"She's my old lady," Ted said.

There also is a poem on the sign Ted made for memorial garden, next to the plastic windmill and the pink flamingo. It's called "Old Dogs Do Not Die" and Ted copied it out of a dog magazine. It tells how a master never forgets his best friend, even if the dog has died, the way "So Big" did.

This is the way the poem ends:

"And only I can see you swim, In every brook I pass. When I call you no one but I can see the bending grass."

In the city, grass bends many ways, but nowhere quite the way it does at 1610 Lodi.                                                      *—1979*

---

# EARL

One thing everybody says about Earl Johnson. He was quiet. Mature for his 16 years, caring, responsible, respectful of his parents, unremarkable, minded his own business, did the best he could in school.

Quiet.

Earl did not strike the people who knew him as the sort of young man they would be reading about in the newspapers. A young man who would die in a flash of gun fire from a Saturday Night Special on a Saturday night in Syracuse.

Two weeks ago, Earl died on a neighbor's front lawn on Fayette Boulevard near Seeley Road. A revolver slug went into his chest in what seems to have been, at this point, a tragic accident.

A while before this happened, Earl, who was in his sophomore year at Nottingham High School, had been hanging around a superette near LeMoyne College that was the weekend meeting place for the teenagers who live between Seeley and the campus. Then he and three friends headed toward Seeley, where a party was going on.

According to the way police have reconstructed the incident, the friends stopped to talk along the way. Shortly, three young women approached on Fayette. So did a car with strangers in it. The young men in the car hollered at the girls, trying to get them to join them. They refused and moved closer to Earl and his friends.

At that point, Earl did something his friends think was uncharacteristic for him; he yelled at the strangers to leave the girls alone. Not everyone I talked to about his agreed, though. One of his teachers at Nottingham said he was just protecting the turf. He was only a block and half from home and may have recognized the strangers as from the South Side. If he did, according to the teacher, he did what she expected an East Side kid to do: tell the invaders to move on.

Instead, police said, one of them got out of the car and went for Earl. They started to fight, and when Earl, who played football and basketball and was in good shape, seemed to be getting the better of the stranger, another man piled out of the car and went at him.

Finally, another stranger emerged. He had a revolver. Shots were fired. The stranger's companions have told police the shots were intended only to scare the Nottingham students. Instead, one hit Earl and he staggered about 100 yards and dropped. The strangers, all of them, jumped in the car and drove away.

They claimed later, when they turned themselves in to police the next day, that no one in the car knew the shots had hit anyone.

Earl lay mortally wounded on the grass. Another stranger, this one an angel of mercy, came up and ripped open his shirt. She tried to keep Earl's heart pumping until the ambulance got there. Everyone struggled to hold on to Earl but he died at the hospital.

The next Monday morning at Nottingham few people talked about anything but the shooting. Some of them talked with tears in their eyes. All of them were asking WHY?

"Why? Why this kid?" Willetta Spease was saying that to me last week when we talked about Earl. She was his physical education teacher the past two years. To some at Nottingham, before that Saturday night, Earl might have been "just a face in the crowd," as one teacher put it.

To Mrs. Spease, he was a very special face.

She told me she couldn't answer her question but that didn't stop Earl's friends at Nottingham from asking it. Tragic coincidence was about all they can come up with. Earl was in the wrong place at the wrong time.

And there was a gun in that wrong place. Maybe if the strangers had been carrying a ball bat instead of a gun, Earl would have been in gym that first period Monday instead of the morgue.

His teacher was thinking about the Friday before.

"Earl usually was very quiet," Mrs. Spease said. "You know, the kind of kid you notice because he's so quiet and make a note to try to draw him out. He was a unique student in that way. Always on time, always prepared, always willing to get going and cooperate.

"That Friday before he was unusually outgoing, though. Smiling and enjoying himself. We played flicker ball and he was laughing all the time when he missed. After class, I said to him, 'Earl, you're having a lot of fun this year. I'm so glad.' He smiled. He was a super kid!"

Mike Conroy is a city police investigator assigned to Nottingham. The school's cop on the beat works in civies and he knew Earl. Quiet was the word Mike used. Never a problem. Never been in trouble with the police. They used to talk about sports when they met in the lunch room.

"You should have been here Monday morning," Mike told me. "A pall hung over the school. In the cafeteria, it was so quiet you could hear the pots and pans rattling."

"Big Sam" Noel, one of the school's hall monitors, was out on the street the night Earl was killed. His nephew was with Earl and he had to check on him. Monday morning, Sam could see the way the kids reacted to the tragic weekend. Another schoolmate, a young woman with a brain tumor, had died between Friday and Monday.

"You could see them walking with tears in their eyes," "Big Sam" said. "Black and white students. Hey, it's a life, buddy."

Tears, but no hate, apparently. Mrs. Spease didn't find any hate for the killer and she didn't expect to.

"Our kids are not that type," she said. "They know how to handle this thing without violence."

On Friday, the day of Earl's funeral, the school was quiet again. The tabernacle on Oakwood Avenue was so crowded with young, sad faces that it was standing-room-only. More than half of the mourners who came to say goodbye to Earl were from Nottingham.

Kevin, Earl's buddy, was in the church. All he could think of was it might have been him. He was with Earl at the superette but he headed home, the way Earl did sometimes, because his parents wanted him there for a family get-together.

"An all-right kid" was the way Kevin described his friend to me last week. He liked sports and played JV football and freshman basketball. Didn't say much to people but had a good sense of humor when it came to ribbing his friends. Liked music and was a sympathetic listener. And responsible, Kevin said. Earl was very responsible, to his family and friends.

He told me about the baby daughter Earl and his girlfriend, who attends another city high school, had last summer. The pregnancy, he said, was a shock, but his friend dealt with it like a 16-year-old kid going on 36.

"He really cared about that baby," Kevin said. "He wanted to stay in school and graduate so he could save money and take care of the baby."

Earl's middle name was Tyrous. His baby was named Tyonna.

*—1982*

---

# MARY

There are times—many times—when Mary, who lives in the city, wishes she did not.

Those are the times she thinks about how it was when she was younger and lived in Marathon where her family owned a big house and she had an uncle listed in "Who's Who." Her cousins bought them a pony and loneliness was something to be read about in the books.

"Do you like to pick strawberries?" she will ask. "Oh, we loved to do that down around Marathon. And blackberries. I learned how to milk a cow. Yeah."

No strawberries here, where Mary lives in a downstairs flat at the edge of downtown. She has just tuned 65, a widow and pensioner, and the fields here, such as they are, seem more battle than pasture.

Mary will recall, without much prompting, about the man who was killed one night right across the street. Stuck a butcher knife into him, they did.

Or the time, when her husband was alive, when they fire-bombed the house, tossing Molotov cocktails onto the front porches and scaring the hell out of everyone.

For 18 months after her husband died, and before she got the dog, she slept days and stayed awake all night, for self-protection.

A neighbor two doors down, a woman in her 80s, had it worse. They broke into her house and bombed from the inside.

"I don't like the city," Mary said. "You're afraid to go out, even go downtown. It costs me $5 for a cab to go downtown and get my checks cashed. It's an awful way to live."

There are ways to cope, though. The house, brown and one step from a lot, is a fortress, looking inward. The signs on the front porch, "No Trespassing," "Beware of Dog," are the city's signs. The postman goes to the back door where a gray-white German shepherd is tied to the porch of the empty house on the half lot. His name is Baron and he barks a lot.

The back door to the kitchen is always latched and inside, Mary is hunkered in the back four rooms to save heat for the winter. It's enough, she says. I'll make do. God won't give you any more than you need.

She is tucked in from the battle here, but like a true fortress, there must be an ear and Mary's is her police scanner, tiny red rectangles of light bubbling through the city's circulation system looking for trouble.

"Car 51—boy friend, girl friend fight . . ."

The radio is on the nightstand next to her bed. She has a jigsaw puzzle on the bedspread, partly done. There's a target pistol—loaded—next to that, and a club on the floor.

"Signal 78," the radio voice says. It is flat, matter of fact, dealing with other people's problems. Just then, somebody needs an ambulance.

Mary says it keeps her in touch. She's a good police reporter. She knows who the cops are and what they are up to.

"Hear about that guy who landed his balloon in somebody's parking lot the other night?" she asks.

After Marathon, Mary spent a number of years in Key West, Fla., where she often took a plane across the ocean and spent the weekend in Havana. She came back to the area in 1952 and has rented the flat for the past 25 years. The people in back moved out and the old woman upstairs died and now the house is hers, as long as the check comes through to pay the rent.

A friend, husband of a woman she knew who died, looks in on her every day and helps with getting out (she uses a walker), fetching groceries and showing that someone cares how she's making out.

"Oh," Mary says, "I know what it is to be lonely."

A lot of little things keep her going.

Mary's radio continues to profile the city "Check a robbery at the store . . . employee is supposed to be chasing the robber . . ."

Mary counts several policemen her friends but she is wary, these days, about calling them if trouble signals. She got into trouble once doing that and they had her in Hutchings.

"You see a lot of things, but you don't dare call the police. They want people to cooperate and then they call you crazy. People are afraid to say anything, anyway. They'll firebomb your house and then have you examined."

Toughing it out is better, according to Mary and she has a few scars from the jagged edge of a bottle in a bar to document that. When thugs come to the back door, trying to fast-talk their way in, she'll put the dog on them and remind them how it might feel to have a shotgun doing emergency surgery.

"Oh," she says, dragging on her Kool, "they tell me I ought to move. But it's safer here than on the North Side. At least, here, you know what you've got."

Red lights dance next to the bed. "Car 59, they're holding a purse snatch. . ."

—*1979*

---

# BLACKIE

Blackie sits on his granite ledge over the news stand, knowing he owns Warren Street.

Almost as good a time as when he was a squeaker and supped on mother's milk in the spires of the cathedral.

Now he knows all he has to do is bide his time and Mike will be out with a fresh bag of Planter's, salted. He knows the one-legged pigeon has made love to the territory and won.

Blackie pulls himself in against the cold. He looks down at the turf and registers the street's piffle. The bankers and their secretaries go in and out, taking back cigars and Gothic romances. Some of the old men want their tip sheets; others are troubled by the late arrival of the dailies.

"Hey, got anything on homosexual turtles?" a man in a black vinyl hat with earflaps asks.

The door flies open and a bum is rushed out.

Humanity ebbs and flows here year around, and Blackie roosts the landscape, part of it, yet distantly observing. Once, last summer, when he came to lunch one man had another on the sidewalk, punching him and tearing at his shirt.

Another time, an old lady tripped on the edge of the sidewalk and an ambulance was called. Nights, when he and the other rock doves hug the walls, trying to pull out heat, they watch the hookers grazing across the street, see the cars from Elbridge cruising.

The perch is clear; he is alone. Down in the vestibule, Mike appears and snaps the bag.

"Hey, Blackie, lunch time."

Mike Zaretsky knows some of his clients think he is crazy. But he and his son, also Mike, want to take care of their one-legged pigeon. Winter and summer, they call him down for lunch on bags of peanuts from Wally's News Stand.

"He's really funny, a real character," Mike said of his pet. "He's here almost every day, usually about the same time. He sits on the perch over the door and when we go out and call him, he comes down. He knows what's going on, and so do the other pigeons.

"I'd like to know who said pigeons are dumb. Why, there's this other one, now he's got both legs, but he tucks one up and walks from side to side just like Blackie. Because he knows that's a way of getting fed. Who says pigeons are dumb?"

None of his friends on Warren Street know how Blackie lost his leg but they can guess; the traps. The city tries to bait them into the snares on rooftops because some people count Blackie and others of his Columbidae family a nuisance in the city.

Maybe 30 a week are gathered in this way and then taken to be gassed. Of course, if pigeons are not dumb, Blackie knew about the DPW incinerators. He knew he could learn to balance on the one pink limb that matched his eyes; he knew his wings were strong.

Another day Mike Jr. is working the front counter. Blackie has just hopped in from the sidewalk to eat before he is flushed by customers and other pigeons.

"One day I went to noon Mass at the Cathedral and he followed me back to the store," Mike said. "We started giving him peanuts and now he just keeps coming back. And before that there was another Blackie and he only had one leg, too."

His father comes up from the back with a stack of women's magazines. "Did you see him?"

"Yeah. He ate and ran before the bigger ones got to the peanuts. That's pretty good chow."

"Sure, Blackie goes first class. We do a lot of business for the peanut people."

Blackie is back over the door, observing again. The tiny eyes dart, recording the familiar heads: the cop from the corner, the women with the transparent plastic shopping bags, three-piece suits from the office towers, nuns, a jogger in a blue sweatsuit, the young man with a frozen beard and armload of library books.

At the far end of Warren, Martha probably has seeded Hanover Square, over the old public toilets. She has her weekly ration of cracked corn for Blackie's relatives who live downtown. But no one up there has this creature's steady meal.

The other way, in St. Mary's Circle near the fountain, a covey has spotted a leftover pretzel bag from a window ledge of the church where the bishop prays. In the city there is always a dole or people to be picked up after.

Is it in thanks that they leave that grimy souvenir in the snow?

This time around Blackie is gone, perhaps to nap against the stone columns, out of the cold, and listen to the cooing of the prayerful in the pews.

"He'll be back," says Mike behind the counter.                              —*1979*

---

# FOXY

Foxy came to Syracuse to look for work. She put on her good clothes and started walking along Warren Street at night, when autumn began to nip.

One night, about 9:30, she was heading north, not far from the big, stone cathedral. She was in a friendly mood, waving at cars as they moved through the corridor where cleaning women had just about finished tidying up after the bankers.

Herb drove by and she waved at him. He stopped. Foxy ran up to the car.

"Wanna have a good time?" Foxy asked.

Herb said sure and they negotiated for a while. Then he showed her a badge he carries and arrested her for prostitution.

Foxy missed her Good Time that night. She went with Herb to the Public Safety Building and was booked.

Foxy didn't give her real name for the arrest report. She said she was 19 and self-employed. The address she gave was a rooming house on West Onondaga, which police had heard of before.

"White female, 100 pounds, brown hair and eyes."

Foxy was pleasant enough with her captors. Said they didn't need to worry, she was clean, had a regular health check. They thought she seemed a little young, but Foxy had an answer for that. This guy kidnapped her in Rochester and forced her to turn tricks for him.

The next morning Foxy went to Police Court and was ordered held for a visit to the VD clinic. After that, she'd probably be released on bail, or pay a fine, and could be back looking for work again in a day or two.

Meanwhile, a man called the police department's Youth Division. He said he was looking for his sister; she'd run away again and was under age. He didn't sound like her brother.

Some calls were made and finally officers figured out that Foxy hadn't been exactly leveling with them.

There was a missing person alert out on her from Rochester. When they checked with that police department, they found out Foxy had been on the street looking for work there, too, and had been arrested.

"Sure, we know her," one of the Rochester cops said. "Send her home."

Herb wasn't too surprised. The vice squad was arresting an average of 15 women a week in downtown Syracuse and some of them seemed pretty young. Three years ago, Herb, who is balding and has been a cop a long time, arrested one that was 12 years old.

He guessed, afterward, that Foxy didn't look 19. Maybe 17.

Sometimes, if they look their age, vice men don't bother arresting a girl who beckons them. They try to get in touch with the family and send her home.

Pretty soon, they see them back on Warren Street.

"Street children," says Sgt. Cathy McAvoy of the Youth Division.

The street empties them into the Public Safety Building offices and the cops try to sort them out. Sometimes they remember names, faces; sometimes faces blur like photo finishes.

One they remember was Little Bit, another visitor looking for work She was arrested three times in Syracuse in 1976 and 1977. Later that year there were warrants on her for parole violation but by that time Little Bit was on the Coast, running after the horizon.

Pleasant enough kid, too. "A nice girl," one cop said of the young woman he arrested for prostitution. "I liked her."

Next thing he knew there was a story about Little Bit in the newspaper. This time it used her real name, Jill. Her body was found on the side of a dirt road in Los Angeles. She had been sexually assaulted and beaten on the face with a rock. Police suspected the "Hillside Strangler."

Little Bit was 17.

"You can't keep them in school if they don't want to be there," Sgt. McAvoy said of her street children.

"All they have to do is tell one school they're transferring to another, but they never go. So they're never picked up as truants."

Then a pimp kidnaps them and they grow up waving at cars on Warren Street.

Foxy's mother was called about her missing child and later that day, she showed up at the Youth Division to take her back to Rochester. She was in such a hurry to get to Syracuse she didn't have time to change out of her shorts.

Yes, she said, Foxy lied about her age. She's 14.                    —*1978*

---

# A.B.C.

At night, the city's center changes moods; three-piece business to leisure suit. Sometimes, leisure is shucked for tatters.

Late, creeping to midnight in mid-January, a man with a camera is standing in front of the creche in the square. He is taking a picture of his girl friend in the glow of the nativity.

A block away, under the tinsel stars and moons, another young woman stands, pulled into a doorway against the wind. She is selling her body, starting at $20.

Maybe that's why there is a sheet over the front window of the old office building at the edge of downtown. Inside, the space looks like the dressing room for a road company. An instant hair setter, vials of make-up, combs, mirrors, shoe bags, ironed uniforms over the chairs.

The three young women, city employees all, seem to be preparing for a night on the town. Their heels are high and black, their slacks tight, the cut of the blouses low. The curls are warm and bouncy and they help each other into short fur jackets.

Each has a small service revolver tucked into her fashion belt.

Finally, they walk into the room nearby and there is a low murmur of appreciation. Forewarned, no one whistles. About 15 young men have been assembled for the night's assignment; they look like a group of friends going hunting.

But this is not a lark, the commander says. It's going to be a bitch. Keep your eyes on those girls. I don't want anything to happen to them.

Any questions? The sergeant will hand off assignments. Some of the men will be funny cars. If not, make sure you have wig-wags. And when the "john" is down, show him the tin and bust him.

Come on. Let's get this thing going.

The cars sweep among the red lights of the squares, which dance in the wind, and soon are part of the street in its leisure suit. There is a call on the radio:

"Letting the first officer off right now . . . OK, A is in place . . . B is out . . . C in place."

OK, give us your passion play, remembering that in New York State, a "john" patronizing a prostitute is committing a Class B misdemeanor.

The cars and the men blend and the women stand as close as they dare to the Warren Street facades to fetch the inner warmth and the johns. The regulars look puzzled at first, and then understanding.

Doors flick open and shut in Hanover, which has a lighted evergreen planted over the ruins of the public toilet. A woman in a frilly blouse steps onto the sidewalk from one of the doors and calls into the night:

"Hey, watch out; she's a cop."

"Looks like some competition," the radio says.

"Cripes, get those broads out of there," the commander says. "If you have to, take them on a ride to Nedrow . . ."

"Yes, sir . . . Lots of competition."

Traffic loops into Warren. It's tight, double-parked. Even some guy in a flat-bed, who keeps circling. Maybe one of the stores is having a midnight surprise sale.

"We've got one on foot . . . Stand by."

At the bank corner, where shoppers had been hours before, a young man in a hunter's jacket is spread-eagle against a car and another young man, also in hunter's jacket, is running his hands up and down his body.

Another night person walks by. A man in woman's clothing. The commander hails him but he doesn't smile.

"Hey, Lennie, what are you doing out?"

"Looking for my friend, officer . . ."

By now Hunter's Jacket is in the back seat of the police car. "Officer," he says, "I don't want to be in this position."

They are coming down fast now. It is past midnight and A, B and C have all the good lines; someone has offered B $60. But it's cold, so C takes a break in the commander's car, which suddenly fills with perfume, kicking stale coffee out the door.

"Wow," says C. "Four in one swing. My mother would be proud of me."

Meanwhile A, bracing against the window of the bank displaying its manger scene, has showed her police badge to a man and woman, who inquired if she flipped both ways.

"What did he say?" the radio voice again.

"$20."

"Take him."

Three shaggy men stalk Warren Street with coffee cups in their hands. Keeping an eye on their women.

"Chief," says the radio. "A has a problem with her toes; we're going over to OCD to get her some socks."

Shortly, A has her corner, again, white socks against black open toes. Then, in a while, B is resting, too, recharging her radio battery. The night ticks away.

*—1979*

---

# VINCE

I dropped by to see the grocer who still wants to treat people with respect, even after he's been robbed six times in three years. He's an institution in the Near Northeast neighborhood around Dr. Weeks School.

Vince Ludovico runs Ludy's Grocery at 106 Oak St. He's owned it 45 years. The turf is Ludovico. He grew up on the lot where the city built Dr. Weeks.

Last week a robber stuck a knife into Vince, grabbed some cash and ran off. Vince and a few of his neighbors chased the robber, but he got away. Vince went to the emergency room for stitches, then returned to Ludy's to cash out. He was back at the store, in his usual white shirt and tie the next day.

"It bled a little, but I'm OK," Vince said to me Wednesday. "You've got to work. That's my choice. I love the business."

Getting bumped off that way goes with the territory, according to him. Inconvenience was the word he used. Vince's 45 years as an independent grocer tell him to get stitched up, cash out and get on with it.

If you go into Vince's back room, where the beer and soda are stored under a picture of The Last Supper—and Vince draws up a chair and a cup of joe for you—it's possible to sit this far from the grocer and look into his soul.

The robber? Vince shrugged. He didn't know who the hell he was. Not a neighbor, for sure. A neighbor wouldn't knock off the neighborhood convenience store.

The only clear picture he had of him was when Vince tried to give him the elbow and the visitor sliced at his funny bone.

"I've been in the war. I've been under fire," he explained. "I looked into his eyes. He wanted to kill me. That's the way he looked at me. I could have killed him."

Now, a week later, the grocer tries to understand the man who could have murdered him for a few bucks.

"He might have a problem," Vince continued. "I wish he hadn't done it. I'd have given him the whole store. People say to me, 'Well, the bad parts of the city are coming into this neighborhood.' I don't know. They're not bad people; they're hungry people.

"Who knows what they want? Dope? Clothing? Food? I get nervous It bothers me. But times change; we've got to change with them."

Vincent Sr. and Rose Ludovico had six children, five of them sons. Vince Jr. took over his father's Mom and Pop store on Hawley Avenue when he got home from World War II. He'd been drafted right out of Christian Brothers Academy when he was 17. He considered going to LeMoyne College, but family tradition had a comfortable strength to it.

"I could have gone to college," Vince said. "I said I think I'll be a grocer."

Ludovico's store sat at 800 Hawley Ave. The Ludovicos lived upstairs. In the '70s, the city wanted to build a new elementary school and community center in the 700 and 800 blocks. Vince said he was stunned, at first.

"They said they wanted to put a school in there," he recalled. "If I didn't sell, they'd go to condemnation. That's the worst law on the books, condemnation. I got excited. I wanted to hang the assessor on a meat hook when he came in.

"But what was I going to do? I wanted to stay in the neighborhood. I sold it to 'em and bought this building I'm in now."

Any regrets?

"I accepted it," he said. "You've got to have a good education."

The school, which opened in 1977, is as much of a landmark north of Burnet Avenue as Ludy's. A while ago, the gymnasium was named for Walter Ludovico, Vince's brother who served on the City Council for years. Vince himself visited Dr. Weeks to give a talk to pupils about the small businessman.

"I stood right on the spot where I used to cut up pork chops," he told me. "And here I was, a neighborhood guy, making a speech at the school. I told them we can still go forward if we make up our minds and do it right."

Vince said he did right by the neighborhood and it did right by him. Forty-five years selling food saw many a tab made at Ludy's and many a tab left unpaid. Ludy's isn't Wegmans, the grocer pointed out, so you do what you have to do to create good will.

And the good will comes back, you bet.

"You have to treat people like people," Vince said. "Shame on us, if we can't live together."

Then, "Thank God, I'm respected."

I'll say.

Lots of neighbors heard about the robbery. They dropped in to see if Vince was OK. He told them he was; bless you for asking, he'd say.

A little girl wandered in on us as we talked. She called Vince "Poppa," wanted to show him the bandages on her hand where she'd been cut, just like Poppa had been. "I got stitches, too," she said.

"They're all my kids," Vince went on. "I got close to 70 godchildren from around here." Not all are white citizens of Italian ancestry, either.

Later, another child approached Poppa. Poppa hugged him. It was his helper Kim's son, Vincent by name.

Vincent's namesake smiled. "Someone left two babies at the house next door. Their foster mother named one of them Vincent. How about that?"

The grocer has rescued neighbors from fires. He baby-sits in the store if a mother needs to go downtown. Makes up food baskets at Christmas. If you come in for a jar of peanut butter and loaf of bread and can't pay until Friday, he'll let you leave without paying, the way he did the other day.

"Hey, I've known that man for 20 years," he said to me. "He's good for it. I don't even write it down."

Most of the robberies have been with a gun, not a knife. Once, a few years back, the piece got so close to Vince's face he could read the serial numbers.

The police caught the man. He did four years in prison. He'd been a neighbor, too; Vince knew his mother. She was a customer of his.

"Oh, the stuff I sent him in jail," the grocer recalled. "Wayne. He's a good friend now. I want to rehabilitate, not disable."

Vince won't pack a gun, the way he did in the war when he was a constable with the 78th Division in Berlin. The scars from a sniper's wound remain on his knee. He's a member of the Disabled American Veterans, but he won't let an old soldier's skepticism turn Ludy's into an arsenal.

"I was the most armed man in the army," Vince continued. "But I always remember what the priest in our unit said to me. I wanted to get a pass to see my grandmother in Italy. He said he'd sign it if I took off my weapons. He said if I had my weapons, I'd be in trouble.

"I'll never forget that. The priest was right. If you don't have something, you're not looking for something."

So, Vince lives with changes. Some go down harder than others, though. He hates the return bottle bill and resents the inspectors who make life miserable for the little business guy.

Vince thinks about retiring, turning over Ludy's to his daughter Joanne. Hey, he'll be 65 soon. I mean, he's got those rental properties. That Social Security. He could sit in a rocker in the yard of his log house in the Adirondacks, and take it easy.

"My dad left my store to me," Vince said. "I want to leave it to someone in the family, if I can. It's been a good business for me. I did well."

*—1991*

# THE ELEPHANT TREE

Burt Van Luven showed me the Elephant Tree the other afternoon. It's one of the natural wonders of Syracuse.

I got Burt going on this when I wrote about old Lodi cemetery, which is buried across Beech Street from Thornden Park. Burt, who is 71, was interested in that because he grew up a whistle away, on Bassett Street. There were 11 kids in the family and Erie Boulevard was still the Erie Canal.

Burt wrote to me about the Elephant Tree, which he climbed as a boy and carved with his initials. The last Burt saw of the landmark it stood at the northwest corner of Thornden near Madison.

He offered to point it out to me and last week Burt and his wife, Vivian, drove in from Messenger Bay to do just that.

Meanwhile, I did a bit of research at the Onondaga Historical Association. Burt had been told the public park once was the private estate of a chap named Davis. The house of the estate used to sit on the curve just past that tree. It was vacant then and the lads prowled around inside, alert for "secret passages."

It turned out Burt was right, except that the personal park was older than we suspected.

The 76 acres which became Thornden Park were assembled by a wealthy saltmaker named James Haskins. He started with 10 in 1854 and ran Thornden up to about 100.

Then he died, in 1873. No one was ever sure if he killed himself or was murdered. A servant found him bleeding to death in the bathtub, his throat cut with two razors. That might account for the ghost stories Burt heard about the Haskins place.

Haskins built an "old house in the woods" which Alexander Davis bought and added to after his friend's death. Davis was an "aristocrat" with money. His father represented Syracuse in Congress.

Davis made Thornden the arboretum it is today while he lived there, between 1875 and 1901 when he "burned his bridges" and moved to London for good. A newspaper story I found at the OHA said he was responsible for planting The Elephant Tree.

The article also gave me the tree's correct scientific name. It's a "fagus pendula," or weeping beech.

I learned The Elephant Tree—I'm going with Burt's name here—was, at the time the article appeared, 30 feet high with a 60-foot spread. It was described as the one tree in the park citizens wanted to carve initials into and perhaps the largest of its kind, anywhere.

The tree remains. Burt thought he remembered a fence around it. That's gone and it surely grew, in the 60 or so years since Burt, "Corn" and Art were all over its gray hide like a flock of wrens. The leaves weep to the ground, just like in the old days.

And it appeared to Burt and me that the Elephant Tree had spawned two new weeping beeches nearby. "Sons of beeches," as Burt pointed out.

Photographer Carl Single and I talked Burt into climbing into the first fork of his old friend for a picture.

"We've been in all these trees around here," Burt shouted, as if to Art and Corn. "We called the top up there the crow's nest. Why, once Art fell from the top. Straddled that branch right there."

Later Burt and I walked east a bit and he showed me where old man Davis' house sat. It burned in 1929, eight years after the city took the whole of Thornden from the Davis estate (he died in London in 1910) by condemnation and started making a park of it. The house was to be a community center.

The rose garden was planted in 1924; the trout pond made into an amphitheater. "That was our old swimmin' hole," Burt said.     —*1988*

---

# ABIE

They found Edward "Abie" Combs on his back next to Canal Street. A man about Abie's age was driving by around 8 a week ago Saturday morning and he saw what he thought was a man spread out on the grass near the fence along the I-690 culvert. Abie was dead, probably for hours.

Syracuse police aren't sure what happened to Abie, who was 67 and had been living in a community-based home in Naples approved by the Veterans Administration. He'd only been in Naples a month or so.

Abie was a traveling man. A wanderer, according to Ellie Havens, his daughter, who lives in Warrensburg, near where the Schroon and Hudson Rivers meet.

Abie was a Warrensburg man. He was born there and ran Abie's Taxi Service for years.

He also played the fiddle. Some people who remembered Abie's fiddling told me it was some of the grandest they'd ever heard.

Ellie hadn't seen her father in two years. Hadn't heard from him in a year. She didn't have a notion in the world where he was when the cop called and told her he was dead.

Dead on the grass next to the interstate in Syracuse? With an arm broken up near the left shoulder and bruises and nasty cuts on the left side of his body, leg to head? And his pockets full of cash? $784.70, to be exact?

"DOA Natural," the police said for the time being.

Police Lt. Tim Mumford said experience told him Abie was not hit by a car. The wounds, the condition of the clothing and the lack of any clue that the walker had met up with a motor vehicle—it all suggested a fall, then a natural shutdown of Abie's electrical system.

The medical examiner, Dr. Erik Mitchell, told investigators he found no signs of foul play at the autopsy and suspected hypothermia. That is the slowing of body processes to the point of death because of cold.

Cause of death on the death certificate wasn't filled in "pending investigation." Cause will have to wait for toxic reports, the police were told.

Abie was an alcoholic, and alcoholics are more vulnerable to hypothermia than people who are usually sober. A drunk doesn't realize something is wrong; his body doesn't know enough to protect against heat loss.

On the other hand, the Syracuse temperature reading at midnight before Abie was found was 34 degrees. There was no wind to speak of and a light drizzle of rain. It warmed to 44 degrees by 8 a.m.

It's hard to figure what Abie was doing there on Canal Street, since no one has been located who saw him after he arrived in town late Friday afternoon by Greyhound bus from Canandaigua. The telephone pole marking the spot where he died is 1½ blocks east of the bus station.

You could speculate for hours about whether he was walking toward the depot or away from it. The cops checked the bars nearby but were told that man hadn't been seen at any of them.

Abie had been living at the Landmark Retreat in Naples since he was released Jan. 8 from the Veterans Administration Medical Center in Canandaigua. He was at the hospital about a week, checking in the day after New Year's Eve.

Investigators found out he went to the bank Friday morning and closed out his account. He told the woman who runs the retreat he wanted to see relatives in Syracuse. She didn't know he didn't have relatives in Syracuse. He left his clothes behind in Naples.

Abie took the bus to Syracuse at 1:30 p.m. He knew the way. He had stayed at the Rescue Mission before, the last time in March 1985. This time he didn't check in anywhere, as far as anyone knows.

His daughter doesn't know, but nothing about her dad's life surprised her anymore.

Syracuse? Rochester? Albany? Florida? Who could say where Abie's feet were dragging him?

The last address Ellie had for him was another half-way house in Branchport. He left there a year ago last December. He had been home to Warrensburg about two years ago.

"That was Dad's way," Ellie explained. "He never stopped in one place too long. When this happened I had no idea where he was. I tried to write to him and talk to him on the phone every opportunity I had, but he'd just disappear. He was a sick man; alcohol got the best of him."

Abie's daughter didn't know her father very well. She is 24. She was 7 or 8 when Abie and her mother split. It was the drinking that did it, she said. He was a different man liquored-up than he was sober.

Ellie does remember her dad's gift for music. He could play just about any instrument there was, including the piano. Had a nice singing voice, too.

"He was a very talented man," she said. "He could have gone a long way except for alcohol."

Abie had the magic in Warrensburg, an Adirondack village of about 3,000 where aviator Floyd Bennett used to live. When I asked some of the villagers about him last week, the only answer I got was, sure, Abie, the fiddler. He was one of the good ones.

There used to be plenty of fiddling in the Adirondacks. Warrensburg was a logging town and loggers loved music. Abie played and sang at the gin mills and restaurants with the likes of the Fuller boys, Maxine Keith, Tex Roberts and Dave Culver.

Abie could play the fiddle under his chin, on his hip or under a chair. "Any place you wanted him to play," according to Chuck Bederian, a townsman from the old days. "Abie could play just about anything there was. Except I never knew him to play blow instruments. Drums, piano, guitar, banjo, fiddle; Old Abie could play anything."

Chuck especially remembered the weekend nights Abie and old Tex Roberts—Tex being one of the hottest woman fiddlers there was—

would get up on the roof of the Esso station there in Warrensburg and play for square dancing right on the blacktop pavement.

He was a dandy man in Warrensburg, Abie Combs was.

Ellie is having a hard time with her father's death. A chunk of hope fluttered out of her life when Abie's heart stopped beating next to Canal Street the other night.

"I'm 24 years old and I never knew Dad," she said. "He'd come home once in a while but he was usually drunk and I just couldn't have him at my house. Then he'd up and leave. He'd call and write for a while and then he'd stop. I couldn't chase him all over.

"I have two small children who never knew their grandfather. I always had a ray of hope we'd get to know him but it's too late now."

Ellie wanted to know everything I knew about Abie's death, which wasn't much. Her friend John Alexander, the funeral director who buried her father, tried to get some information from the medical examiner's office but couldn't, even though he used to work in Syracuse.

John told Ellie he thought Abie might have been sideswiped by a car, perhaps from behind.

"We're just waiting to hear something," Ellie said. "There are too many 'ifs' and 'ands' in this. I loved him dearly; I hope he knew that. I want to know why he's gone."                                     —*1988*

---

# MEL

The kids told me when I got home the other night; Mel had been hit by a bus. He was dead.

Melvin R. Antone was a free spirit of the city's South Side. A colorful figure of the neighborhood, you might say. We'll miss him.

Tuesday, Mel had gotten on the 8:03 Centro, northbound from Nedrow. Fellow passengers told police after Mel was dead he appeared intoxicated to them. It was not unusual for Mel to appear to be intoxicated.

The cops determined Mel took a seat behind the driver. As the bus approached the Interstate 81 exit ramp, he stood up and told the driver he wanted to get off. The driver said he couldn't get off at the ramp, which ran next to the house where he had a room.

The bus stopped at the next cross street. Mel started to leave, taking his time about it. Two riders saw him standing on the sidewalk. The driver pulled back into traffic and the next thing the passengers knew, Mel had fallen under the wheels.

He died of a heart attack. He was 57 last April.

Mel was an Oneida Indian from Canada. He moved to Onondaga County about a dozen years ago from Oneida Settlement, the reserve near London in southwestern Ontario. He told his friend, Ray Elm, his wife kicked him out because of his drinking.

Ray is Oneida, too. He lives at Onondaga. Ray told me Thursday that Mel was a friend of his, although they were better friends when Mel first came to live at the Onondaga Nation.

Mel was a carpenter. A pretty good one, according to his friend.

"When he first came down, I figured we had a good one here. He wanted to work as a carpenter and he had some jobs. He was a smart man, in some ways. He talked good. Talked good Oneida, too. We'd talk Oneida.

"He stayed with his relatives at first. Then he was drinking pretty good, and they got sick of it. Told him to get out. He went downtown to live."

Mel's turf roughly extended from the Brighton neighborhood of Salina Street to the Onondaga Nation territory. Here he spent a lot of time hitting people up for money. He did it with a mixture of humor and graciousness which made him few enemies.

"He was a gentleman, even when he was drunk," Ray said. "He never bothered anybody."

After Mel gave up on carpentry, he was a man of the streets. He owned a mattress, but often slept in doorways and front yards. Two of his pads were the city park near my house and the alcove of the old bakery shop, next to the bank. Sometimes when he stopped to catch a few winks, neighbors worried about him and called the Rescue Mission wagon.

Mel was looked after but not cured by the social workers. He had a streak of independence which might have been explained by what many pints of Richard's White do to the brain cells.

You could set a clock by Mel. I often passed him on my way to work, moving slowly south on Salina, toward Nedrow. The plastic bag he used to collect empty soda cans dragged behind him. His chin was sunk deep into his chest.

"He was sure-footed and slow," his friend Pete Farsaci at Pete's Barber Shop said to me Thursday. Mel liked to duck into the shop near the turnpike to get out of the weather and tease Pete a little. Pete teased back.

"He said he wanted to get his hair styled," Pete said. "How much? I said it would be $5.50. He said no, he had a place he went where it cost him $18."

Mel roamed. He did Pete, and Jean Wright at Valley Package Liquors next door. Summers, he'd hit the ballgames at Meachem Field across the way. Or he'd rest under a tree along Salina and wait for the kids to get out of school so he could ask them for money.

Sometimes the kids gave it to him. Sometimes they took up collections among themselves for their pal.

One time Pete asked Mel how much mileage he got out of his shoes. Three months, he replied.

The last several weeks, Mel's friends of the street worried more about him than they had before. They thought he looked too thin. One neighbor couple took him out to eat. He seemed to have trouble getting up and down steps to the shops. The forward motion was less sure than it had been.

Still, Pete said he was shocked when he heard about the accident.

"He was like a politician who knows everybody and everybody knows him," the barber said. "He never made any waves. The guy enjoyed himself."

Mel was taken back to the Oneida reserve Thursday. He will be buried Saturday afternoon in the yard of the First Oneida Baptist Church near Mount Brydges. There to see him off will be Robin, David, Connie, Leona, Jasmine, Jane, Janice, Roderick, Marilyn, Roswell, Wallace and Roxanne Antone, his 12 kids.        —*1988*

---

# THE GUILFOILS

The New York Central Railroad rode the shoulders of downtown Syracuse 30 years. The main line east to west was raised from Washington Street in 1935. In 1965, they tore up the elevated. After a while, I-690 was put down.

The Central line had 13 tracks. The 14th was down the embankment from the right-of-way, at 501 Burnet Ave. The Depot, by name. In the old days, when the trains were running, the bar at the corner of Howard was "the 14th track."

The railroad is gone but The Depot carries on. Even the real depot —the train station—died and turned into a bus terminal. The Depot survived as a working landmark.

The green and white sign that hangs over the sidewalk reads "Guilfoil's Depot Grill."

Inside are the Guilfoils who work the landmark; Helena and her son, Michael, who is known as "Mickey," or sometimes Mickey Jr." They have been going at this corner 42 years.

Mickey Sr. was Michael Francis Patrick Guilfoil, who seems to have been one of the grandest men ever to live in this town, in stature and stature of reputation. Mickey died in his sleep the day after Christmas 1964. According to Mickey Jr., his father was called "King of the Taxi Cabs" in Syracuse. He was an independent.

Also, according to his son, Mickey was drawing green beers in Syracuse long before that other chap started his St. Patrick's Day custom on Tipp Hill. Mickey Jr. and Helena are very precise about the day, in fact. It was March 17, 1945, the saint's day after they took over The Depot, which was, in fact, Aug. 10, 1944.

Mickey's widow well remembers opening day, after Himself had bought the business from the Burns family. The Depot goes way back, as a bar and a building. Mickey Jr. knows for sure it used to be down the street, westerly, and was moved to its present location.

Anyway, Helena said, "I was pregnant for our daughter the day we opened up. I remember that. I also remember we took in $50 the first two hours. We were amazed we made that much money."

Helena still comes to work at The Depot. She is 74 and does not believe it is a good idea to sit around thinking about how old you are. How old she is isn't reflected in the spirit that shines out of Helena's face. She comes in early and makes chili, goulash, roast beef sandwiches and hamburgers for lunch.

"Nothing fancy," she said.

There is nothing fancy about The Depot, really. It is one of our last family-operated corner bars. Two rooms and a kitchen, apartments upstairs. Dart boards and a jar of pickled eggs, a quarter each. There is a toy train set, modeled on the DL&W, above the bar. Mickey Jr. bought that for his dad 32 years ago. Just below are two framed photographs, at either side of the mirror. Franklin Roosevelt on your left, John F.

Kennedy to your right.

"Big Mike cried like a baby the day he died," Helena said of FDR. "He loved that grand old man!"

There is a likeness of Himself too. A drawing done by a Depot patron after Mickey died and then put into a frame with a small cross of Palm Sunday fronds and one of Mickey's lucky shamrocks. The King of the Taxi Cabs was drawn in his fedora, which made him look so much like his dear friend, Frank Costello, mayor of Syracuse.

The Mayor was a large man with a capacity for many pints. He drank at The Yates too. Helena said without any effort at all she could see Himself and The Mayor over there at a table in the corner "talking about the old days."

The portrait hangs at the crest of the doorway into the dining room. It is in black and white, which is unfortunate, in a way, because Mickey was such a colorful guy. Helena sees to it that this lack is corrected at least once a year on St. Patrick's Day when one of her husband's green bow ties is attached under the portrait's chin.

Oh, I said. He wore a green bow tie on St. Patrick's Day?

"And a green suit, green shoes, green cane," Helena said. "Don't forget his green topper," Mickey Jr. said. "And then he'd parade down Warren Street and up Salina in his green," his mother said. "And I'm sure making a stop or two along the way."

I was ready to guess that Michael Francis Patrick was born in Ireland when Helena said no, Rome. Rome, N.Y. Yes, his parents were from Over There. Helena is from Pennsylvania. Mickey ran cabs first, before he went into the saloon business. He kept a cab or two after that. Mickey Jr. hacked it for 10 years.

The Depot was one of those places where a free lunch once was served at the bar. Oh, the bean sandwiches and the hot dogs they used to put away at 501 Burnet! That was before the liquor authority said no, you have to charge for food.

The place opens at 8— "Good morning, Mickey; a bit of an eye-opener, if you would" —and closes at 2 the next morning. When the trains were going past the roof at 501 (coal soot may still be found in the attic window frames), there were plenty of railroad men at The Depot. Then it was the kids from SU. Now it's, well, a middling-aged group of mostly regulars who play a lot of darts and yak about winning the lottery and buying fishing boats in Tampa.

"It's mostly the same people, 365 days a year," Mickey Jr. said.

"Decent customers. Like a family. If someone's in trouble, they help out. We have a Guilfoil's Athletic and Social Club here. Every year, we give a $500 scholarship for college. When we need to have the walls washed in here, everybody pitches in.

"Some of the people have been coming in for years."

Mickey Jr. mentioned one very steady patron, Eddie, who is retired from the post office. Mickey and Helena do not believe Eddie has missed a day coming to The Depot since they opened in 1944.

*—1987*

---

# CLARK

Consider Clark Morehouse, the man in the white apron and matching sneakers sitting in the Rescue Mission dining room, where he appears to be a small place of tranquility in a building with a permanent hangover.

Clark's eyes are closed; he is playing Chopin on an old upright Claredon piano.

The Rescue Mission is not a place you expect to find a former sales executive, who once owned his own company, playing Chopin on the piano.

Clark smiled as I pulled up a chair.

"A little rusty, huh?"

"I'm no music critic. Sounds pretty good to me and your audience seems to enjoy it."

"People seem to like to have music while they're eating and so they don't mind if I sit down and practice when I have time. People like it, except some of my friends who want me to 'play Melancholy Baby.' I'm not much on that kind of music. I like classical."

"Adds a little class to the joint."

Clark lives at the Mission and works for his room and board in the dining room, three servings a day. He's there because he's down on his luck right now—out of a job—and making music at the old upright makes him feel good. The Mission is a place where it pays to feel good, especially if you look around and see someone who is worse off than you are.

Clark pointed to a shadow figure with a cane walking down the hallway behind us. "That's my friend. He started drinking again and got beat up pretty bad the other night. They beat him up and took his money."

Clark knows what it's like out there and he doesn't want to go back.

"I'm 14 years off booze and 13 off smoking," he said, with the confidence of a man who found out the hard way the difference between a glass of good cheer and a fifth of poison.

"A friend told me I shouldn't try to do both at the same time and I didn't and it worked out fine. You'd have to tie me down to get me to take a drink now."

Clark hadn't been near a piano for more than 20 years when he came back to Syracuse some time ago looking for work. He settled into the Mission and one day, out for a walk, he passed Onondaga Music.

"I looked at that sheet music and decided to take a chance and see if I could still play. I bought some and started playing. Actually, I was quite surprised. It came easier than I thought. It all came back."

Actually, Clark explained, he spent about 15 years of his youth studying the piano while he was growing up in Utica and Lake Placid. When he was in prep school one of his teachers had played with Les Brown and the pupil got so good that the two of them used to hire out to play for civic groups.

After high school, Clark attended St. Lawrence University, where he earned a degree in chemistry and zoology. At graduation, he went into naval aviation, flying Navy planes onto aircraft carriers for six years after the Korean War.

Following discharge, he worked as a sales executive for several chemical companies and had a home on Long Island. He also started his own photographic company in Florida, got married and raised three children.

In time, however, booze took its toll of man and marriage. By the time Clark was succeeding in an alcoholic rehabilitation program, his wife, he says, "had had enough of me." They divorced. He sometimes talks with his children by phone but hasn't seen them in some time.

A bell rang and chow line was beginning to form in the dining room, where Clark had just cleaned up after breakfast. There were pea soup and sandwiches for lunch and residents walked in looking for fuel to help them through another day of sobriety.

Clark put his hands down and started playing again. This time it was Debussy that came out.

He stopped for a minute and looked around. Everybody seemed to be eating soup.

"You know, it takes a tremendous amount of practice to do this well," he said. "I'm glad there's a piano here because I can come in when I'm not working and play. I'll never play with the symphony, but I will stick with it."

Clark closed his eyes and nodded back into the notes. The sound was soft.                                                                     *—1980*

---

# THE BIG, GRAY FUTURE-MAKER

The big, gray future-maker with the blue curtains and the red throttle sat there at the west end of the Davis greenhouse all day. For 15 hours, the Automatic Voting Machine sucked up all the attention in that space.

Hey, babe, I will tell you who the next mayor of Syracuse will be.

So it did.

At 9 Tuesday night, the door to the polling place of Ward 8, District 7, was locked. The coffee maker placed in a shopping bag. The blue curtains folded up. The American flag unstuck from the overhead door. The front of the machine closed and locked, and the two back sections, closed and locked. The seal removed from the lid of the pizza carton.

Then "Moon" Gilmartin opened yet another panel and started reading the numbers, column 1 to column 13. He moved through the dull stuff like a Democratic ward chairman who wanted his old friend's son to be elected. They wanted the stats back at the satellite headquarters pronto.

"5-A," he said. His nephew, Marty Masterpole, 12, put the count onto one of the sample ballots. "5-A, 296 . . . 5-B, 119 . . ."

5-A was his old friend's son, Tom Young, Bocko's kid. Our new mayor. 5-B was the other guy, a candidate who would be interesting to Moon only if he had more votes than 5-A. If Moon's man didn't hit one out of the greenhouse, Moon might as well fold. Ward 8, District 7 is Bocko turf. Tom's old man is dead many years, yet he is all over Tipperary Hill.

Off and on, all day, I sat there wondering if he wasn't in the big, gray future-maker, too.

District 7 runs like a 2 by 4 at the north edge of Burnet Park. It takes in pieces of four of the poet streets: Whittier, Coleridge, Byrant and Lowell. It looks at the zoo. On election day, the district held 577 registered voters. Exactly 439 of them voted. More are registered as Democrats than Republicans. Moon conceded that since he took over as chairman after Bocko, Democratic registrations fell back, here and there.

But, of course, Bocko's 2 by 4 isn't the same neighborhood it was when Tom was a kid, either.

Yes, I heard that all day. There's only one Young left in the district, for crying out loud. Kevin, the candidate's brother. Kevin—saints preserve him—bought the old family house at 394 Coleridge from Kate, his mother. The homestead was as busy as an Irish undertaker's all through the weekend. It was Moon's satellite. Tuesday, volunteers were in and out of Kevin's getting registered Democrats and irregulars off their duffs and down to the greenhouse at Byrant and Wilbur.

Moon said they hit some houses five times. Five times! Marty, who goes to St. Pat's, swore he was at one door when the phone rang and the resident excused himself. When he came back, he said it was another volunteer wanting to know if he'd voted yet. Now, that's organization.

Kevin Young voted about 15 minutes after Eloise Kelly, Mary Snyder, Gilberta Guerin, Mildred Troendle, Moon and I opened the place at 6. The florists arrived later.

The women are inspectors. The district has voted at Davis Florist for as long as anyone—including Al Davis, whose father started the business in 1903—remembers. A year ago, Al opened an annex, where the really big, expensive plants—some of them trees, really—are stored. District 7 moved in.

The inspectors, who were there 15 hours, said it was like working in a rain forest. The women sat facing a large cactus the color of lime soda with very large spines.

Tom Young laughed when I told him that later in the day. Sure, the greenhouse. He voted there before he moved. They all did. Went to Mass and then voted Democratic, just the way he did Tuesday.

We were in the main headquarters, next to Matty's and the paint store on Washington. A good pick. City Hall is but two blocks west. Tom had his suit coat off. He looked pleased. There was a sign on the wall inviting us to a "victory celebration" at the hotel that night.

Yes, it was a good day. He had a little pasta at Our Lady of Pompei's election day lunch—surely, a candidate would lose if this rite were not carried out—and he went next door to try the lunch special at Matty's:

Tom Young chili with bread, $2.35.

No, as a matter of fact, Tom said after I asked him. Bocko didn't want to be mayor. Turned it down. Yes, he did.

I walked over to the Public Safety Building. Lt. Bill Finnie was by himself in the Uniform Bureau. His fingers were close to the phone. He had the election detail. Usually did. In at 5:40 a.m. for 16 hours of distant poll watching.

How's it going? OK. A few minor problems. Dunbar Center was locked when it wasn't supposed to be. John DeFrancisco's people were taping balloons to the parking meters. The Republicans said the Democrats were campaigning closer than 100 feet of some polling places because of the sheet cakes with Tom Young's name on them.

Sheet cakes? Sheet cakes, Bill said.

The Mayor had the flu. Can't seem to shake it. But he was at the office, feeling a little overlooked, a little nostalgic and packing his bags.

"I'm pleased," Lee Alexander said. Yes, a sweet 16 years. "Difficult, but good," he continued. Next year at this time, he will be practicing law with his son, Jamie. The old man's name will be three inches higher than the kid's on the shingle.

Yeah, I said to The Mayor, ask Tom Young about the size of the letters in his old man's name. *—1985*

---

# MACIEJOWA

Ah, the West Side!

A senior citizen and still passing out surprises.

Just as we get to the crust of the babka bread, at least one tender morsel of candied cherry remains. I walked around it the other day. It's called "Maciejowa," meaning "the place where Matthew lived."

Maciejowa (pronounced Ma-*chee*-o-va) is a tiny neighborhood north of I-690 and south of Hiawatha Boulevard. It's shaped like a flower pot and contains no more than 50 homes and a few businesses. The main drags are two: Pulaski Street and Giminski Drive.

You've got the Little Gem Diner at one end and Hogan's Radiators on the other. Not to mention the Idle Hour, Pachek's Grocery, your bowling league, the Sacred Heart choir, blacktopped front yards, flower gardens, house foundations painted silver and statues of the Infant of

Prague in the living room.

And the names on the mailboxes, the i's jingling the sounds of Warsaw and Danzig. Zdunk, Jaskulski, Wiskleski, Czajak, Pikolycky, Renckoski, Jurkiewicz, Borowski, Grudzinski, Filipkowski, Kashuba . . .

Years after it first came together, Maciejowa still hangs in there with an identity, which is ethnic Polish.

Recently we rediscovered Matthew's Place with the help of the Syracusans who live there. They, in turn, had recently rediscovered themselves. When I got the news, I couldn't stay away.

One of the activist neighbors is Barbara Kowal, an accountant who lives in the house on Pulaski Street her grandfather bought in 1910. In the past few months, Barbara's become a campaigner for the preservation of Maciejowa.

"We're trying to reconstruct ourselves," Barbara explained. "We're that group on the West Side with the funny name. Now people know who we are."

Yes, there are homemade t-shirts marked "Maciejowa," petitions, letters and phone calls to elected officials.

Maciejowa began around the turn of the century when Maciej (Matthew) Bulawa, a Polish immigrant land broker and house builder, started selling lots and renting rooms to other Polish immigrants. They honored their benefactor by naming their enclave for him.

Matthew lived in Maciejowa from around 1900 until 1922, when he sold his lots and relocated across the railroad tracks to West Belden Avenue. The family home remains, on Giminski Drive, next to the grocery.

Maciejowans first rallied as neighbors in the summer of 1940, when a huge fire broke out in Richfield Oil Co.'s storage tanks, across Bear Street at the edge of the little community. Things got so hot that the fire blistered paint on the houses of Maciejowa.

The neighbors were terrified but they held their ground. They wouldn't let Oil City devastate Matthew's Place.

"One lady grabbed her two small children and pushed them up the street in a carriage to get away from the fire," Barbara Kowal said. "She got three blocks away and decided that if the whole place blew up, the distance of three blocks wasn't going to save them. She turned around and went back home."

That mother, Genevieve Latocha, still lives in Maciejowa.

In 1940, the residents formed up and went to City Hall. Their benefactor then was John Giminski, a West Ender who was city treasurer.

The Giminskis were into funerals and coal. Turtle Street had been renamed Giminski Drive in their honor.

The Maciejowans of 1940 told the city they wanted the tanks to keep their distance. They oughtn't to be close enough to blister the paint on a man's house, for heavens sake. Oil City backed off.

Now, it's Oil City again, trying to gobble up Maciejowa, 50 years later. And again, the neighbors cohere.

"It started when we got a postcard from the city March 9 of this year," Barbara explained. We sat at her dining room table drinking coffee and eating muffins. Frank Borowski later joined us from across the street.

"The card said there was to be a hearing to consider a special permit for an indoor amusement establishment at 233 Pulaski St.," Barbara continued. "We got together and wrote a letter to the city. Every neighbor signed but one."

The establishment turned out to be The Pump House, a night club that had opened in the old rigging company building with the bakery outlet shop at one end. The club brought more noise, traffic and insensitive strangers to Maciejowa than the neighbors wanted.

"This had been zoned industrial since 1926," Barbara said. "Don't ask me why, but it was. But we got along with the businesses. Most of them are very good neighbors. They close at night and it's no bother. The night club's going till all hours. We're here to live, not to make money on our property."

Maciejowa worried that a night club in the island—a night club?—was but the first change of many. Barbara and her helpers from down the street and around the corner, including her sisters and a couple of cousins, dug in and researched their challenge.

Shortly they discovered Maciejowa had been made part of the big picture of Syracuse's "Lakefront Development" project. When they read in the papers last February about "new housing" planned for "Franklin Square"—several blocks to the southeast—they'd been reading about their own flower pot piece of Syracuse.

"Franklin Square meant us," Barbara said, motioning past her Infant of Prague in summer dress to the southeast. "From my back yard east to Van Rensselaer is marked for housing in the Lakefront Plan. They've promised us they won't alter existing neighborhoods, but we figure we'll be gone in 10 years. If the project goes, they'll flatten us."

If so, Maciejowa will go under in one piece. The letters, phone calls and meetings with city officials got the neighbors what they wanted. Last month city councilors rezoned Maciejowa residential.

The city cartographers drew their new lines around existing businesses. The night club stays, but it can't expand its parking into a vacant lot next door. "All in all, we managed to encompass most of Maciejowa in the new zone," Barbara said.

But more than an adjustment to the official instruments happened, according to her. The issue brought neighbors together, reenforced the sense of community reaching back four generations in a few families and gave residents the notion that unity is strength.

"We're a force down here now," Barbara said of the neighborhood association, which has yet to formally form. "The councilors were impressed with the way we organized ourselves. We're starting to think of other things we'd like to do."

Later we hit the street. Barbara showed me Maciejowa. It took about 15 minutes.

"You know, most of us care for the area," she said, walking along. "We've been here since early 1900, which is longer than any business. The businesses come and go, we remain. Not everyone's last name is Polish but the spirit is here."

In Matthew's Place, grandchildren move into a grandmother's house when she dies. A daughter returns home when her husband dies. A son reclaims a family heritage.

Barbara's grandfather, John Kowal, bought her house on speculation. "They thought Solvay Process might come in here; they didn't," she said. When his wife died, he moved from Park Avenue to Pulaski. "In those days, they had the Polish spelling, 'Pulawski,' on the street signs."

When Grandpa died in 1936, his daughter and her husband moved into 114 Pulaski. Two more sisters lived upstairs. When the daughter's husband died, Barbara, who'd grown up "on the other side of the tracks on North Geddes," moved in with her aunt and eventually bought the place. Now she lives there with her two sisters . . .

"Yeah," she said, as we crossed a neighbor's finely-cut back yard, "I used to get mad at the kids on my side of the tracks. These were the poor kids down here. They made fun of 'those Maciejowa kids.' I'd say 'Hey, those are my cousins.' "

We went into Pachek's. It's the size of my living room. Stanley Pachek stood behind the meat counter, under the sparkling varnished wood of his ceiling. His sister, "Honey," was at the cash register. Their parents, Anna and Vincent, opened this Mom and Pop 75 years ago.

On our way along Giminski Drive, Barbara pointed out the house where Matthew Bulawa lived. She found out about their founding father from Jean Renckoski, who has the nice, big, white house facing Spencer Street. Jean remembered Matthew.

"She came here from Poland when she was 3," Barbara said. "Her parents rented a house on this same street. When she got married, they bought a new home. She's 87. She's been here all that time."

The roots to the old country are long.

"Even before they came from Poland to Syracuse, they knew where to come," she continued. "They were told to come to Matthew, he would take care of them. And he did. He had a boarding house for men, only Polish men. He loaned money. He found them jobs.

"It was a tribute to him that they called this place Matthew's. When he was here, he was like a king on a throne."               *—1990*

------

# THE SMALLEST HOUSE THERE IS

This is a short story about John Weda's short house at 812 Danforth Street.

The house is 12 feet wide and 16 feet long.

According to John, who's been there 23 years, 812 is "the smallest house there is in Syracuse." Most people seem to think John is right about that. Certainly, the place is the wonder of the North Side, which isn't exactly poor for unusual buildings.

"Oh, it's quite a place," John said when I dropped by to say hello. "People stop and take pictures. Sometimes the cars are lined up. They yell out of the buses, 'Hey, that's a nice house you've got there.' People who go into Weber's (the well-known North Side restaurant a few doors away) are always coming up here for a look. I've never heard so many comments. Some times they ask me if I can build them one like it. Well, I didn't build it."

The house, of course, is smaller than most apartments—living room, kitchen and lavatory—but as far as John is concerned, it's just right. He is 66 and has been a bachelor all of his life. Small houses are good, he told me, because you aren't tempted to buy a lot of things you don't really need.

Of course, John knows there are people who wonder why he has three TV sets and two clocks that chime in this super-efficient space, but that's none of their business, really. He likes to watch TV, when he isn't hiring out to do chores for his neighbors or riding one of his two bicycles (an English rig and a 40-year-old one-speeder) to fetch the monthly groceries.

John gets his house a toasty warm with a gas heater, which is right across from the daybed where he sleeps and next to a sink and the water heater. The kitchen isn't much more than a way to get out the back door but there's room for a warmer oven and a three-coil "hot plate."

The house has a small back porch, handy by the utility shed, where John keeps his two snowblowers. Then there's the plot where he raises vegetables in the summer, including 200 tomato plants. That's between the house and the two-car garage, which is bigger than the house.

John grows plenty of flowers in the modest yard too. Geraniums out front, across the flag pole, where the U.S. banner always flies. Out back, zinnias and asters.

There's more time than there used to be for the yard, John said, since he retired five years ago from Aunt Josie's, another North Side landmark, where he worked as a handyman for 20 years. Before that, he did the same thing at Tubbert's, the restaurant that used to stand at Salina and Court. "I lived in the attic up there," John told me. "Rose Ryan, the boss, she was like a mother to me."

John was born in Utica and his family moved to Syracuse when he was a child. The Wedas lived on Burnet Avenue and John once worked at W.T. Grant's downtown.

In his present place, he seems to be almost as well known as his house.

"He's a super neighbor," said his landlord, lawyer George Raus Jr., who lives next door. "He keeps up his yard beautifully and helps people out. Why, some days, when there's plenty of snow, he'll plow the sidewalk all the way down to Salina Street!"

George said the family that owned the property before his family probably built 812 Danforth as a business place next door to their home. Before people started living there, it was a shoe repair and a beauty shop. John painted it the red color it now carries and he likes to add "little touches" to keep a glow on the house's reputation. His latest touch is a literal glow—strings of Christmas tree lights.

"I bought these last year but didn't get a chance to put them up," John explained. "I turn 'em on every afternoon as soon as it gets dark. Brightens up things a little." —*1984*

---

# HATTIE

Hattie Sage may be the last person still holding out in a private home in downtown Syracuse.

Hattie hangs on in a gray house between Onondaga Creek and the railroad tracks on Adams, around the corner from the fire house. She's been there more than 30 years and although there are times when trouble tries to batter down her door, she endures, sitting in her warm kitchen with the dog nuzzling her and a picture of Franklin Roosevelt on the wall next to the refrigerator.

"Oh, it's changed, all the way through," Hattie says. "It was nice when I moved here; now everything's gone."

Her husband is gone. Dave. Her second one. He died Flag Day 1948, just 11 months after they bought the house from the Champlains. The house next door where the Kings used to live? Torn down. The ones across the street and around the corner, too. The blind factory? Closed and moved out.

Unity Kitchens' in there, with all of its randy spirits looking for a way through another day. The train tracks were elevated. When Hattie came there, they were flat, right on Clinton Street. Now the freights go clanking by over her head, while weary travelers roll down the banks into her back yard.

Hattie is tucked in this old house, with its high ceilings and white wooden mantels and she's doing just fine, even if things do change outside. She has a dog, a cat and the men who board with her, including George, who is outside right now clearing the walks with the new snowblower Hattie bought.

The furnace is new, too, and she's had some redecoration done around the place. She had her chairs re-covered.

This makes things cheerful inside because Hattie doesn't get out much, anymore. Her niece comes and drives her to the grocery store when she needs provisions, but Hattie hasn't been downtown in maybe 10 years, even though the business district is just around the corner.

Sure, things changed outside and she says she's afraid of going around like she used to. But if you were 94, the way Hattie is, maybe you'd be a little cautious, too.

Hattie didn't want to let me in when I first came to the door. Can you blame her? "I've been taken four times," she kept saying. Later I found out a couple creeps with a pickup truck got in and conned her out of some money for doing the driveway. Another time it was the men who came to do work in the kitchen.

I went next door and got Peter King, one of the guardian angels of Unity Kitchen, who had told me about Hattie. He came over and we went in, with his dog, and sat in the kitchen talking.

Peter is concerned about his neighbor and looks in on her now and again. He thinks she is a remarkable woman, not only for her longevity but for her spirit, which does not spend a lot of time looking over its shoulder at the past.

Peter asked me if I knew anyone who was 94 who had had their chairs re-covered and bought a new snowblower.

He's also amazed that Hattie is such a good neighbor to the Kitchen, which is nothing like living next to a home for maiden school teachers.

Hattie often hears the cries of pain. Her boarders bring in stories about throats being cut and old men getting rousted and robbed up on Seymour Street. Bricks have sailed through her bedroom window and odd creatures sometimes appear at the door. Jim Welch, the Kitchen's environmental sculptor, builds things in the side yard, but Hattie, who has lived in the city a long time, knows this is part of living in the city.

"They help me out," she told Peter and me. "I get along with everybody. Say, do you remember Johnny? The fellow who put the brick through the window . . . ."

Peter and I thought someone who was born the year Grover Cleveland was President and Geronimo surrendered would have interesting things to say about the passage of time, so we finally coaxed Hattie into talking about what it was like when her family came over from Germany and settled in the salt flats near Liverpool.

"My father worked in Galeville, in the salt yards," she said. "In fact, all of the family—there were nine of us kids—had shares and used to help out. In the summer, when the bell rang, no matter what time it was, we'd have to go out and help pull the covers over the salt tanks (where brine was drying) if it was going to rain. Even if we were in school, we'd go out and then go back.

"We lived in a little house behind the Moyer's place, where the candle company is, at Greenpoint and the canal was in the front yard. I'd go out and catch a fish for supper. It was only a little town when we came there. There was a toll gate out on the road.

"In the summer my father worked on the salt and in the winter he used to cut willows—the ones they used to make baskets—and we'd strip them for people. He'd bind them up and take them to the people who made baskets. Later, we moved into the city, over to Apple Street."

That was about the time Hattie, who says she was "fat then and passed for 18," went to work making lanterns at R.E. Dietz Co. It was 1901 and she was 14. Her brother worked there, too, and some of her sisters.

"I worked on a bench, assembling lanterns," she told us. "I enjoyed it there. When I retired in 1959, I had worked 58 years and three months. I was the oldest one that ever worked there."

Hattie must have put together lots of those old "Vestas," I thought. That's the old trainman's lantern, that used to swing on the long, looped handle along the New York Central Railroad.

"Yes," Hattie said, "I earned $8 a week and I used to walk home for lunch. I liked to walk. When we moved over here, I still walked, up West Street. Sometimes the train would be stopped across the street, so they'd let me climb up through the cars to get through."

It was all going be like an old movie, speeded up. Hattie sat there with her hands folded onto her flowered apron and kept talking. We smiled over the history lesson, Peter and me.

On the way out, Hattie said she was feeling fine, except for the scratches on her arm from the cat. How do you do it? I asked.

"Oh, I have my cereal every morning and a beer once in a while," said Hattie.                                                                    —*1981*

# Chapter 4

# COUNTRY

---

## ONCHIOTA

Ray Fadden told me about the bear with one paw who used to read Ray's thoughts. A trap took the paw. After that, the burly king of the forest came to Ray's back yard—the landlord here calls his feed lot "Ray Fadden's Restaurant"—to eat the meat scraps Ray puts out for his friends.

Ray and his family live in the woods along County Route 30, in Franklin County north of Saranac Lake. The post office is Onchiota. Ray is a retired schoolteacher. He runs Six Nations Indian Museum, across the road from the house where he lives with his wife, Christine. His son, John, an artist who teaches in the Saranac school system, lives with his family a quarter-mile away.

The notion of a peaceable kingdom comes alive when you step out of the car at Onchiota.

Ray talked about his friend, the bear, as I followed him around the lot behind the house. Here, and around the museum buildings, are 135 feeding stations for the creatures who arrive flapping their wings or padding on all fours. My friend insists he owes it to them to provide them with extra food. This hobby costs Ray an arm and a leg—more than $1,000 a year for sunflower seed and cracked corn, by his estimate —but it must be done.

"I can't ignore my friends," Ray said to me.

Yes, the bear was his friend He showed up at the back stoop one night and Ray knew what he'd come for. He has a butcher friend who provides bones and other scraps.

This feeding has been going on for years, so the Faddens have a modest bone yard out there beyond the porch that winds half way around the house.

Ray spread some seed out on the top of a tree stump for the birds, squirrels, chipmunks, skunks, porcupine, whatever. We heard ravens yelling at us from the trees. A large bird with the wing spread of an eagle took off from a crown nearby.

"They'll be licked clean by morning," Ray said. I picked a black fly out of my ear.

"You know," he went on, "it is possible to talk to animals. You can communicate, read each others' thoughts. I had a bear who came in here with a bad leg. It never healed. He let me pat him on the head. He licked my wrist. The last time I saw him I know he came to say goodbye. I let him go back to the earth."

The bear with one paw—Ray called him "Gimpy"—had a way of snorting which his benefactor interpreted as a greeting. Ray would bow in return. Gimpy would bow back.

Bears are bolder than some of Ray's other friends, of course. They'll come right up to the door and knock, looking for food. Ray showed me the slashed window screens to document that. Sometimes a mother bear will send a cub to wake up the Faddens in the middle of the night.

Once Ray had a young boy visiting him who wanted him to bring the "nice black dog" he'd found into the house.

"The dog was a bear cub," Ray said, chuckling. "I didn't think that was such a good idea."

They keep coming; Ray keeps feeding. A chipmunk rushed up to Ray, and he popped him a peanut. "I wonder what he's doing over here," he said after a minute of staring at his friend's twitching tail. "He belongs over on the other side of the road."

"Nobody feeds 'em like I do," Ray continued as we headed for the museum. "Ray Fadden's Restaurant, that's what this is. But what else can I do? They're starving."

Ray sees things going wrong in the Adirondacks, where the Faddens have lived nearly 30 years. Hungry creatures are part of the picture.

The flora is starving, as well, according to Ray. The pines aren't dropping the cones they used to. Acid rain, he believes, has weakened trees so that they snap when years ago they would have thrived.

Ray wouldn't have that many tree stumps around the house if it weren't for acid rain, he said.

"We're all having a hard time in the Adirondacks," Ray explained. "Either the developers want to cover the whole thing with cement or the acid rain will kill all of the fish and trees.

"Why, at the beginning of last winter, we got the worst storm I've ever seen. We had heavy snow, and it just snapped off the trees. Acid rain made them weak and they just broke off. I lost plenty of trees out back. You look around, and see those trees along the roads just slumped over."

Ray was getting fired up , the way he does. We got to the front door of the museum and it started to rain, of all things.

Ray worries about his own environment and everybody else's.

Foresters might argue with him about the trees. They don't think the chemicals in the precipitation that kill lakes in the Adirondacks has done equal damage to trees. If those trunks are curled over, or snapping off, the experts contend, it was the weight of the snow that did them in, not the poisons out of the Ohio smoke stacks.

Ray excused himself to go back to the house for pipe tobacco. Look around the building, he said. I did.

The Faddens built the museum themselves, and Ray either collected or made all of the exhibits, which is a considerable number. I'd been at Six Nations before, and each time I got dizzy, trying to take in everything. It's impossible to appreciate in one sitting.

When Ray quit teaching school—most of that among the Mohawks at Akwasasne—he and his wife, who is Mohawk, scouted out this spot near Buck Pond to teach Indian children about their own culture and show white people Indian ways and history.

Ray is just as emphatic about how Native Americans ought to be portrayed in history classes as he is about acid rain and feeding bears. He feels we have taught our children lies about the first settlers of the Americas.

The Fadden's museum is a small, Mom and Pop effort at putting the record right, by their measure.

Ray returned with a can of Union Leader tobacco. He sat in a chair he made from a deer hide. He lit his pipe and there was a knock at the door.

"Probably some Indians," Ray said. "They just keep coming. Won't let me do my work. Actually, I've turned this over to John. I'm just the janitor."

The visitors were a man and wife and their two daughters. They said they were from Korea. They didn't speak English well enough to explain to us how they had found their way to Onchiota.

All four headed for the sales counter, which Ray told me later should have been built at the back of the museum, not the front.

"Everybody wants to buy something," he said. Ray stocks a mix of cheap trinkets and fine crafts, including Mohawk baskets. The pamphlets and other printed materials, graced with drawings by Ray and John, who uses the Mohawk name "Kahionhes," are sold to buy "feed for my orphans."

"I had a woman out West who sent me money for seed," Ray said as one of the Koreans examined a rubber tom-tom. "But she died, unfortunately. I could use a few friends like that to help me out a bit with my seed money."

Ray asked the visitors if they'd like him to tell a story from one of the many story belts he made for the museum. I was relieved he didn't pick the longest piece of bead work in the world, which circles 75 feet of the museum. He grabbed a stick he uses as a pointer and moved it among the pictographs of a belt.

"One day an old man came into the village," he began.

The story concerned an ugly stranger who stopped at each of the clan huts and was turned away. Finally, a bear clan woman welcomed him into her house.

The Koreans were looking at the clocks on their wrist. "Have to go," the father said. Ray understood; they didn't know what on earth he was talking about. "Thanks, grandpa," the man said.

"Sensai," I corrected. "Teacher."

Ray finished the story for me. In thanks, the ugly man showed the woman all of the herbs of the woodland and how to heal with them.

This inspired my host to try out his monologue about the contributions of Native Americans on me. He mentioned baked beans, Irish potatoes, rubber, popcorn, peanuts, chewing gum, Egyptian cotton and democracy.

"That's why there's racism in America," Ray declared. "They don't teach the gifts of all of the cultures. Kids think everything came out of Europe. No wonder they think whites are superior. Truth is, every race has contributed."

Ray walked me to the car. I asked him if he had any wounded creatures he was nursing just then. No, he said; and no thanks to the "so-called hunters." He can't abide strangers who want to go into these woods and kill for no reason.

Nor the cruel sportsfolks who kill mothers and leave the babies to starve to death. Or the lousy shooters who wing a crow or an owl, then leave the bird to make its way; maybe to the Fadden place, maybe not.

Ray reminded me that Indians killed animals only when they were hungry. I remembered the Christmas card I got from Ray one year. It was decorated with pictures of the family's forest friends. In one corner, a Native American hunter was quoted, speaking to his quarry:

"I am sorry that I had to kill you, little brother, but I had need of your meat. My children were hungry and crying for food. Forgive me, little brother. I honor your courage, your strength and your beauty."

No one of us is going to fix what needs fixing in the Adirondacks. That shouldn't keep us from honoring the courage, strength and beauty of a man who's trying.                                          *—1989*

---

# BILL AND JOHN

Bill Rodriguez met up with John Witbeck a year ago last October. It is a distant acquaintance at best. John probably had been dead 68 years at the time. They found his skeleton under a tree in a wooded ravine next to Cayuga Lake, in the Town of Genoa.

Bill is a forensic anthropologist who works for the Onondaga County medical examiner's office. John was a farmer. Officially, he'd been a missing person since 1920.

The anthropologist got very interested in the farmer and the mystery of what happened to him. Very, very interested. I'd stop short of saying Bill is obsessed by this strange circumstance.

Yes, he's made quite a study of the case. A couple of weeks ago, in fact, he presented a report on his research to the 42nd annual meeting of the American Academy of Forensic Sciences.

Bill's paper on the Witbeck case was one of four picked by the academy for its Last Word Society. It made quite a big hit, according to him.

The paper was titled "What Ever Happened to the Farmer in the Dell? The Disappearance of John Witbeck."

The Witbeck case is one of those oddballs of forensic science. One of the few times when it's really true that a mystery may have a solution out there waiting to be found. This time, a solution was found, only to generate yet another mystery.

John was a prosperous farmer who lived on those flat lands along the lake about half way between Auburn and Ithaca. The records contain two spellings of his last name; often it appeared "Whitbeck." We can't be certain, from the evidence, which was preferred.

His wife, Grace, was 18 years younger than her husband. They had one child, a son named Henry. "Lee," as he was called, died of a ruptured appendix in 1913 at the age of 14. It was said John took the boy's death hard.

Grace Witbeck had her own wealth. She'd inherited a farm from her parents and that was the one John worked, after they were married in 1897. She attended Wells College and was an artist. Neighbors recalled both the Witbecks as being single-minded people.

Then, one day in May 1920, Genoa learned John had "up and vanished into thin air."

State Police were told by his wife he'd left the house with his .22 hunting rifle and she hadn't seen him again. Neighbors searched without luck the next morning.

There were extensive searches, for several days. No trace of John could be found. Townsfolk walked fields and woods all the way to the lake—about a mile—and back.

The Genoa Tribune, the local weekly newspaper, reported the missing man was "said to have been despondent at times since the death of his only son, six years ago, and it is thought that this accounts for his disappearance."

The paper also noted the Witbecks were just back from California, where they spent the winter. Had John fled to California? Or somewhere else?

"Others even entertained gossip that Grace killed John and burnt him up in the furnace," Bill Rodriguez reported in his paper.

Finally, the searchers gave up. Grace sold the farm and eight years later filed to become administrator of her husband's estate. Five years after that she remarried. She died in 1952.

Grace was the last of the Witbecks in Genoa. The mystery of John Witbeck faded; fewer and fewer people remembered it. Eight months before the bones were found a local history book, "South of Auburn," presented the story again after many years. Only a handful of folks knew it firsthand at that point.

And then, in October 1988, a family took a walk in the woods near the old Witbeck farm. One of the children saw a badly deteriorated pair of leather boots sticking out of the forest floor. A little digging turned up parts of a human skeleton.

That's when state police called in Bill Rodriguez in Syracuse. He was asked to go to Genoa to excavate the skeleton and conduct an examination.

When Bill did his inventory, he saw several parts of the skeleton were missing. The most important element wasn't there, he explained. The cranium, the top of the head. The only thing he found was a jawbone minus its teeth.

The bones were old, Bill concluded. Not only that, they were consistent with an adult white male, more than 60 years old who stood about 5-foot-7. He found healed rib fractures and arthritis in the spine. A special dating technique called "osteon counting" was used on the skeleton. The age came back 61 years, plus or minus 4 years.

John was 62 when he disappeared.

Local historians provided Bill with pictures of the Witbecks. He found the remains conformed to the old photographs too. He looked at John's jowls in a snapshot and compared them with the jawbone in his hand. Yes, this could be the man.

Interviews with townsfolks told him John broke his ribs while busting a horse. That fit. So did the rusted tobacco can found next to the bones. And the old farmer boots and the rifle.

Yes, the gun Grace mentioned as missing from the house along with John back in 1920 lay there next to the body in the woods in 1988. Bill identified it as a "Stevens Crack Shot" made in 1910 and available in the Sears, Roebuck catalog. X-rays revealed an expended bullet in the chamber.

The pieces fit John Witbeck and his time frame. If only he had all of the skeleton, Bill said. He went back to that ravine in Genoa twice looking for the top of John's head. Nothing.

"That really upset me," the anthropologist explained to me later. "I thought it would turn up if I looked hard enough. Animals took it. The skull has to be out there. I couldn't find it.

"There I was, over there yelling, 'John, where's the rest of you?' "

Bill worked with a modern state trooper who was assigned to clean up the Witbeck case after 68 years. Investigator David Gould agreed those were John's bones. He had the same problem Bill did; neither one of them could say, for sure, what happened to him.

"Unattended natural death," the trooper concluded.

Genoa finally got to give John a proper sendoff. There was a small, quiet funeral service at West Genoa Cemetery. Don Powers, the sexton, built a small pine box for the bones. The anthropologist and the trooper were there, along with Gordon Cummings, the town historian. As the box was lowered into the grave, the old leather boots were placed on the lid.

What did happen to John?

Heart attack, suicide, murder, maybe?

Bill shrugged, in person and in the paper he read to the academy.

"This case really got to me," he said when we talked about it recently. "Did he slip and fall and just die there? Did he have a heart attack? Did he kill himself? Was he murdered? It's a mystery I can't solve."

The ravine where the skeleton was found is one bother. It's a hard place to get to, yet it's just off the straight line path from the Witbeck place to the old railroad station on the lake shore. There was talk in 1920 that the farmer skipped to California. Did he?

Gordon Cummings, the retired Cornell sociologist who is town historian, is puzzled by the location. Searchers were all over the woodlot in 1920. And plenty of hunters since then. How could the body be there all that time and not be seen?

Bill's research report included a conversation with Jane Myers, who lives nearby. Jane told of a summer day in 1948 when she was walking along the lake shore when an elderly man drove up in a "car of ancient vintage bearing California license plates."

The man told Jane he was 93 and had come East for a last look at his home where he grew up. He had a long white beard and plenty of accurate information about Genoa. He said he knew Jane's mother.

Jane said she kept at the old-timer for his name but he refused. "'Tis best that it is not known," she said he told her.

Could that have been John Witbeck? "Based on skeletal analysis, I think not," Bill wrote in the paper.

He does, he explained to me, have some questions about Mrs. Witbeck's story. When he disappeared, serious arguments between John and Grace were recalled by neighbors. On the day he vanished, it was said they had a bad spat about some trees John wanted to set out as a memorial to his dead son. Grace didn't like the idea.

"Remember," Bill continued, "the only version of how he disappeared that day is the one Grace Witbeck provided at the time."

When I was in Genoa in 1988, I talked to Lula Fiorenzo, a shirttail cousin of Grace. She said she was bothered by her cousin's long silence about her missing husband. "I lived with her at one time and I never heard her say a word about it," she explained. "Ever."

The missing cranium probably would solve the mystery. It might contain a gunshot wound, which would rule out a heart attack and rule in suicide or murder. More than likely, suicide. Although . . .

"What if we found a skull fracture?" Bill asked.

Maybe John didn't walk to that ravine. Maybe someone dragged his body to this first crude grave.

That's why we'll see Bill Rodriguez back there, looking for the top of John's head, as soon as the snow clears and the weather's decent.

"I'm going in for another look," he explained.     *—1990*

---

# THE HARRISES

There are ghosts in Ellis Hollow. Oh boy, are there ghosts.

Two weeks ago today, the Harris family was murdered at The Hollow. We still don't know who did it, or why. Linda Brady has been baby-sitting the Harris house nights for the state police. She's had a few odd, uncomfortable minutes out there by herself in the country darkness.

This 29-year-old state trooper is a native of Tompkins County. She lives five miles over the hill from the Harris place, which sits at the edge of a large hillside of evergreens and hardwood in the town of Dryden.

Ithaca is another five miles to the west.

Linda pulls the duty inside her troop car on a little turnoff drive opposite the house. The black and gold car points out, toward Ellis Hollow Road, with the lights on and the motor running. No. 1886 Ellis Hollow Road is empty and locked. Bulbs burn in some of the rooms and in the lantern fixtures along the Harrises' rail fence, next to the road.

Linda sits and watches. When it's light enough, she copies down plate numbers from cars that pass. Most of the time, her only companions are the police radio and the wind.

And the house, with its big gray shadow stretched across the yard.

No. 1886 used to be a home. The beautiful dream place for Tony and Dolores Harris and their two kids.

Now it's a gruesome "crime scene" to be "processed" by cops and stared at and photographed by strangers such as me.

A corpse of a dream with a DOA tag on it.

And a cop sitting up nights with it.

Days, the state's evidence experts are on the house like ticks. They've been inside every day since Dec. 23. The commanders can't get to a point of thinking their job is finished.

"We're processing with extreme methodicalness," Sgt. Bob Parlett said at the command post. "We do with every homicide, but this time we're giving it a little extra."

Linda's challenge is fighting off the ghosts during the solitary watch of hers, which has stretched to 14 hours, night and day, a few times this week and last.

"You sit there, and your mind plays tricks with you," she said to me. The trooper was back at zone headquarters in Varna having a cup of coffee at the time. We talked amid the chaos of tracking the Harris killers.

"It's so quiet, so still out there," Linda continued. "I get a different feeling. Not exactly eerie, just different, sitting there where a brutal crime occurred. Especially when you were one of the people in the house right after the murders were discovered."

Linda came to work at 1:30 p.m. the day before Christmas Eve and was sent to the house. She walked into the oversized salt box with the Christmas wreath on the front door and left a piece of her innocence outside, never to be reclaimed.

How did the experience leave her?

"Shocked," she replied.

"I know I don't have that much experience, but I've never encountered anything like that before. Other troopers with more time in than me said the same thing."

The Harrises, their son and daughter were abused, shot and later doused with a flammable liquid and set on fire. Even the family dog was killed. Only Shadow, the Harris kitten, made it.

The first thing that hit Linda was the smell in the house. The smell of gasoline and burning wood.

After a while it dawned on her: Hey, this isn't a place where people lived. It's an abattoir.

"I used to drive by," Linda explained. "I was always impressed with how nice it looked. It's a very beautiful house. But I try not to dwell on that. All I think about is what happened there. It didn't feel like a home to me. It's a place where a horrible crime occurred."

I asked her about sitting there alone through the nights—when the mind tricks are played.

Sure, they happen, Linda said. Other troopers said so, too.

"Some of the guys say they see the outside lights flicker," she continued. "I haven't seen that, but I know what they mean. When the wind blows, the trees in front of the house move. The lights are on out there by the fence. It looks, well, sort of like a man walking by the house. At least it does when you've been sitting out there hours and hours alone."

Another trooper told Linda about the life-size Elvis poster hanging in one of the bedrooms upstairs. The crime scene team leaves the light on in that room at the end of the day.

"He was patrolling outside the house one night and looked up," she said. "He thought for a minute he was seeing a man walking by the window. It was the Elvis poster."

Ellis Hollow Road runs from Ithaca to Slaterville. Houses are fewer as you close in on Slaterville. Most of them are dream places, like the Harrises'.

This isn't a main drag. Still, the road is much-traveled these two weeks. Linda's observation is that a lot of the traffic has to do with No. 1886 and its role as a curiosity.

"I did a 12-hour shift one day and counted more than 400 plates between 7 and 3 in the afternoon," she said. "New Year's Day it was more than 200."

Most of the travelers keep moving, after slowing down to look at the Harris house and the gift shop that sits next to it. A few of the neighbors stop and talk to the trooper-sitter.

"One woman stopped and asked me if I wanted some coffee or something from the store," Linda said. "The first week, I had people stopping to ask me about the rumors they were hearing. They wanted to know what really happened. I tell them I really don't know and I don't. I don't know all that's going on."

At the same time, Linda, a neighbor herself, feels the neighbors' concerns about the tragedy.

"They have a right to know what we're free to tell them," she said. "They are concerned. Everybody in this county is concerned."

I drove by the place on Trooper Mike Burling's watch. That was afternoon. The school bus came down the road as we talked. It didn't stop at No. 1886 the way it used to. Three unmarked troop cars and a crime unit van were parked in the circle drive that goes by the front door. Another was around the corner, in front of the two-car garage, next to the basketball hoop on a pole.

I got out and stood looking at the place. It's hard not to, knowing what we know. I focused on the fat chimney for the three fireplaces in the kitchen, living room and game room. Smoke and fire, I thought. But no warmth.

Linda was right about those mind tricks.

I thought about Kansas.

Several years ago, I was out there on an assignment that had nothing to do with murder. My hosts gave me a tour. The tour included the Clutter place at Holcomb.

I looked at an empty house in the country at the end of a circle drive-way.

It was exactly 30 years this past Nov. 15 that four members of the Clutter family were murdered in that house. The parents and their two kids, bound and killed with shotguns by two ex-cons.

Maybe you remember the case. It lives on because Truman Capote wrote a book about it called "In Cold Blood."

The last time I'd thought about what the folks showed me in Kansas was 10 years ago, Nov. 14, 1979, a day short of the 20th anniversary of the Clutter tragedy at Holcomb. That was when the four members of the Carl Bachman family were murdered in their home at Lee Center, north of Rome.

Remember? A man and wife and their two kids found in their large handsome house in an affluent suburban neighborhood? Bound and shot to death?

In time, three men were convicted and sent to prison for those moments of horror.

Ghosts in Ellis Hollow?

Oh boy, yes, Linda.                                                  —*1990*

———————

# THE NORTONS

Continuity.

Features of the landscape along the ridge south of Seneca Turnpike have changed since Augustus Norton came from Connecticut in 1807 and started cutting trees to make barrels in the Town of Onondaga. Yet there still are Nortons in his house, wood still burns in the stoves and the smell of pumpkin baking for pies fills the kitchen.

Arthur Augustus Norton is the cooper's great grandson and time has given him the patriarch's look. The white beard flows down his flannel shirt and the hair has settled into a crown. The goloshes are buckled, ready to test the morning, and his harmonicas rest before him on the table.

He will be 88 the day before the next Fourth of July and his years have been good to him. He still considers himself a farmer.

Myrtle Norton is the farmer's wife, "a few years younger," she says, but in place and more than making do. Last fall, Arthur and Myrtle had their 60th anniversary and then settled in for the winter.

Arthur used up the cords the grandson had cut for him and stacked on the porch and Myrtle read aloud to him from "Little House on the Prairie" and Deacon Doubleday's book and Myrtle baked and Arthur cut and carved ax handles on the couch in the living room.

Don't mind the clutter, Myrtle said; Arthur never could throw anything away. And this winter he brought the tools into the house so they wouldn't rust.

More than 100 acres here, sloping down steeply in places to Pleasant Valley; pond, woods, sugar bush, ravines, barns, the sap house, mailbox in front of the house Augustus built with Arthur and Myrtle's names on it. Even the road has the name Norton.

"My great grandfather settled here and built a log cabin across the road," Arthur explained from his kitchen chair. "He started clearing the land gradually and then built this house. There have been Nortons here ever since."

The generations are close by, too. Children just up the road. Thirteen grandchildren, and six greats in the offing.

"Oh, there used to be Nortons all over here," Arthur said.

This is a pocket of the past doing just fine, in the present, thank you.

The city is just over the shoulder; climb one of the slopes and you see it glowing at night. There is a TV set on a pile of newspapers in the kitchen but the water supply is pumped outside the back stoop. When Myrtle wants one of her famous elderberry pies, Arthur picks a pail of fat fruit from the patch in the yard.

Winters, though, the Nortons hear the snowmobiles circling their fields and find the messes they make breaking into the sap house. After the snow melts, they come in on bikes and perform their rites among the trees Grandpa Augustus cut his hoops from.

The farm has returned, in kind, the Nortons' care. Lumber, food, sap, and then some. For over 30 years, Myrtle churned 30 to 35 pounds of butter a week from the 10 cows, then went to the Regional Market with the salt-free bars, along with eggs, pies, maple sugar, syrup, sometimes a head of livestock or two.

She was a Kelley from the valley, but she learned to drive a team and milk and split wood and on the winter breaks, weave rugs on the loom upstairs. During the war she subbed at the post office and when she was 70 she still was driving a rural route, stuffing bills and catalogs into mailboxes.

Arthur, meanwhile, worked the farm and got interested in steam and gas engines. He helped found the societies to commemorate the devices that moved everything from logs to top soil on the farm. He and Myrtle still go to the meets and it doesn't take much encouragement to get him to fire up his specialty, the dragsaw, which does with engine power what two men once did with a crosscut saw.

The Nortons started tapping their maple trees about 45 years ago. At one time, they had nearly 2,000 buckets out and school children would come in buses from Syracuse to watch the colorless sap boil down into amber syrup over the arch Arthur built himself on the edge of the ravine half a mile from the house.

This spring, for the first time, they didn't feel up to tapping and boiling, even though most of the flow came to the arch in gravity tubes and customers still waited.

"A good sugar is like the goose that laid the golden egg," Arthur said.

Then, with a little prompting from Myrtle, he fished out his biggest mouth organ and whistled up a jig. There was a time he fiddled, too, and his wife worked out the chords on the piano.

"Oh, he'll be up at the Grange for St. Patrick's Day," Myrtle said. "Would play the violin, too, if it didn't get stuck in his beard."

*—1979*

# THE PROPHET

Joseph Smith was the son of a farmer. He lived near Palmyra at a time when myths were believed. He had this hardened piece of earth he carried in his britches. It was called a seer stone by some, a peep stone by others. Joseph said it gave him the gift of seeing "where hidden treasures in the bowels of the earth were."

In its time, it would reveal the most enduring of treasures for Joseph.

Some people said they remembered the day in 1822 when the stone showed itself to him. One neighbor wrote:

"I was engaged in digging a well. I employed Alvin (Joseph's brother) and Joseph to assist me . . . after digging about 20 feet below the surface of the earth, we discovered a singularly appearing stone, which excited my curiosity. I brought it to the top of the well, and as we were examining it, Joseph put it in his hat, and then his face into the top of the hat.

"The next morning he came to me and wished to obtain the stone, alleging that he could see in it."

The stone had the shape of a high-instepped shoe. It was about as big as the small egg of a hen. It was composed of layers of different colors passing diagonally through it. Chocolate in color, one person said, and very hard and smooth.

Joseph was not alone in his belief. Money-digging was a passion in that strip of land between Ontario and the canal. Buried treasure guarded by spirits was spoken of. It is still spoken of.

People spoke of Joseph too. It was said he could find not only treasure but lost possessions. Once, someone said, he found a pin in a pile of shavings with the help of the stone. Word got around about this boy who looked into his hat.

There was an old gentleman in Chenango County by the name of Josiah Stowell. He farmed on both sides of the Susquehanna River, around Bainbridge and farther south in Harmony, Pa. He heard Joseph could "discern things invisible to the natural eye." He heard too about a silver mine opened by the Spaniards around Harmony. He wanted Joseph to come to the river valley and get the treasure for him.

Joseph wrote Josiah a letter:

"You Should not dig more untill you first discover if any valluables remain. You know the treasure must be guarded by some clever spirit and if such is discovered so also is the treasure. So do this: take a hazel stick one yard long being new cut and leave it Just in the middle and lay it asunder on the mine so that both inner parts of the stick may look one right against the other one inch distant . . .

"If there is treasure after a while you shall see them draw and Join together again of themselves. Let me know how it is . . ."

Later Joseph went to see about the treasure himself. He and Josiah's "other hands" dug "for the silver mine at which I continued to work for nearly a month, without success in our undertaking . . . I finally prevailed with the old gentleman to cease digging after it."

Today, in the river country around South Bainbridge, which became the village of Afton after Joseph left, a visitor is told about the skepticism, and even the envy and hate, felt for the man. Once, the story goes, he announced he was going to walk on water. Some local lads discovered planks hidden under the water of a local pond. They removed the supports. When Joseph tried his feat, he sank, thrashing, into the water.

We also have the record of Joseph's trial as a disorderly person. This came about a few months after he abandoned Josiah Stowell's empty holes in the ground. Some of the diggers were mad; they brought Joseph up on charge before the Bainbridge justice of the peace.

Josiah Stowell was sworn: "He positively knew the prisoner could tell, and professed the art of seeing those valuable treasures through the medium of said stone . . . he did not exactly find (the mine) but got a piece of core, which resembled gold, he thinks . . . That he and prisoner had (searched for buried money) and prisoner said that it was in a certain root of a stump five feet from the surface of the earth, and with it would be found a tail-feather . . . said Stowell and prisoner thereupon commenced digging, found a tail-feather but money was gone; that he supposed the money had moved down . . ."

Howard Stowell swore Joseph had looked into a hat, "pretending to tell where a chest of dollars were buried in Windsor . . . marked out size of chest in the leaves on the ground."

Jonathan Thompson told the court Joseph used his hat in another search for a buried chest. This, he insisted, had been put into the ground by two Indians who quarreled. One killed the other and threw the body into the pit with the trunk. When Jonathan and Joseph dug, they failed because of an enchantment:

"The trunk kept settling away from under them while digging . . . they continued constantly moving dirt, yet the trunk kept about the same distance from them . . . (another time) prisoner said that it appeared to him that salt might be found at Bainbridge and that he is certain that prisoner can divine things by means of said stone and hat; that, as evidence, prisoner looked into his hat to tell him about some money witness lost 16 years ago and that he described the man that witness supposed had taken it, and disposition of money."

The court record concluded:

"And thereupon the Court finds the defendant guilty."

Joseph may have stopped digging for money then. He didn't stop dreaming. The stone stayed in his pocket. The visions began. In a short time, another sort of gold was found. This happened in a drumlin, near Manchester, Ontario County. It was said if it were not for his stone, this would not have happened.

An angel appeared to Joseph and "told me where they (the golden plates) were; and gave me directions how to obtain them."

According to Joseph, the plates contained the history of an early civilization of our hemisphere and an appearance of the resurrected Christ.

Joseph dictated his revelations to a secretary. Sometimes this was his wife, Emma, who he met while working for the Stowells. The manuscript grew over months, as Joseph moved farm to farm, Pennsylvania to upstate New York. One witness left us an account of how Joseph worked in a farm house at the north end of Seneca Lake:

"(He) would put the seer stone into a hat, and put his face into the hat, drawing it closely around his face to exclude the light; and in the darkness the spiritual light would shine.

"A piece of something resembling a parchment would appear (to Joseph), and on that appeared the writing. One character at a time would appear, and under it was the interpretation in English. Brother Joseph would read off the English to his principal scribe and when it was written down and repeated by Brother Joseph to see if it was correct, then it would disappear and another character with the interpretation would appear."

Joseph's manuscript, The Book of Mormon, was published in 1830 at Palmyra. April 6, 1830, he began The Church of Jesus Christ of Latter-day Saints. From that day, he was known as Joseph Smith, the prophet. Fourteen years later, he was assassinated by a mob at Carthage, Ill.

The church today has nearly 6 million members around the world. Every summer, at the end of July, many of the prophet's people—we call them Mormons—return to Ontario County and the other places Joseph lived when he was a boy and a young man. They hold a pageant at the drumlin south of Palmyra, which they know as Hill Cumorah. The houses Joseph lived in have been turned into museums, which Mormons call shrines.

And in a safe in Salt Lake City, in the office of the first president of the church, rests another souvenir: Joseph's stone, chocolate in color.

*—1985*

---

# LAVERNE

Laverne Kelley had come to Cooperstown from Milford on one of those days it seemed that half of the people of North America were in town to see Babe Ruth's old uniform at the National Baseball Museum. A few of the visitors wandered into The Smithy, where Laverne sat on an old church hall chair in front of the cold blacksmith's hearth with a battered breadboard on his knees.

Laverne is a farmer who carves wood. The Smithy, which is considered Cooperstown's oldest building, is an art gallery. The sign to his right read "folk artist in residence." A goodly pile of wood chips sat at the carver's feet.

Laverne had on his undecorated white T shirt and his cap. He would wear them to cut hay or fix the barn, which he had been doing. That wind in June took down one of his barns.

When I came in, his jackknife was in his hand and a look of great concentration covered his face. Laverne has but one eye that works—he lost use of the other in an accident a few years ago—so concentration is important when you work at the precise scales of the careful carver. His knife has the look of a silver dagger; years of working wood wore all of the finish off.

The man is 58. He has worked wood since he was a kid. At that moment, Laverne had his knife on the model of a 1925 Ford touring car. Later he would put sandpaper to it. He estimated to me he has made close to 1,000 models and figures in 50 years or so.

Laverne has been carving figures only a short time, when you consider how long he did those models. Yes, this is a hobby, still, although the carver admitted to me that he is giving very serious thought to quitting the farm he and his brother, Roger, work near the Oneonta Airport and becoming a full-time, well, artist.

The news release I had from The Smithy referred to Laverne as a "senior folk artist."

That means that Laverne has not been to art school, nor does he care to go to art school. What he does is purely Laverne Kelley. If someone started messing with him, it wouldn't be.

On the other hand, the sign says it; Laverne has been discovered. They've got him in Cooperstown carving in an art gallery instead of at the farm, where he raises veal calves and his brother has a dairy herd. The few figures by Laverne on view at The Smithy have red dots on them, meaning sold.

In New York City, these pieces of Otsego white pine from the town of Milford, worked on and painted with Rustoleum by a veal farmer, sell for several hundred dollars. Maybe a grand, for a figure of a woman scaled ¾ inch to the foot.

The truth is, Laverne no more finishes a carving, than someone wants to buy it from him. The orders are ahead of the work. He was a little awed by this at first. That was last year, when Sydney Waller, director of the galleries in Cooperstown, invited him in to show in a group exhibit of older artists.

Now, he's getting more used to the notion of being a "senior folk artist" who is interviewed by folklorists and journalists, and photographed, at work, by fine arts professors. John Knecht of Colgate University was recording Laverne on video tape the day I was in Cooperstown.

Everyone told me this attention hadn't changed Laverne, merely his perspective on what an interestingly turned out piece of pine does to some people. He remains the shy bachelor he was before a man he knows who is an antiques dealer was at the farm a few years ago and saw some of his models.

"I didn't realize my models (and figures) were that great," he said. "I did them because I wanted to. I didn't think they'd mean anything to anyone but me. But I'm mighty glad they do!"

Laverne said he is really impressed when a professional artist shows an interest in his carvings. And sure, the notion that he gets his time back in money is pleasing. It wasn't that long ago he was selling off an old barn-full of models for a few dollars a piece. He had something like 400 when he decided to do that. Success takes getting used to.

That's why Laverne lets his new friend, Sydney Waller, take care of the orders, for the most part. "I didn't know what to charge," he said.

"That way, I'm relieved of dickering with customers. She knows about those things; I don't."

• • •

Laverne and his brother grew up with trucks and tractors. Laverne himself was partial to tractors. He knew what farm machinery was all about because he had to fix it.

When Laverne and Roger were kids, they had this whole miniature community set up in the dirt down by the creek that runs through the farm. First Laverne did his models in cardboard. That wasn't durable enough. He turned to wood scraps, old venetian blinds, crate bottoms, sawmill edgings, pieces of metal—anything he could get his hands on.

Laverne said to me he started modeling because he admired the look of a fine machine and he wanted a replica of it he could hold in his hand.

As he got to be a man, the carving improved and turned sophisticated. He worked out a scale and used books for precision. He was working from a catalog of Fords, 1905-78, that cost him $30, to keep that touring car authentic.

The models are sawed, carved and sanded— "you can do a lot with a piece of sandpaper," according to Laverne—and then fitted together with nails and glue. His favorite carving wood is dead white pine, cut from the Kelleys' 251 acres of land. Basswood is used, and red pine too.

Several weeks go into each carving, especially the large ones Laverne is being asked to do these days. He guesses he may do six of those this winter. Smaller ones, whittled and unpainted, don't take as long.

Those figures came into Laverne's repertoire slowly. At first, he had a team and wagon that needed a man on the seat to drive. He took a block of pine and cut himself a man. He did the same thing for one of the many John Deere tractors he has cut. Then a woman in Brooklyn wanted him to carve 16 men, women and children.

Before Laverne knew what had happened, he was a discovered folk artist.

One of the interesting things I found out about Laverne that Saturday in Cooperstown was the photograph albums of his work he has kept since 1963. He takes his own pictures and the pictures, in a way, are as remarkable as the creations themselves. Since Laverne is so high on scale and authenticity, his models were photographed in settings so they appear to be real things!

Laverne said he is open to ideas for carvings, and will do what his clients want, but there are two subjects he will never carve. Those are naked persons and reptiles.

That's why he wanted me to see how he met the challenge of a friend who insisted he had to have a Laverne Kelley carving of Adam and Eve. The finished work sat there on an anvil at The Smithy. The first man and woman were wearing what the carver described as "designer fig leaves" and a large tan snake was curled in front of them.

"I won't do a nude figure; no way," he said. "This man who wanted me to do Adam and Eve said, 'OK, show them after the fall, with fig leaves.' So I did. He said there had to be a snake so I did it but that's it. Never again. That's my first and last snake. And I'm not going to charge him for the snake."                                                        —*1986*

---

# THE CHIEF

We stood in West Kirby Street to say goodbye to Sam Johnson. Right in front of his house. Across the way from Dexter United Methodist Church, where the funeral service for the police chief of Dexter was held Tuesday morning.

In front of me, a collection of iron the likes of which never will be seen in this village on Lake Ontario again. Cops, brothers and sisters to Sam, from all over. Some of them in uniform, some in civies. All of them sad and angry.

The cops stood in the street and under the trees on the side lawn of the church. No room in the little white church for 1,000 badges of that magnitude. Their cars were in the streets, double, triple and quadruple parked.

Behind me, Sam's house. It's the one with the plastic butterflies on the front wall. The one with the cute little mushroom sign marked "Sam and Joan Johnson."

Sam was shot dead Friday night down at "The Point," the peninsula that sticks into the lake, along Black River Bay. The county prosecutor will accuse a man from Syracuse of the killing.

First the man's friend died of gun fire. Then the chief was ambushed. Just now, the investigators haven't the slightest idea how the tragedy got started.

Tuesday they had to deal with the ceremony where you bend over and begin to pick up the pieces.

The streets around the chief's house were barricaded to get the police cars in and keep a way cleared. The hearse was parked at the front door of the church. Some of Sam's neighbors stood with the reporters and the cops, looking at the front door. Others were on their front porches or inside, watching through the windows. One family had the wash out on the line between two maples.

The flags around the village were half way down the poles, most of them. There was a good breeze off the bay. Plenty of clouds. The boats were on the water too, filled with fishermen who must have been strangers. Dexter was busy mourning Tuesday morning.

Diane's Coffee Shop had a sign in the door: "Shop will be closed all day Tues. due to funeral."

No need to say which funeral in Dexter, which had about 1,000 residents the last time they were counted.

The words of Sam's minister were sent into the street on wires. The mood, Leon VanWie said, was "anxious and fearful." Dexter was angry, he said, and frustrated, because of what happened to Sam. "He laid down his life for us," the preacher said.

A kid rode by the line of cops on a pink bicycle. Then Sam's sisters and brothers began a walk-through of the church. Up the front steps, off with the hat—place it over your heart, please—and up the aisle and past the coffin. Out the side door and return to ranks.

All the time the organ played. Up at the end of Kirby, where you can see the bay, two dogs were fighting.

They rolled Sam's box out to the hearse, and the cops were dismissed. The kinspeople got into their cars. The friends from the service waited, hugging each other. The cops went back to their cars and turned on their red lights.

The whole sorrowing street—Sam's street—was lit up with flashing red lights!

Bill was standing on Brown Street, which is Dexter's main drag, next to Tony's Service Station. The guys from the garage were out there watching the procession of red lights as it moved slowly toward Limerick, making a northern loop back to the cemetery so traffic wouldn't be a problem. Bill and his friend Mert were counting cop cars go by. Their eyes were as big as their calculations.

"Mert counted 117, and he didn't get them all," Bill said to me. I asked him if the chief was a friend of his. He nodded. "Everybody's friend," he explained. "The only ones who didn't like him were the ones who got into trouble. Almost the whole town is out here for this. It's stopped the clock."

We filled C Section of Dexter Cemetery, a mile away. We friends and strangers. There was a little green tent over the hole dug for Sam next to the Randalls, the LaRocks, the Frashers and the Sweets. The minister said a few more words, and two deputies folded the flag from the coffin. A state police helicopter flew right over the tent at that very moment.

After that, some of the friends and Sam's kin went down to the municipal building, where the chief's office is, and had a lunch fixed by the fire department auxiliary. Sam had been fire chief too.

Being police chief was a part-time job. Dexter, Brownville and Glen Park shared three part-timers. They worked nights, mostly. Days, the chief worked for the water department in Watertown. The man the DA thinks killed him worked for the water department in Syracuse.

"Sam was the backup when all hell broke loose," the minister had said. The Point is six miles out of Dexter. In this case, Dexter understood. A call for help didn't have a territory for the chief.          *—1987*

---

# DOWSER

John Sager didn't waste any time showing me how to witch water when I stopped to see him in Freeville one morning.

He had a half dozen crotched cherry sticks hanging over a roof brace on the side porch and he pulled one off and beckoned me into the yard. "Of course, we already know there's water here," he explained in a salty upstate twang. "But you'll see how it goes."

And I did. He gripped the stick, palms up and knuckles white, so that the small point of the V arched upward. Then he walked slowly toward his butternut and the point bobbed in the direction of the grass.

Once, twice, five times.

"That's about 15 feet," he said, grinning. "Three feet for every time it goes down. It found the vein running out of the kitchen."

John is an 83-year-old bachelor who lives by himself in a white farmhouse with green shutters in the Tompkins County village south of Cortland. It was his grandfather's place and there have been Sagers on the lot, he figures, for about 150 years.

There is an ample vegetable garden at the other side of the butternut, plenty of bird feeders propped here and there. John, who retired 13 years ago after a heart attack, spends his time puttering around the yard, listening to the fire department monitor in his kitchen and, now and again, helping people locate water.

"I tell everybody I ain't always reliable," he explained. "Sometimes I'm off. I always find some water but maybe it's not enough or too roily."

John has been dowsing about 40 years, he said. A neighbor farmer, Rollo Schultz, taught him how back in the 30's: "He said get yourself a crotched stick and I'll show you how to do it. Well, it worked then and it's worked ever since. I've probably done it 200 or 300 times, all told. I have about 35 so far this year."

We stood in the yard and sun danced off John's Freeville fire police badge.

The practice, despite that record, is informal. John says he never charges for the service but will take a donation, if it's offered. Since he feels most professional drillers don't trust a dowser, most of his contact is with residents or farmers who want him to "locate a vein" before they hire a rig and drive a well.

"Somebody will come along and say 'Hey, John, get your stick.'"

John depends on his stick to tell him not only where water creeps below the surface but at what depth. He believes water flows everywhere under us, spreading in a circulation system that sounds, the way he tells it, like the human body's.

He claims all he needs to find water is a forked twig, or similar divining rod, and two feet on the ground. "I can sit in a car along the road and locate a vein if it's under the car," he said. "Or on blacktop, it don't make no difference."

In fact, the only thing that doesn't bob John's wand is water we can see. "If you ride over a bridge over a creek, it won't turn," he told me. "Creek water won't show at all. It's got to be in the soil."

Nor will the stick perform for John if he goes back to a spot he's witched just before.

All this may puzzle some, and amuse others, but John is comfortable with an ability he sees as a special gift, but not particularly supernatural.

"It's electricity," he said. "That's what a chiropractor I went to for rheumatism told me. He said there are two kinds of electricity, positive and negative; you either got one or the other. It's the stick that makes the connection. They say water is a great conductor of electricity."

The ability, which he figures some people have and some don't, has nothing to do with heredity or tuning into other planes of existence, as far as John can tell. "Up at the spiritual ground (the Central New York Spiritualist Association farm at Freeville), they claim it's a medium who can do it, but I'm not much on that."

John's rods aren't special either, he insisted. The greener the better, because they sometimes snap under the required firm grip, but anything will do. John prefers cherry. "As long as it's a crotched stick. Why I've done it with a stick of timothy hay or a metal rod. Trouble with them is that you can't hang onto them. You've got to hold them as tight as you can.

"I've tried every kind; they all work," he said. Then he took the ends of the V again and started walking toward the garden. The twig dipped.

"There's a vein under the garden that runs up to Main Street all the way to the creek."

Was it getting on to lunchtime? John didn't know. "I've never been able to wear a watch," he explained. "I wear them for a while and they stop. Electricity." —*1976*

---

# BOB

The first time I went to see Bob Snyder on Tug Hill I found him bouncing along a hedgerow on his farm, a load of windfall apples on his back.

He was strapped into a large pack basket of his own making and there was a big smile on his face. "Apple sauce for winter," he said, pointing to his cache.

"There are lots of foods in the woods," he told me that day. "And what I don't find out in the bush, I grow in my garden. Hell, you can live on bean sprouts. They're better than the ones you get in the store."

He laughed and tipped his load onto the floor of the main room of his old house, where Bob is out of touch with just about everything but himself in the Town of Denmark, near Copenhagen.

He buys salt, sugar and Pepsi at the store. Beyond that, Bob does for himself. In an age when independence often is declared but seldom practiced, this stubborn North Country Yankee lives by himself a few miles from a main road, without what we think of as modern conveniences and savors almost every moment.

"If I can't buy it, I make it," he tells visitors.

The next time I stopped to see Bob he was working again, with an axe on an ash log in his front yard. He was softening the sappy flesh to prepare for basketmaking, which Bob has been doing "better than 50 years," he figures. He started at age nine after "listening to the old fellows" and picking up a "few tricks from the Indians."

He has made "all kinds of baskets," each one a little different, off and on ever since.

We walked into the house and pulled chairs up to the wood stove. The room smelled of linseed oil, which he uses on finished baskets, and herbs, which he gathers in nearby fields for himself and others.

Here and there, among books and rolls of ash splint, pans of new plants are growing. Those he sells to nurseries. He showed me a pile of squaw vine bark spread out on a newspaper to dry.

Nearby was a bottle of prickly ash berries. Bob opened the jar and laughed, running his hat back through his hair. His medicine chest is just outside the door, hiding to be recognized.

"I got all I need, out there," he said. "Who needs a dentist? I got it here in the bush. Just chew on one of these and it will knock out a rolling toothache. Oh, sure."

Squaw vine tea to perk you up. High bush cranberries to help you relax. Monkshead for a dying calf or sick dog. Willow bark for a headache.

"Just take your jackknife out and strip off some bark," Bob says. "And while you're out there, make a basket, too."

He smiles again and hauls out an experiment. He had been in the woods the other day and made a basket out of willow twigs.

"Oh, sometimes," he continues, "I sit here for 18 hours and make baskets and then I get bored and go fishing. It's an enormous amount of work but I take it as a pleasure."

Pleasure is much with Bob these days, he says, since he decided, in 1967, that working for a living was killing him. He decided to stay in the old house at the end of the road and make baskets, fish and hunt, gather weeds and seeds and consume as much of nature's bounty—from the dancing grosbeaks on his bushes and to the apple-red sunrises—as a man could stand in a day's time.

Bob bought the farm in the 30s but independence and bachelorhood (his children are grown and his wife left), is comparatively recent. It allows him to spend full-time on things he only did as hobbies before.

"This is a good place to study," he told me. "No interruptions. Oh, I get kids out here once in a while. Some of them want to learn how to make baskets and I teach them some, but not everything. It helps to learn something yourself."

Bob supports himself with his baskets, collecting and selling herbs and supplying plants to nurseries. He says he works just as much, or as little as he likes.

"Oh, I have more business than I can handle. I could have 10 men out picking weeds if I wanted to."

Besides his natural medicines, he borrows honey from the bees, maple syrup from the trees and runs a large organic garden with beans, squash, corn and potatoes in the front yard.

"Everything tastes better," he explained, reflecting "but now maybe I have time to taste it."

Bob does his own gathering, farming, housekeeping, cooking (a "mess of chicken" boiled on the stove as we talked and a cake was promised), doctoring and cottage basket industry. He also traps, cures his own hides and makes buckskin jackets, builds drums out of old logs ("it's a shame to waste them"), paints and reads himself toward self-education ("I never went to school.").

Bob's main contact with the rest of us is a daily drive in his '47 Chevy out to the road for his mail.

"All I need is the mail," he said, "and to go down to Copenhagen once in a while."

Once Bob told me about taking a trip to Lowville. He held his nose. "If I go down again, I'll take a gas mask," he said.

Still, the man isn't a hermit. He lives alone, with a woolly black mutt, and amuses himself by ignoring routine. He hunts on his land, fishes, and prunes his Christmas tree farm.

If the World calls on him, he's usually home.

"Oh, I'm here," he said. "If I'm around and they want to find me, that's OK. And if they don't, that's OK, too."

They come in more than they used to, Bob will admit. People who want to buy his baskets, or talk about making some themselves. People who want to ask him about his plants. Women from town who come down the dirt road and wonder at the bounty of his vegetable garden.

"You know," Bob said. "There was this woman out here and she saw the garden and couldn't believe it. She wanted to know what I did with all the stuff. Hell, I use it all myself."

The shelves are stocked with provender against winter on the Hill. Apple sauce, canned trout, pickles, venison, dried berries, small jars of crushed herbs for tea and big jars of beans.

Once he told me, "There are lots of foods in the woods. Made some cider with the grandchildren this fall. Now that's good, fresh cider. There was a guy out here wanted me to help get out a honey tree he'd cut. Got it out, too. Honey was still hot. Good, but you've got to watch yourself and not eat too much. I think the guy got sick."

Another day when I got there, I found a note on a paper plate on the door latch: "In the plantation. Follow the path."

A well-stripped ash log rested in Bob's yard. He was getting ready to winter making baskets when the snow got deep enough to put him on snowshoes to the mailbox. It was so deep last winter that he had to tunnel out the door and just sat by the wood stove for hours weaving strips into carriers.

I followed two sets of boot marks in the light snow into the back lots. I could see the dog's feet, too, prancing ahead, running a path with his nose.

After a while I heard voices at the edge of the quiet bowl formed by Bob's evergreens. My friend and his granddaughter Sherrie came up over the hill and Bob hailed me with the blade of his old saw.

"We cut a Christmas tree for the church," he said. "Fine tree, too."

I turned around and we put some more tracks onto the snow back to the house. Bob had been listening to the news on his battery radio from the Canadian stations. The Hill is a long way, miles and living ways, from that odd clearing in the jungle of Guyana but he was trying to make some sense out of it, like the rest of us.

Bob had a connection. "Suicides," he said. "We've got suicides here, too. These people out on the roads with their cars. You tell me what the difference is? Driving so fast you kill yourself."

The cold air rushed us to the house and Bob shut the dog in the stoop and threw come slabs into the stove. Then he made a cup of tea, boiling the kettle on "my 50-cent stove" and we ate the ham sandwich I had brought.

Bob said he was ready for winter.

"Another bad one?" I asked.

"Hard to tell," Bob said. "You just wait and see. I notice there's no muskrat houses on the ponds but who knows what that means? Let it storm; I'll eat my beans and make baskets."

As I started home, the little village square was bare of snow in Copenhagen and the creche was up, next to the statue of the Civil War soldier and the cannon, pointing away.                                    —*1978*

---

# WILMINGTON

Hardly a morning comes when Francis Betters doesn't wake up awed just because he's here. It has been 50 years and he still feels that way.

Now the world is looking at his mountain as he sees it from the front window of the Adirondack Sport Shop 10 miles from Lake Placid. Old Whiteface Mountain, 4,867-feet, her top passed by clouds, her chest covered with long white fingers of man-made show where Austrians and Japanese in ski caps try to become international celebrities in the Winter Olympics.

There is a quick flicker on the TV screen. "Wilmington, N.Y.," it says. "Alpine events."

But possession is law here and soon Wilmington will have its mountain back from Lake Placid. Tonight the Olympic Games end. Francis will go back to remembering to be in awe of his mountain, go back to tying trout flies.

Just now, though, the world seems to be beating its way along Route 86 into the hamlet at the Whiteface base. Francis woke up yesterday to find cars and buses jamming his solitude. There were strangers on 86 in backpacks and in restaurants looking for bagels and copies of The News. Copters made noise over the woods where he hunts and the West Branch of the Ausable River, 1,000 feet from his kitchen table, where he talks to the trout with little snatches of woodchuck tail wrapped around hooks.

Buses growled toward Olympia and the troopers had their sirens going.

Francis wasn't doing much business this week. He hopes all the fuss would be worth it. So does Wilmington.

When the Winter Games are over, people here want to be able to make a living out of the leavings.

Francis is known all over the U.S. for the dry fishing flies he invents and makes in his cluttered kitchen-living room behind the shop. The most famous of the lures is his Ausable Wulff and the other night, when we sat in rockers drinking scotch and talking, there was a pile of plastic boxes of them next to us reaching toward the ceiling.

"Got about 6,000 in there," my host said. "Takes me two or three minutes to do one. I tie about 20,000 a year and make 40 to 50 fly rods. That keeps me busy."

If it weren't for those cars out there, and international press in the motels down the road, Francis probably would have tied a few thousand more this week. There have been distractions. Usually this is the slow season, even with the weekend skiers. Trout season is the best time for Wilmington, April to November; the river is rated one of the best fishing streams anywhere. Francis, and maybe his town, are a little like bears waked from winter sleep.

I asked him about after.

"Well, one thing; we're hoping people don't rape everyone so they won't come back. That's a problem, the price gouging down in Lake Placid, especially. But we're hoping for a big spinoff. This is beautiful country. The skiing's going to be good on the mountain with all that artificial snow; we've got the number one trout stream. Only thing is, people aren't aware of it."

That's the problem. people aren't aware. Wilmington hopes to get its mountain back and with it, recognition.

A while before I walked down 86 from the Falcon's Nest, where I'm staying, across the bridge over the river, to the town hall, which has become an Olympic Information Center. I passed Whiteface Market, with its hot coffee and sandwiches to go; the diner, where visitors may park for $4; the doctor's office, the real estate shop and Church of the Nazarene, with its billboard "You have friends in high places."

The clusters of birch, the liquor store, the Cloudspin Corner shop, "Olympic Hours, 7 to 9"; the little fireplugs, little post office, little one-story white houses with inner tubes hanging from trees.

I found Pam Winch working in the town hall for the Whiteface Mountain Chamber of Commerce. She was stuffing "Wilmington Welcome" kits to be left on car windshields at the parking lots. "Introducing New York State's Best Kept Secret" one of the flyers said. The secret, to those beyond the town lines here, is the mountain, of course.

Pam, who is Wilmington born and raised, said the center has been helping Olympic visitors find housing, tickets, bus rides and other conveniences but the generous array of literature, posters and other promotional gear in front of me was designed to try to get them to return, when things are less of a hassle.

"There have been a few people who were mad about the experience —mostly because of the buses," Pam said. "But most of them said they want to come back. We hope they will. Most of the people around here live on tourism."

Olympic inflation didn't get too bad 10 miles out of Placid. Meals and rooms could be had in Wilmington without pain, with a few exceptions. Pam frowned over the few. The restaurant that wanted $4 for a hot dog, with bun, plainly was taking advantage.

"It's people like that who give us a bad name," said Pam.

Wilmington has a lumber yard, where some of the people work, but some of the houses are shabby, some boarded up. There are jobs in Placid, in the mills, the college and the prison, but people worry about their kids. They hang around down at the bridge, steal their neighbors cars and don't look forward very often.

What was I to read into the billboard on the graceful old brick Whiteface Community Church? "Father, forgive them," it said.

Meanwhile, Frank Stevens wonders when he will get his campground back. He is Wilmington, like Francis and Pam, and the state used its powers to get his 21 acres away from him for an Olympic parking lot. Some of the buses said "Stevens" but Frank wants his Adirondack Campground back so he can get a piece of the action. Right now, it looks like a place the bears used for wrestling matches.

"The way they just moved in and took it bittered a lot of people," Frank told me. "They sure offered me an ungodly low amount of rent for it. Now it's all tore up, a mess. They're supposed to fix it up before I get it back but they got until July. That kind of cuts into the camping season, doesn't it?"

The campground was new. Frank came back here to develop it, and he hopes the promises he heard about Olympics Fever come true. "I sure do," he said.

Some of the people in Lake Placid call Wilmington "Winky-Town" because they think they own the mountain. They made LeRoy Beane move up here and he knows better. They raised the rent on him in the village, where he grew up, so he moved his wife and kids out here, where a man doesn't have to pay an arm and a leg for a house. Even though he is making a pretty good Olympic buck, working seven days a week for ABC as an electrician, LeRoy knows the difference between greed and justified compensation.

"Greed, that's all it is," he said into his Miller's at the Falcon's Nest bar. "I was born here and I'll die here but things like that make me think about moving away. Greed."

"Yeah," the girl behind the bar said. "I had to get out of my cabin down there too. I worked a deal with the landlord. I didn't make out too bad, but I had to get out for a minister from Argentina."

LeRoy shook his head. He will do OK, but he really doesn't know about the future of the place. He really doesn't.

Francis Betters sits in his rocker in front of the plastic boxes of Ausable Wulff and waits for the ice to go out on the river. There is a pile of manuscript next to his typewriter on the kitchen table. He is writing a book. The last chapter is waiting.                    —*1980*

---

# PERRY'S MASTERPIECE

The first time I saw Perry Daniels' map of his farm it was flat on the floor of Lou Moon's cottage on the hill above Cazenovia Lake. We walked over it.

Years ago, in the 1940's Mrs. Moon figures, the Lewis County farmer began to work on a project that was to be his master creation. His ceiling of the Sistine Chapel.

Except that Perry Daniels worked in wool and cotton rather than gesso. And instead of Another World, he laid out his own universe in fabric. He hooked it into a rug.

Actually, three rugs, I learned as my hostess walked me around two rooms of her comfortable home, fires perking in the grates.

Here the Black River runs in wool under the chair and around the highboy. There are the cattle, the deer, the crops, the rail fences, the flowers and the people. Perry's hooks followed the plot lines over the Daniels spread and into the Wheeler and Ford places where the river flows past farms along the road from Boonville to Port Leyden.

Mrs. Moon, who grew up in Lowville, has had a summer home near the Daniels farm for years and has known of Perry and his rugs all of that time. But, she recalled, she was stunned when she first saw his rug map. She bought it—it measures 15 by 19 feet—and, with regret, had to halve it to fit into the two rooms of the cottage at Cazenovia.

"It's remarkable," she told me. "I don't know how he ever made it. But then Perry Daniels is a remarkable person."

Part of the extraordinary creation is the man himself, an unschooled farmer who turned 78 last summer.

Perry, I learned from Mrs. Moon, neither reads nor writes and has spent all of his life on that riverbank plot. He communicates barely except through his stitchery, since an illness during infancy left him with impaired speech.

One of his kin, niece Lillie Kohler, explained it this way: "He was sick when he was a baby. And one side was paralyzed. They said it might have been epilepsy. But they couldn't let him go to school. He stayed home and grew up here."

There was no special education for a child who seemed odd in the turn-of-the-century district schools of the Black River region. So, boy and man, Perry did what you can do without words, tended the farm, and spent winters learning to sew from his mother. When she died, and his niece came to live with him, he was, by then, an accomplished and prolific craftsman.

"Oh, he makes an effort to talk," Mrs. Kohler said. "You can understand him if you relax and listen."

A few months later I saw the rest of Perry Daniels' rug map. This section, as large as Lou Moon's, is on the floor of the main room of the old Wheeler farmhouse just up the creek from the Daniels' farm.

Like its counterpart, this rug is full of the farm as the artist saw it, flattened and stretched and pulled through burlap with a bent wire Perry fashioned from a piece of metal found in the barn yard.

"His mother taught him to sew," Mary Wheeler said as we picked the landmarks out of her rug.

"She was a beautiful person. His father used to gather rags and mill ends for him and he worked on the rugs during the winter, when he couldn't get out. I'm told he stretched the rug over sapling rods he cut on the farm and then rolled it up as he worked on it."

She urged me to stop by the farm on my way back. Perry, she said, had given up hooking rugs—he did a lot of smaller, more conventional pieces which he sold to tourists and neighbors for years—but still was working at sewing, she thought.

I did stop, walking up to the little farmhouse next to the barn to talk with Lillie Kohler. Across the road, nailed to a tree, was a handwritten sign: "For Sale, Croched rugs. Come to House."

Mrs. Kohler, of course, remembered Perry's map rugs. It must have taken him six years, working off and on all winter to make them, she thought. He used to take some butcher paper and wander through the fields, sketching ideas, and then come back into the house, go up to his room over the kitchen and work away at his frame.

"He has some imagination, I'll tell you," Perry's niece said with unconcealed pride.

Perry, as he often does, moved in the background along the river that day. I could see him out the window, a browned, small, grizzled figure, piling scraps of wood into a old wheelbarrow. Letting others try to reason out, in words, what he had done in silence.

In that little two-room bachelor's quarters, up the narrow stairs and duck not to bang your head, I found Perry's fingers continue to weave. Not nimble enough to hook, maybe, but to patch quilts, make mittens and sweaters and crochet heavy rag rugs.

Lou Moon was right, "Maybe you can't understand him," she told me, "but Perry Daniels is a very bright and gifted man."         *—1976*

---

# Chapter 5

# HISTORY

---

## THE WIDOW

Twice in her life, Betty McKeever has answered the door to a newspaper reporter. The last time it was me.

Thirty-nine years ago, another stranger arrived at 4 in the morning. The children were asleep in their cribs. The bell rang, Betty ran downstairs.

"Do you have a picture of Jimmy Diamond?" the man asked.

Jimmy Diamond was dead. He was a Syracuse fireman, working the night shift out of Engine 1 across from City Hall.

He answered an alarm and went around the corner and died under the rubble of the Collins Block, Feb. 3, 1939, at the age of 31.

Betty came down the stairs a wife and fell back a widow. The reporter brought the message the chaplain should have carried.

And then, after Betty had gathered up the children and went next door, the man got into her house and stole Jimmy's picture. She saw it in the paper.

Mrs. Jimmy Diamond remarried more than 30 years ago. She is a handsome, happy senior, living in a white and gold-trimmed two-bedroom apartment in the western suburbs of Syracuse. Her second husband, another Jimmy, retired, helped bring up those two kids, who now have kids of their own.

"God has been good to me," Betty said.

Yet the widow's scars hang on. She may remarry, the years may smooth out the pain, memories and names may flicker, but the widow of the Collins Block is a fireman's widow forever. Syracuse's worst fire tragedy is part of us, a spectre frozen into the city's soul.

Betty is the last of the widows made when the restaurant on Genesee fell in on eight firemen, a ninth died of a heart attack at the scene. She knew how it felt April 9 when four more widows were made in an inferno at 701 University Ave.

"Oh, Lord," she said, wiping her eyes as if to remove an old memory film. "My heart aches for them. We feel so deeply for those women and children."

Jimmy Diamond had been a fireman about 10 years when he died. He and his brother, "Lukes," were known to the town as athletes. There were two children, Marilyn, 4½, and Jimmy, 2½, and a house with a mortgage.

The first alarm when the Collins Block burned came in about 2 a.m. The building adjoined the State Tower on the west. It was 80 years old and had been weakened by the Bastable fire in 1923. The main occupant was Ada Keep's Restaurant.

The source of the fire never was identified, but it was put out quickly. The walls collapsed after the men went in, maskless, among the debris.

"Hyco" Moore was right in front of Jimmy in the basement. He got out, barely. Years later, they said his voice was permanently hoarsed by screaming for the men to free him.

When the walls collapsed, "Hyco" told the widow, he dove and his partner was struck by a two-by-four. He was asphyxiated but they didn't get the bodies out for three days. Three days of listening for voices that weren't there, the women and their families sitting in front of the frozen shell in fire trucks, waiting. The priests.

"Oh, after that first minute at the house, I was surrounded by priests," Betty recalled. "I'll never forget what Monsignor Brady did. If ever there was a saint . . ."

Then, on Sunday, the last victim was removed and "everyone just walked away."

But only in fact. The community gathered in the widows and children and made them its own. There was a survivors' fund which helped pay off the mortgage and friends from the engine company to paint the house when it needed it. When young Jimmy needed a left-handed catcher's mitt, the firemen in Gloversville heard about it and had a special one made for him.

A plaque was placed on the site. It's now a drive-in bank office.

In time, there was a monument to the Collins Block dead in Fayette (Fire Fighters) Park. And every cold, windy February, widows, sons, daughters, brothers and sisters came downtown for a few minutes and watched a mayor and a fire chief lay a wreath.

After the insurance and the fund, Betty received $25 a month widow's benefits from the city. The children got $5 each. That wasn't much and she had to go to work.

"I didn't have any choice," she said. "With two young children. But we got along. My family helped out with the kids and on June 1, I went to work as a secretary at the Board of Education. And no one handed me that on a platter. After that, I worked at Porter School until I remarried."

Then the payments stopped. But not being a fireman's widow.

The son, Jim, became a Syracuse policeman. The daughter married. A third Jimmy, a grandson the fireman never saw, loved sports, in the family tradition. He's an All-American lacrosse at Ludden.

And there's an heirloom, maybe to give to another Jimmy Diamond: the helmet his grandfather died in.

Betty got by. She hopes the new widows won't have to work, as she did; "They owe them that much."

Nor endure the chilling moment when she got her husband's last paycheck. In it, Betty said, the pay for Jimmy's three days under the debris had been deducted.                                                    *—1978*

---

# GLADYS AND HARRIET

Gladys Bryant and I visited Harriet Tubman's stone at Fort Hill Cemetery in Auburn Saturday. That was when Gladys told me about the little Christmas tree that grew to be bigger than just about anything else at Fort Hill.

Saturday was the 12th Harriet Tubman Pilgrimage in Auburn. Every Memorial Day weekend elders and members of AME Zion Church from all over come in and pray and have a good time with the memory of "Aunt Harriet," a woman most of us think was one of the greatest Americans we've had.

Aunt Harriet spent the last 50 years of her life in Auburn after she made herself a place in history by guiding blacks out of slavery, South to North. "Scout" was the word used to describe her by the Empire State Federation of Women's Clubs when it bought a new monument for Aunt Harriet in the cemetery in 1937, 24 years after she died.

William Henry Seward, that other distinguished Auburnian, had found her a piece of land near the city line. There was a house and Harriet married Nelson Davis, a Civil War veteran like herself. The name on the front of her stone is "Harriet Tubman Davis." That's all. Her story is on the back.

She planted apple trees in that plot on South Street and wanted to open an old folks home. That didn't work out. Now the house is a museum, with a new library next door.

When she died at the end of the winter of 1913, Gladys Bryant went to the funeral, right there in Fort Hill. Gladys, who is 80 and lives in Skaneateles, is her Aunt Harriet's great-great-grandniece. In case you're counting, Gladys' great-grandfather, William Henry Stewart, was Aunt Harriet's brother.

The AME Zion pilgrims went to the house Saturday. Then to Thompson Memorial Church, on Parker Street, where you can see Aunt Harriet's burial place from the front door. She had a hand in starting the church too.

There was a bus charter for the weekend. Some of the women wore long skirts and red bandannas, which was the way they were told Aunt Harriet dressed. They did this as a memorial to their Moses and because part of the pilgrimage program is a "Miss Harriet Tubman" contest. A good number of the visitors were ordained ministers of Aunt Harriet's church.

The pilgrim in charge of the memorial service at the cemetery—and indeed, the pilgrimage itself—was Bishop J. Clinton Hoggard of AME Zion. The bishop is a handsome man who wore the purple vest of his office and arrived in a car. When he reached the burial lot, he greeted an old friend, the Rev. Emory Proctor of Syracuse.

The stone markers that were on this Stewart plot when Gladys was a girl are gone. Her grandparents, Emma and William Henry, are in there, but Gladys isn't sure just where. Aunt Harriet's monument is a simple rectangle with two geraniums growing right next to it. It is in the cemetery's western quarter, over the hill from the graves of an Indian chief, a presidential assassin and a calvary officer who died with Custer at Little Big Horn.

Aunt Harriet rests among the Smiths, Staffords, Jennings and Elliotts.

The bishop moved us into a semi-circle under a large spruce and got right to the prayer, which was said by the Rev. Andrew Gibson of Rochester. He mentioned our debt to Aunt Harriet. The bishop suggested two hymns, "Steal Away," and "Climbing Jacob's Ladder." He said they were favorites of the woman whose dust we stood on at that moment.

That also was where Cicely Tyson, the actress who played Aunt Harriet on TV, knelt and meditated when Gladys brought her to Fort Hill.

More pilgrims joined us as the service continued. The women in the bandannas walked up to the spruce in a group and started singing. They had children with them who had Harriet Tubman buttons on their chests. The bishop seemed pleased by the size of our congregation. He had us sing the two hymns again. Then he asked another bishop to lay the memorial wreath next to the geraniums.

Around the cemetery, a lot of survivors had been laying memorial wreaths and pots of flowers that didn't need much watering. None of them were singing the way we were, though.

When the service finished, the pilgrims had the bishop stand with them for pictures. They put a line up to the back of Aunt Harriet's stone. The bishop rested his hands on top of the stone and smiled.

When that was happening, Gladys pointed to the spruce. From where we stood, you had to back up and shade your eyes to see the top. This mean piece of shade for Aunt Harriet is taller than anything else close by that grows.

"My mother, Alida Stewart, and my Uncle Charles planted that tree," she said. "It was after Aunt Harriet died, probably 1914. It was a little Christmas tree at that time. And there were no other trees here. It just grew and grew. I think it's amazing. Why, one time, someone cut off a piece out of it, and it still grew."

We both looked up again, at the old spruce's crown and the sky.

"Harriet Tubman's bones," Gladys said. "That's why it's the way it is."                                                                                 —*1980*

---

# THE MOTHER

There isn't a Gold Star hanging in the window of the house on the North Side. Who needs a Gold Star? No one inside is going to forget

Bobby, who was killed 15 years ago in Vietnam.

Bobby was just a kid out of school, working his first job, when he was drafted in 1966, a year Vietnam had a lot different meaning than it does today. He thought about enlisting in the Marines, but his girl friend talked him out of it. They were thinking about getting married.

So, he waited, and finally the letter came and Bobby was ready. Somebody's got to help out those people, he told his parents. He thought of going to war as part of the dues you paid for citizenship; he would go over there, do what had to be done and come back to the house on the North Side and pick up the pieces where he'd left them.

Bobby had bought two new suits, but never got a chance to wear them. Those were two of the pieces he'd pick up when he'd done what had to be done.

Bobby, who probably never thought of himself as a patriot, turned out to be one, in that silent squad of kids from North Sides all over the country, who did nothing at all before they became soldiers to prepare themselves to kill people.

He volunteered into the paratroopers and, when he came home to Syracuse on leave, he looked like a man of war. His mother and father were very proud of their son.

But before Bobby left for Southeast Asia—to a place the teacher probably never had time to teach him about in social studies—he said something to his brother that showed he understood that what he was doing was more than wearing a snappy uniform and spit-polished boots.

He told his brother he was learning to live with the thought that some of them weren't going to come back.

He didn't. He had been in Vietnam only six weeks when the young PFC went out on a search-and-destroy mission and charged a machine-gun nest. Bobby died, and so did one of the enemy.

The Army gave him a Silver Star, and he came back to Syracuse in a casket and was buried the day after his birthday.

Everybody said he was a hero, but when the man in uniform came to the door of Bobby's house, as the family knew he might, his mother couldn't answer the door.

It was Armistice Day and all Helen could see was the eerie glint of the man's buttons and she couldn't answer the door.

Helen, in 15 years, has come to grips with the death of her son. She knows, in her heart, he was just a boy following orders.

She feels the same way about the faceless soldier on the other side who killed Bobby; he was just a boy following orders too. She is a religious person and she prays for that kid, the same way she prays for Bobby.

She also has, in time, come to terms with the war itself, and what it meant to us. The political part of it doesn't bother Helen; best leave those wounds to heal, if they will. She is concerned—she told me the other day—about how America has tried to turn its back on Vietnam's memory and, in the same way, on the boys who were luckier than Bobby and came back.

Sometimes Helen wonders if they were so lucky.

"It's been terrible for the ones who came back," she said. "All those boys in wheel chairs, the pain. It's bad enough to lose a son, but he's dead; it's over. But to have to deal with all that hate when they came back."

Helen and her husband learned to cope. But even after 15 years, it's hard to believe Bobby is gone. Not a day passes that she doesn't think about him. Not a single day, Helen said. She never will forget. Not until she's in the ground herself.

That's one memorial, the kind you can't see. After a year of mourning, Helen joined the Syracuse chapter of the American Gold Star Mothers, where grief is shared and part of the therapy is setting goals. Just now, the chapter is working with Gold Star Mothers nationally to help raise funds for the Vietnam Veterans Memorial, which will be placed near the Lincoln Memorial in Washington, D.C.

Helen and her friends are pushing for the memorial, because they don't want us to forget Bobby and the other sons and daughters.

"Actually," she explained, "they told us that the Gold Star Mothers shouldn't give directly to the memorial. They say we gave our children and that's enough. But we're glad to help."

That's why Helen, and her friend in the Syracuse chapter, another Helen, are spending time handing out brochures about the memorial, which needs $5 million in corporate and private donations, in shopping centers around Syracuse.

"Some people are very receptive," Helen told me, "but some don't even know what Gold Star Mothers are. I guess we want to forget about things like that, pretend they didn't happen."

Helen can't, of course. Just before I left her, she brought out Bobby's Silver Star, which the Army gave her in a plastic box with a photocopied letter from command headquarters explaining how he got to be

a hero. She wanted me to see it, but then she apologized.
"Just like a mother," she said.                              *—1971*

---

# ISABELLE'S HOUSE

This is about how Isabelle Miller had her way with Syracuse University for 35 years, even though she was dead at the time.

At SU, this is called the "little old lady story."

Isabelle was the widow of Holly Miller. She lived at 229 Euclid Ave., at the corner of Ostrom. This was close to the action, you might say.

The house was free and clear. The Millers had bought it about 35 years before, when they moved to Syracuse. Isabelle was from West Virginia. She lived alone and sometimes rented rooms to students. Her daughter lived in Illinois.

At the time that Isabelle became a figure of considerable impact on University Hill, 229 Euclid stood out in its neighborhood. When the Millers moved there, the block was filled with private, one-family homes. In the late 1940s, many of them had been sold to the university for use as "cottage" dormitories.

All but Isabelle Miller's place. It sat there like a wood frame fortress, with the drawbridge up.

You see, SU wanted to build a new dormitory along Euclid between Comstock and Ostrom. This had been in the works since 1949, when a wealthy widow named Mary Margaret Shaw left the university $1.5 million to build a dormitory with her husband's name on it. Her husband was Robert, a very successful baker in Chicago.

University officials approached Isabelle about her house. Lot No. 229 was the last piece in the package that would give them a new $2 million dormitory for women in a two-acre tract.

No, Isabelle said. I don't want to sell. Apparently nothing her neighbors from SU had to say convinced her to change her mind.

Well, no way was SU going to throw away plans for a dorm. Eight of the old cottages had been cleared from the block. Lorimer Rich, an architect alumnus who was famous for his design of the Tomb of the Unknown Soldier, had drawn plans for a 340-bed brick dormitory of three wings.

The wings spread east and west, Comstock to Ostrom. The east wing cut 10 feet into Isabelle's back yard. How about selling us at least that little squib? SU developers asked. No way, Isabelle said again.

Then we will build around you, they replied. Which they did.

Construction was about to start in August of 1951 when a newspaper reporter visited Isabelle to see if she had given in. She hadn't. The house was paid for and she wouldn't stand for it being torn down.

"I will not sell," she said. "The university has not made any attractive offer and it is a disgraceful thing to try and make me move. There are plenty of wide open spaces for the university to build on. I'm sick and have no intention of making a change."

Robert Shaw dormitory was built with the baker's money but it wasn't built the way Lorimer Rich drew it. There was a certain lack of symmetry. The central wing had to be moved back. The southern section of the east wing couldn't be built at all. The lawn and terrace along Euclid would stop at Isabelle's lot line.

We'll make some adjustments later, William Nicholls, assistant SU business manager, explained.

Shaw was finished in a year. It was dedicated Nov. 16, 1952. And 229 Euclid stood where the east wing and the terrace would have been.

Isabelle died at her home 14 days later. She was 81. She was buried down Comstock at Morningside.

A while after 229 was sold to SU. The house was demolished; the wing went on in its wounded state. Now, 35 years later, Shaw dormitory will be finished in the spirit of the original Rich design.

A couple of weeks ago SU announced it was going to spend several million dollars to update and expand student living centers, Shaw among them. The work at Shaw alone probably will equal the original in cost.

"In the course of planning this," Harvey Kaiser explained, "we dusted off some old drawings. When we looked at the Shaw drawings, we discovered a wing that wasn't built. No one around here seemed to know why. I guess it was lost in institutional memory.

"Well, finally, when we brought it up at a trustees' meeting, someone remembered the little old lady story."

Harvey, an architect, is SU's senior vice president for facilities administration. The Shaw wing, he said, will follow Rich's design outside but will be updated inside with fewer rooms and more lounge space. "We're lucky," he explained. "The brick they used still is being manufactured. After two or three years, it will look like the original. I guess 35 years is a long time for the next step to complete the building."

And when the new Shaw wing is dedicated in a year or so, someone ought to suggest a name for it. Right. The Isabelle L. Miller Wing.

*—1987*

---

# JACQUELINE AND MARY ANNE

I'm driving down a shaded street in North Syracuse. I'm driving backward, into a tunnel. It's Aug. 22, 1967.

Jacqueline Saunders and Mary Anne Marzullo were 14 and very good friends. They'd be in the ninth grade at Roxboro Road Junior High School in Mattydale that fall. Jackie lived with her mother in Mattydale; Mary Anne's family—she was one of five children of Linda and Salvatore Marzullo—had a home in a quiet neighborhood north of the Northern Lights traffic circle.

That night the chums had a date, with themselves, to go to the Mattydale Fire Department's Field Days behind the fire barn on Molloy Road.

The carnival was a big deal for the neighbors. A tradition, a thing to do on a hot weekend in the middle of summer. Mary Anne and Jackie had been talking about it for days.

They left for the evening with $8 between them. They'd be back at Mary Anne's place by 11, to spend the night. About 10:30 p.m. they called to say they'd be a little late. A friend saw them walking north, along the east side of Brewerton Road (Route 11), near The Roost Restaurant, toward North Syracuse, about 11:30 p.m.

Jackie and Mary Anne didn't make it home.

The next morning, about 11, three fishermen headed for a day on Chittenango Creek, near where it flows under Oxbow Road. They came upon their bodies.

They lay at the edge of a farm field, at the end of the dirt path into a lovers' lane-fishing hole. They had been strangled, probably by their killer's hands.

The Oxbow is 12 miles east of Mattydale.

The pals in life died together. A single length of quarter-inch rope had been used to tie their wrists, then bind the manacles to one another.

The murders happened 24 years ago today. They remain unsolved.

The crime stunned and troubled Central New York. It's a disturbing piece of unfinished business that won't go away after nearly a quarter of a century.

"I think about it all the time," Public Safety Commissioner Owen Honors in the Town of Clay said to me last week. Owen was one of the first investigators at Oxbow Road.

Owen retired as a state trooper 14 years ago. A hundred officers, or more, worked the case 24 summers ago. A rough guess is that 1,000 interviews were conducted.

Since then a dozen state police investigators had personal charge of the investigation, which was worked, reworked, reworked, then reworked again. Cops retired, cops died, and file number HH 727-728 passed to the next one. The investigator assigned the case had to write a report to his supervisors four times a year about what had been turned over.

Lots and lots of information turned over in those files. Yet the murders aren't much closer to a solution than they were that Saturday when Owen Honors walked into the field next to the creek.

"Every time we turned around, we'd run into a stone wall," Owen explained. "It was very discouraging."

And this week?

"We've run out of leads," state police Investigator Richard J. Sauer said.

Well, almost.

This is Rich's case since September 1990. He's in his 11th year as a trooper. In the summer of 1967, he was 11 years old and living in Taunton.

Rich got me to that street of shade trees and quiet neighbors in North Syracuse last week. He wants us to know a homicide case remains open until an arrest is made. He wants us to know it's his job to find the killer—or killers—of Mary Anne and Jackie.

He wanted Linda Marzullo, Mary Anne's mother, to know that, too.

I knocked on Linda's front door and we went inside. She poured me a cop of coffee. We sat at the dining table, next to the cabinet filled with her china and crystal bells. She opened a white box and Aug. 11 flew out, again.

The box is full of news clippings about Mary Anne and Jackie.

"My family thinks I'm crazy," Linda said to me. "I kept all the clips. Every once in a while I take them out and cry."

You put a tragedy such as theirs behind you, Linda explained, but you never forget it.

I asked her about Rich Sauer's work. Yes, he'd talked to her, and to Bernadine Saunders, Jackie's mom. Both families are pleased that troopers never give up on a case as horrible as this one.

And yet.

Maybe it would have been better if the girls died in a car crash. They could be buried, mourned and remembered, but in closure.

We loved them and it's over. Let's get on with it.

Linda knows that some of her kin feel that way. But Linda? Well, honestly, she doesn't know how she feels that her daughter's murder goes legally unavenged.

"I have mixed feelings," she said finally.

Jackie and Mary Anne were normal, sheltered, suburban kids, on the edge of lives of their own. Linda knew something was wrong the minute she got home that night and the girls weren't there. Soon she was off in the car, driving around looking for them. And after that, at the carnival lot, looking, asking questions.

Rich Sauer's working theory is that the girls were driven from Route 11 in a car. They were picked up as they walked toward North Syracuse, perhaps by someone they knew. Or maybe they were forced to go. There's a reason for those rope handcuffs.

Rich thinks the killer knew the Oxbow.

Yet what did the captor have in mind? No signs of sexual contact were found on either victim. They died struggling to get away.

Didn't anyone see them on Route 11? All reports of the girls in a car, or elsewhere, went nowhere, according to Rich.

"It's like they fell off the earth," he said.

"There's usually something there to tell you why it happened," he went on. "There's no starting point in this case. It's a non-motive crime. Why were they killed?"

Did Linda have a theory?

"I don't think they would have gotten into a car with a stranger," she said. "I think it was someone on dope, who didn't know what they were doing. What else could it be?"

Rich has made a study of this case. Years ago, as a new trooper pulling desk duty at the Cicero station, he'd take out a notebook of reports and read it.

When he took over the files, Rich went back and read them again. He went to the library and checked microfilm newspaper accounts of the murders. He tried to contact all of the investigators who've owned the case over the years.

"I wanted to know if they'd remember something that didn't fit back then," he continued. "Something they might do differently now. Maybe there was something they'd missed."

He also spent an afternoon reviewing the files with Dr. Humphrey Germaniuk, an assistant county medical examiner.

Rich has to keep working the case, even though the rest of us put it aside. Maybe there's someone out there who has the answer this cop is looking for.

"I want to bring it back so people remember it," he said. "Maybe there's something they didn't think of at the time. It's not going to go away."

I leave Rich to his questions and hit Route 11, back to Syracuse from Cicero. On the way I'm drawn to 2610 Brewerton Road, the spot where the friend passed Jackie and Mary Anne before they fell off the earth. No. 2610 is a house, painted brown, with the shades pulled tightly over the windows. When I pull into the driveway, a hand draws back a curtain, then closes it.

At the Seaco Convenience store at 2616, the clerk is making pizza. Did she remember the girls from Mattydale who were murdered 24 years ago?

Sure does. Everyone was frightened out of their minds. They said one friend of the girls never left her house for a year after that. They said the firemen closed the field days and didn't have them again in Mattydale for 10 years.

That was a bad time around here.

I turn and look at the sign on the door on my way out. The Mattydale Fire Department Field Days are on this weekend.

Did the killer of Jackie Saunders and Mary Anne Marzullo confess to police in 1968?

In that year, a 39-year-old man was arrested in Cicero for sexually assaulting a young man he picked up hitchhiking. The man told his victim he'd killed "those two girls in Mattydale." When questioned by troopers, he said he took them to his house in Cicero, tied them up, then drove them to Oxbow Road and strangled them.

He showed investigators the exact spot where the bodies were found in 1967.

He also told them something that wasn't generally known, that the only thing missing from the victims was the pair of brown, cat's eye spectacles Jackie always wore.

He said the glasses fell off and he'd hidden them in a cubby hole in his garage.

Troopers searched house and garage—literally tearing them apart in some places—but they couldn't find the Romco/Rochester size 38 eyeglasses.

Nor could Rich this past June when he returned to the house with two technicians from Welch Allyn Inc. and a fiber-optic device which could probe into the walls.

The man had a hereditary brain disease at the time of his confession. He died in 1975 at a state hospital in Odgensburg.

Do his condition and the still-missing eyeglasses eliminate him as a suspect?

Rich Sauer shrugged. "I can't eliminate him until I arrest someone else," he replied. "Right now, I can't eliminate anybody."        *—1991*

---

# KENYON HOLLOW

This glorious adventure began on the most beautiful day of fall 1985 when I picked up Red La France at his house at the foot of Arab Hill, Town of Fabius.

Red, who was born Albert La France, is the Fabius dog warden. Before that, he specialized in raising championship cattle. He is president of Beauchamp, the Onondaga chapter of the New York State Archaeological Society. As an amateur archaeologist—he seems to have been self-taught in his arcane specialty—Red has few peers. He really works at it.

He is an expert in antique Iroquois ceramics but hardly anything that lies buried under the ground escapes his attention. He works with school children a lot. He teaches other amateurs. Recently, his interests included digging for an old Indian village and a canal tavern, both near Liverpool. He also is compiling a survey of old cheese factories in our region.

Old cheese houses got Red into Kenyon Hollow, a tiny community that once sat on Arab Hill in the far southeast corner of Onondaga

County. Kenyon Hollow was why Red and I headed for The Hill that morning; he was going to show me Kenyon Hollow's leftovers.

Arab Hill, as a point of orientation, is one of the spurs of the Allegheny range rising from the gulfs of the Onondaga-Cortland line, east of Fabius. The National Geodetic Survey marker we found makes Arab 1,900 feet above sea level. That's 100 feet short of the next roll of landscape, Morgan Hill, which is said to be the highest point in Onondaga.

Arab, since 1930, has been part of Highland Forest County Park. It used to be quite different from what it is today.

Red and I keep asking people where the name "Arab" came from. In Fabius and Cuyler, the pronunciation heard is "A-rab," with the strong "A." Some claim "a bunch of A-rabs used to live there," although there is no evidence of this. The first recorded white settlers were New England Protestants. Another story has to do with a family named "A—rab," but I'm not sure I believe that one, either.

Red is sure of but one thing; he found a little settlement up there that almost everyone else, including the formal historians, had forgotten or overlooked. He means to correct this oversight.

Red lived close to Kenyon Hollow for several years without knowing it was there. But then it wasn't, really. The county, in its zeal to plant trees on what had been a mostly barren hilltop that had run out of soil for farm land, eliminated most of the pieces of the settlement. Those that remained sat waiting for Red to rediscover them.

This took place first on an old map. Red consulted it while in the midst of research for a paper he had to do when he was trying to get an academic degree from Empire State College. My friend realized years ago that a degree many speak louder than field work in his adopted profession, but he has had a devil of a time getting those papers that cry "I am." According to him, he has been too busy earning a living and digging trenches in the ground to satisfy academic requirements.

So, there was a cheese factory marked on a map of the middle 1800s. The site looked to be south of the survey bench mark of Arab Hill, maybe halfway between Kamikaze Hill on the Onondaga side of the park and Cowles Settlement, on the south, or Cortland County, face. Highland Forest's main road, which meanders into a dirt path toward the end, passes right by the old cheese house site.

Red turned himself around and took to The Hill for a look. He found the foundation of the cheese factory where it was supposed to be. He found more too. In time, between 20 and 25 foundations. When there were buildings on those old stone walls, Red learned, the place was called Kenyon Hollow.

This may not seem to be a startling revelation. It stunned Red, however.

That day, as we drove and walked just about every corner of the park, he kept coming back to that first surprise. How come nobody knew about this place? It's really shocking there wasn't a record kept when the county bought the land and wiped out Kenyon Hollow. I mean, they just burned down the old farmsteads and pushed the debris into the cellar holes.

Curiosity and pride took over Red. Kenyon Hollow became what he said to me was "my private campaign at preservation." He has been at it four years and the end is not in sight at all.

The first day Red led me though Kenyon Hollow we started at the north end, where a hiking-ski trail covered what had been the road up The Hill from the gulf. Red knows enough about old land signs to be able to chart Kenyon Hollow Road as it crossed Arab. You look for a line of trees planted along the road. You look for the remains of berms. When you get to the farms, maples and lilacs from the yards tip you off to a foundation, or two.

In his months on The Hill, Red has found traces of houses and barns, as well as the cheese factory, school house No. 17 and a cemetery. In time, these will be plotted and marked. The county is interested, again, and some of Red's research is being financed by a grant. There is a geographer to help.

Everything he and his friends learn about Kenyon Hollow, and the artifacts they collect, will end up in the little museum Ray Benson, the former park superintendent, started on The Hill years ago.

Red determined that Kenyon Hollow, as a community, began at the north, just past the park gate next to the horse barn. Most park visitors don't get beyond this point because of the rough road which deadends at the county line.

At the south end, the settlement seemed to have wandered over that line, without regard to it. After all—as it was pointed out to me by Candace Svendsen, the Fabius historian—there wasn't always a line and folks didn't pay heed to a mark on a map, anyway. Candace's family name was Craw. There were many more Craws than Kenyons in The Hollow.

But failing to worry about town and county lines meant the settlement's history—what there is of it—belongs to Onondaga and Cortland, Cuyler and Fabius. It blends into Fabius and Cowles Settlement, a Cortland County community still marked on maps just south of the park border.

Candace's parents lived in The Hollow. She has many stories she heard from the family. We also lucked out in finding Ralph Abbott in Fabius. Ralph lived in Kenyon Hollow the first 13 years of his life, from 1899 to 1912, when his parents moved to a more prosperous farm near Syracuse.

The Craws lived next door to the Abbotts in The Hollow. Ralph went to school at No. 17 and his teacher was "Dama" Partello, Candace's mother.

I met Candace and Ralph after Red showed me the foundations of the Craw and Abbott farms. We walked around in the cellar holes and picked family possessions such as tinware and busted pots out of the crags. The renewal process of nature is slowly reclaiming this evidence of man living on The Hill. Gradually the earth folds back around the stones of the foundation while the winds fill the holes with turf. Grass, weeds and trees come in.

The evergreens were planted by the first foresters of the 30s. This 50 years of growth covers Arab Hill so well, it is hard to see what it was like when Ralph Abbott lived there. Ralph has those contrasts in his head; Red and I have to work at them, all the while getting help from maps, pictures and peoples' memories.

That picture of the old school Ralph has hanging in his dining room helped quite a bit.

It took Red months to find some of the old foundations. Even last fall, when he toured me, the overgrowth of small trees and weeds was a powerful obstacle for a couple of amateur historians.

I thought we walked a mile east off the park road to find what had been the Van Dusen farm. Red said he had had a heck of a time locating it last year. Later Ralph told me he could see the house from his front yard.

We pushed through a thicket and around a stream that Red pointed out had been enlarged by a family of beavers. The Van Dusen foundations were hidden in a grove of golden rod. I ate an apple from the Van Dusen's tree in the yard. Next to the house was a 10-by-10 cellar that puzzles Red. He can't figure what it was.

A mess of household and farm goods was dropped in there when the county wiped out the farm. Red has done some digging. He found an old bottle of embalming fluid in there. He can't figure that, either.

We pushed a little farther south along the beaver's stream bed to the grove at the edge of the park where Red found the cemetery one afternoon when he was out with a troop of school kids. So far, he's located only two old markers, cut with dates of 1823 and 1844, but he knows there are more, perhaps just below the surface.

There are stories about how rough it was up there in the old days. Stories of farm boys going down to the flats to get grain ground and then having the wolves tear open the bags when they tried to get the flour home. In 1795, when an early settler, Susannah Potter, died, her husband made her coffin out of the door of their log house. Years later, one of Ralph Abbott's playmates, one of the Vosburgh boys, was killed when a tree fell on him.

It was subsistence farming, at best. The wind blew pretty good and the pastures weren't much to begin with. Erosion carried the soil to the valley and only tough grasses survived. Families moved to Cuyler and Fabius, looking for better deals. Farms were rented and then abandoned.

These days, according to Ralph Abbott, if he mentions the name Kenyon Hollow, "nobody knows what I'm talking about."    *—1986*

---

We had quite a time at the Craw reunion at Highland Forest County Park. For a few of us, it was sort of a home-coming.

Years ago, there were Craws all over this highest ridge in Onondaga County. Now the best a family member can do is drop by for a Sunday picnic with a mess of kin.

Arab Hill, and environs, became a park in 1930. By then, the last of the Craws—it is said that was Herman—had moved off The Hill. What use the land had been for farms was worn out in 100 years or so. Some of the farmers just left, without bothering to deed the lots to someone else.

The county gathered those lots into a parcel, burned the houses and barns and planted trees. The look of The Hill changed. Years later, as the Craws sat down for their 80th reunion, or so, it was hard telling this once was a little farm community in the farthest southeast corner of Onondaga.

Ernie Craw and I had a devil of a time finding a few tracks left of

Ernie's kin, in fact.

Actually, I'm not a Craw, according to the best information in hand. Ernie married a cousin of mine. I came to the reunion as a guest. Three years ago I was introduced to Ernie's homestead by Red La France.

There were others up there too, of course. But the name Craw appeared most often on old maps I looked at. Not only that, you have the intermarriage factor, which drew several neighbor families onto the Craw tree.

A good example of this was the interesting discovery we made after Julia, Ernie's sister, opened up the second Craw reunion book on one of the picnic tables at Torbert Shelter, where we were drinking coffee and eating doughnuts from Chittenango. The book carries reunion minutes, and lists of Craws in attendance, from the 19th reunion in 1930 to the present.

Ernie and I noticed the 1930 reunion—the one that pivotal summer when the foresters and park-planners took over The Hill—was held at the home of the president of the family association in Cuyler. His name was Clayton Case!

We started giggling. You have to understand that Ernie's wife, Marilyn, is a Case, through her mother. Had Ernie married a distant cousin, by accident? Well, no, probably not. Marilyn's Case kin lived in another part of the county, around Marcellus. I knew of no cousins in the Town of Fabius, but we'd check it with the Case genealogist.

We moved on to more serious matters, such as why they called this place "A-RAB Hill."

The Craws assembled at the shelter agreed this always had been Arab Hill, or just The Hill, among Craws. The name had something to do with a family that lived over on the back side of The Hill, the Albros. We couldn't figure what, though.

Hilda, Ernie's mother, said the grade getting to the Craw farm was so steep they'd have to get out and push the cars when Hilda and her husband came to visit his parents.

Julia remembered those trips. "We'd come up on Sundays and pick wild flowers," she said. "They had an old ice house on the farm. Anyone remember the old ice house?"

No one answered. This is the challenge, among contemporary Craws. The old folks passed on without being seriously questioned about life at Kenyon Hollow. About all Red La France had to go on was a dozen sunken building foundations he found. Just now there's plenty of back-filling to be done as far as family history is concerned.

The professionals will help some. Red scratched the surface literally and figuratively; the reassembly process has started among the Craws. The county hired researchers to look into life on The Hill between 1830 and 1930. Some of that information will be woven into the new exhibits at Pioneer Museum at Highland Forest.

The pioneers of the museum will be the Craws and their neighbors in Kenyon Hollow.

Cousin Candace from Fabius is part of this. Her mother was the last teacher at School No. 17, next to the farm of Ernie's grandfather, Everett Craw. We all shut up when Candace had something to say at the reunion because of the valuable information she carried with her.

Candace and Ernie got to talking about Everett, who weighed about 300 pounds and was built like a wedge. Candace had heard they buried Grandpa in a casket specially-made to accommodate his stature. Ernie shared the story of Everett picking up a huge keg down at the store in DeRuyter when no one else could even budge the thing.

Ernie wanted to see the home place, what is left of it. I offered to try to find the foundations Red toured me though three years ago, right after he started finding them among the trees the county planted. He dug out artifacts too—glass, crockery, wire, nails, roofing, machinery parts, horseshoes, bricks. These will be shown at the museum. Red recommended the foundations be exposed, bermed and marked.

We set out down the park's main road, which used to wind clear over the hill, from the old turnpike (Route 80) to the county line and Cowles Settlement on the south. A county fence stops cars at what had been the north end of Kenyon Hollow.

We left the road and picked our ways through the trees, to a house foundation Red marked No. 1 on his map, which I saw later. I was pretty sure that was the one that used to hold Grandpa's house. Ernie got pretty excited. I knew how it was. A man can't help but be worked up when confronted with his own history, no matter how meager a shambles it is.

We could almost see Everett up there in the vanished doorway, filling all of it.

We ducked among the trees and weeds, all the time the bugs snapping at us and the sharp branches grabbing at our faces. The barn must have been up the hill to the side, probably. Yeah. We couldn't find enough old foundation stones to say for sure.

The old Abbott farm and the school house were down the way a bit. We checked out those too, and I pointed into the woods, where I thought Red had found the old cemetery, with two stones left above ground. One was John Barber's, who died in 1844 at the age of 14. The second marked Anny Austin's grave. She died in 1823.

On our way back I noticed Ernie'd picked a broken china cup out of the foundation of Grandpa's house. He had the memento in his hand. The old dish will be Everett's grandson's start toward putting his memory back together.                                         *—1989*

---

# FRANCINE AND ABE

Francine Bizzari said she has an affinity for Abraham Lincoln. Affinity, as in kinship, attractive force, spiritual connection.

Every Feb. 12, which was Lincoln's birthday, the slain Civil War president wishes Francine happy birthday. Feb. 12 also is Francine's birthday.

Francine is 46. She lives in Auburn. She is a wife and mother. During the last 10 years or so she has been a professional psychic. She had the feelings of an unusual ability years before that.

One day in 1980, Francine decided she wanted to visit the William Seward House, at 33 South St., Auburn. She had lived in the city all her life and never had been inside the mansion, which is a public museum. No. 33 used to be the home of the man who was Lincoln's secretary of state.

Francine made the visit with her husband and a friend. Her husband brought his camera. That day it was loaded with infra-red film. Infra-red film is useful in recording images that may not show up on regular film.

"The minute I got inside the front door, I was drawn into this room," Francine told me the other day at her home in Auburn. "I wanted to see if William Seward's spirit is there. Of course, Betty (Lewis, the director of the museum) was skeptical."

I was familiar with the room. It is the north library. The last time I visited Seward House I spent some time sitting in a side chair next to Seward's whist set talking with Paul McDonald, the caretaker, about "Henry," as the former owner is called. One of the decorations in the library is a huge bronze bust of Henry.

Francine said she felt the need to go into the library and sit on the couch at the west end of the room, next to the bust.

"I could feel William Seward immediately," she recalled. "He was lying on the couch. He was sick, very tired. He had some congestion in his chest. He pointed to his chest."

I knew, because Paul McDonald told me, that was the couch where Henry died, during the afternoon of Oct. 10, 1872.

Francine continued:

"I felt the presence of another man in the room. I turned around and I saw the bust of Lincoln (at the east wall, next to the window). I felt a cold chill and I knew someone else was there. It was Abraham Lincoln.

"I got into communication with Lincoln. I asked him if he ever had been here, in Auburn. He said he was. He was here for a special anniversary party for the Sewards. It was a surprise They didn't let anyone know about it. Both he and his wife came, he said."

The secret has kept well. I checked several Lincoln books and none mentioned a visit to Auburn. A 1972 collection of the letters of Mary Todd Lincoln recorded a "courtesy call on the Sewards in Auburn" in the summer of 1861. Her husband was not with her for the trip.

Betty Lewis said as far as historians at the Seward House knew, Lincoln never visited the Sewards in Auburn. She also said she was not aware, as Francine was, that Mary Lincoln had attended a seance at the National Hotel in Auburn.

Mrs. Lincoln's interest in spiritualism is documented. It has been suggested seances were held at the White House while the Lincolns lived there and that the president himself sometimes attended these sessions. Mary Lincoln did have a number of meetings with spiritualists. This was part of her recovery from the death of her son, Willy, in 1862.

Books of ghost lore contain reports of Lincoln's ghost at the White House over the years. Teddy Roosevelt claimed he could feel Lincoln's spirit. During Franklin Roosevelt's time, a woman staff member saw Lincoln's figure in the Lincoln bedroom. The ghost sat on the bed, pulling on a boot. Eleanor Roosevelt also told friends of Lincoln's presence.

Francine said she made a couple of other discoveries during her visit to Seward House. One was a carriage in the garage behind the mansion.

"There was a buggy out in the garage," she explained. "I could feel it even before we got there. There was an accident with that buggy. Someone was trying to kill Mr. Seward."

Betty Lewis told me that was the carriage Seward was riding in a few days before the assassination plot in 1865. He was thrown and seriously injured. That was why he was in bed when one of the assassins found him the night John Wilkes Booth killed Lincoln.

Francine said she also felt the presence of Seward's wife, Frances, around the piano in the parlor and outside, in the gardens. Frances died a few months after the assassination attempt on her husband. Francine felt she liked to give tea parties in the gardens.

The snapshots taken that day are in Francine's scrapbook. There are three. Each show what appear to be splashes of light on the print. One shows a light spot at the piano, another next to Francine as she sat on Seward's death couch and the third around Lincoln's bust.

This might strike some people as pretty creepy but Francine said it isn't, as far as she's concerned.

"The house is not haunted," she said. "The house is full of love. I could feel comfortable there. There is lots of activity, though. Lots of spiritual activity."                                    *—1980*

---

# BIG BILL

If ever there was a man of legend in the Finger Lakes, it was Big Bill. Stories survive him still.

The record shows him born in Columbia County, on the Hudson's eastern shore, into a family that had immigrated from Germany a generation before. His father was a dirt farmer who soon moved farther inland, as the wilderness frontier began to lengthen in the York State. That was nearly 200 years ago.

In the beginning, the family was unnoticed, but Big Bill apparently soon fixed that. Stature turned some heads; that was why they called him Big Bill. By all accounts, he stood over six feet and had the sort of build that made him look like he had an oak barrel under his shirt. His eyes flashed and when he laughed, it was good and loud. He liked to tell stories and, as he grew older and found ways to afford them, sport flashy clothes.

Bill's father, Old Godfrey, moved the family deeper into New York in the 1830s. A story preserved in the family had it that they really were headed for Michigan but got to northeast Tioga County. They stopped overnight in Richford and the hotel keep asked them where the pike would take them. When they said Michigan, to go into lumbering, the Richford man said there was good timber right there, on East Hill.

They looked around, liked it and stayed. That's why, even today, the family plot is known as Michigan Hill. Down there they say it Mich-a-GAN, though.

Big Bill settled in, bought 50 acres of land for about $50 and married a red-haired, blue-eyed Cayuga County girl, Eliza, from Niles, in 1837.

Life was tough in the little frontier settlement. Children and mothers died early, churching was little thought of and pioneers lived day to day, hustling the best they could. Since Big Bill was a hustler, he did better than most.

Big Bill and Eliza had three children while they lived on Michigan Hill. In the 1840s, they left, moving again with the frontier into the Finger Lakes. This time the little farm overlooked Owasco Lake, north of Moravia.

It was during this period of his life that legends began to bulge around Big Bill. This is what a family account said of him, modestly:

". . . of roving disposition. He was engaged in trading and selling merchandise. He would be gone for months at a time and would then come home unheralded, either astride a good horse or driving a good-looking rig. He was a good story teller, telling of trips through New England and upstate New York. He used no liquor. He kept his business to himself. He hired a man to do the work on the farm . . . he provided well for his family. He taught his sons to be sharp in business."

This role, family man and traveling salesman, sat strangely with the quiet, stay-at-homes around Moravia. That's one of the things still told about Big Bill—how he'd be gone for months, then suddenly pop up in a new rig and suit. It is said the roll of bills in his pocket seldom was less than $1,000 and the trousers usually were silk.

He swam like an Indian, they said. Wrestled bears. Jumped backwards over fences. He loved to sing and played the fiddle tucked into his hip.

Some said he was a ventriloquist, hypnotist and speculator in horses and land. Quite a fellow, Big Bill.

One of his grandsons once said of him: "He was a very entertaining man. All the family loved him. He came and went when he felt like it. He lived a detached kind of life and I didn't know much about it."

That was part of the lure of Big Bill, then and now. Nobody knew much about him.

One of the things that has been verified is that he was a medicine peddler. That may have been what he did on those trips away from the farm. Some said he turned into a different person when he hit the road, with a new name and personality. They said he pretended to be deaf and dumb and sometimes traveled with a fellow who pretended to be an Indian.

Not everyone loved Big Bill. Sparks flew from his electricity and in the summer of 1850, Bill moved his family (by now there were six children) out of Cayuga county to Owego. He lived there about three years, when the family re-established in Ohio.

One reason for selling the Moravia farm may have been an indictment returned by a county grand jury against Big Bill. It charged him with the rape of a hired girl who worked for the family. Anyway, they never came back, but the charge was not pursued, either. A family historian said merely "he was forced to absent himself from home for fear of criminal prosecution."

In Cleveland, where the family settled, the children grew up and prospered—some say prospered very well—and Big Bill's feet were looser than they'd ever been. The frontier had been rolled even deeper into the West and he was out at the edge, fiddling and swapping and making more mysteries.

Finally, after a while, he disappeared from Ohio altogether.

When Eliza died in Cleveland in 1889, at 79, she was described as Big Bill's widow. But by another account, her husband couldn't make the funeral because he was living in Illinois, with another wife and another name.

The two story lines branch from the southern Finger Lakes region where Big Bill, in this version, is said to have married a Canadian woman named Margaret Allen in 1855. In time, they set up housekeeping in the river town of Freeport, Ill., where Big Bill, the "celebrated cancer specialist," became Dr. William Levingston, physician. Eliza still was his legal bride.

"Doc" Levingston and his Margaret lived in Freeport the last 34 years of his life. Folks there remember him as a tall, strapping man—later deaf and bent by age—who was known to travel a lot in his early days. He boasted, told stories and always wore a large diamond pin at his collar in place of a tie. Most of his life before he came to Freeport was not mentioned.

When he died in 1906, at the age of 96, he was buried in the city cemetery under a stone that carried the name "Levingston."

But later, a funny thing happened. His son, whose name was John D. (for Davison, his Niles grandfather), became a very famous and controversial figure in American life. He made it big in oil, and reporters, who were called "muckrakers" in those days, began poking around in his biography. They found his father, Big Bill, and published pictures of him. When people in Freeport saw the photographs, they blinked. Wait a minute, they said, that's "Doc" Levingston.

And yet another legend was woven into the life of Big Bill Rockefeller.                                                                                                    —*1980*

---

# JERRY

We know the story of the fugitive slave named Jerry in Syracuse in 1851.

The raucous rally in Clinton Square. The angry white guys battering down the door of the jailhouse nearby. Jerry, in drag, getting out of town at the bottom of an empty meat wagon.

Then hiding in the village of Mexico two weeks before he hid in a second wagon—this one empty of hay—for a trip to Oswego and Lake Ontario.

And finally, on a steamer, across the lake and into the St. Lawrence River, a freed man in Canada.

A monument was dedicated to the event 139 years ago this October. One day there might be a remembrance in Canada, too.

I'd always wondered what happened after Syracuse to the man born William Henry. Others had too, including Chet Whiteside, the Syracusan who was father to the Jerry Rescue Monument.

Last month I went to Kingston, Ontario, to try to find an answer or two. Before I left that sparkling city on the river, I stood in the grove that seems to be Jerry's final resting place.

The "Jerry Rescue" took place Oct. 1, 1851.

Jerry died in a Kingston hospital Oct. 9, 1853. He was 41 years old.

Only a few fragments of his life as a free man in Canada survive in 1990. One of them is in the collection of the Onondaga Historical Association. It's the "Jerry Chair."

This well-worn, fragile antique—in the style of a captain's chair—has been in Syracuse since 1922, when it was donated by the Wheeler family of Union Springs. It comes to us with a story.

Jerry seemed to have gotten by with the help of friends in Kingston, which was no stranger to liberated black men and women from the United States. One, Harriet Powell, fled to Kingston from Syracuse in 1839.

A helper of Jerry's in Kingston was a man named Joseph George.

According to the late Elizabeth Simpson of Oswego County, author of the 1949 history "Mexico, Mother of Towns," the fugitive found "friendly shelter" with George, "who wrote his letters for him."

He also got a job in Chester Hatch's chair factory on Princess Street in downtown Kingston. The Hatch shop is well-documented in the files of the Kingston public library. One newspaper ad described "elegant chairs at the sign of the fiddle" in 1817.

A Syracusan, Edward Wheeler, found Jerry at the chair factory "near the old market building" when he moved to Kingston to run a saw mill in early 1852. He knew Jerry because he'd helped him escape.

His son, R.E. Wheeler, wrote of seeing Jerry when he went to the shop with his father. In a letter to the historical association in 1925, he said:

"It was in this city (Kingston), at that time as a boy of 8 years of age, that (I) saw the ex-slave, at work in his shop . . . and it was here that he made the chair for my father by whom it was highly cherished during his lifetime and was in the possession of the family for a period of 70 years or more.

"In our family, it was always known as 'The Jerry Chair.' "

On Oct. 17, 1853, the Syracuse Standard published a letter from Wheeler in Kingston which commented on Jerry's death. He mentioned a few things about his friend's life in Kingston:

"About a year ago he became 'converted' at a revival held in Kingston (the Baptists we believe) and during his residence in Kingston we understand his conduct has been quite as good as that of the generality of men of his rank in life.

"Some accounts represented him to have had occasional fits of despondency and loneliness, but he was generally cheerful and contented with his lot."

Elizabeth Simpson's account of the rescue of Jerry in her Mexico history is reinforced by her family connections. The historian, who died in 1967, was a great niece of Wheeler's.

She also wrote that Jerry was "said to have married" in Canada.

I couldn't find any record of a William Henry in Kingston between 1851 and 1853. Neither could Chet Whiteside, when he went there to check out traces of Jerry in 1988 and 1989. Nor could Richard Wright, retired president of the historical association, before us.

Enter Ruth S. Riggs of Kingston, an archivist with the Anglican Church's Diocese of Ontario. The Herald-Journal hired Mrs. Riggs to search her archives, and others in Kingston, for clues to Jerry's last two years.

She found a record of his death.

It was in the parish register of the church that became the Cathedral Church of St. George for the Anglicans in Kingston.

Under burials, the funeral at St. George of "William Henry, 40," Oct. 9, 1853, was recorded. Jerry was sent to rest with the prayers of an Episcopal priest.

And where was he put to rest?

The register didn't say, according to Ruth Riggs. She and I made additional checks at Cataraqui Cemetery, Kingston's municipal burying ground, which opened in 1853, the year Jerry died. Cataraqui's files do not mention William Henry, or a name close to that. Or even "Jerry McReynolds," as he was sometimes known.

However, Mrs. Riggs said last week she is sure Cataraqui was Jerry's burial place. In fact, Elizabeth Simpson said it was in her Mexico history:

In Chapter 18, we read, "He died of consumption in the general hospital Oct. 8, 1853, and was buried in Cataraqui cemetery three miles from Kingston."

I visited Ruth Riggs at the diocesan center in Kingston. We talked about the other man from Syracuse and then she directed me to Cataraqui, which is about four miles north on Princess Street. There I met Marjorie Simmons, president of the cemetery board, and Gordon Raymo, the superintendent.

Cataraqui, which was the Indian name for Kingston, sits on a hill next to a shopping mall and a busy highway. Once inside the gates, I was reminded of our own Oakwood Cemetery.

Many of the worthies of Kingston made their way to Cataraqui—including Jerry's wood shop boss, Chester Hatch, and his wife.

"You're nothing unless you have three generations up here," Marjorie Simmons explained, with a laugh. Yes, she qualifies.

Canada's first prime minister, Sir John MacDonald, was buried in Cataraqui.

Marjorie Simmons and Gordon Raymo apologized for not being more definitive about William Henry. Early records are spare. They agreed with Ruth Riggs that it was likely Jerry was in the cemetery's first "common ground," a modest plot of unmarked graves near the front gate.

I walked to Section A with Mrs. Simmons. She pointed out the McDonald plot, at the top of the hill. Close by is the cemetery's first burial of record, the grave of Henry Cassady, April 23, 1853. Cassady drowned in the St. Lawrence off Kingston. He was the son of the mayor.

We stood next to a metal statue of a goddess with an urn. Mrs. Simpson and I looked at the swatch of uncluttered grass. "Oh, if you could only turn back the clock for an hour," my hostess said. "If he's in there, I hope he's at rest."

A small footnote to Jerry in Kingston:

In 1890, when he would have been 78, had he lived, the Syracuse Journal published an account of the rescue which had the principal "alive but quite feeble" in Colorado.

The story claimed Jerry had left Canada for Colorado, invested in land and prospered. He wrote letters to friends in Syracuse, the Journal reported, but "for some unknown reason they had not been received."

It also was revealed Jerry had been reunited with "four of his children" after the Civil War. His grandson, identified in the story as Thomas Blackhurst, had just graduated with a degree in medicine, in fact.

Jerry was born in North Carolina to a slave mother and a white, slave master father. When he escaped, to end up in Syracuse in the late 1840s, he lived in Missouri and may have had a wife and son.

Chet Whiteside was interviewed by the Whig-Standard newspaper in Kingston during his visit in March 1989. The story mentioned it "would be a big thing for him" to find William Henry's grave "or a great-great grandchild."

Chet told me last week he never heard a word from anyone in Canada about his wish list.                                                          *—1990*

# GRACE AND CHESTER

I went looking for a thread of history in the central Adirondacks.

I found it at the Higby Cottage near South Bay of Big Moose Lake, in the living room, next to the window. The thread was held by Roy Higby.

Roy is 91. He is a survivor. Big Moose has changed mightily since Roy was born a few hundred feet away in his father's cabin. Roy has changed, too. He has outlived people and events. The people are gone. The events keep coming back.

Roy, I would say, is an expert in recycled time.

For example, an afternoon in July of 1906, when he was 13 years old, keeps coming back at him. That was the afternoon he was on the steamer boat "Zilpha." The craft belonged to his uncle. Roy was the purser. That afternoon he went out on the lake to help the engineer handle machinery. They anchored in South Bay where an overturned St. Lawrence skiff had been found. First thing Roy did was to look over the side.

"Almost at once I discovered a light blur on the bottom of the lake," he wrote in a book called ". . . A Man from the Past," published in 1974. "I called the engineer . . . he then took a long pike pole off the roof of the cabin and started to probe the water with it . . . a hook line was dropped down which caught on part of the girl's dress and she was brought to the surface.

"I can remember exactly my first sight of the body . . . She was dressed in a white shirt-waist, light green skirt and button shoes and stockings . . ."

Roy was there for the beginning of what came to be called "An American Tragedy Murder Case." The girl in the lake was Grace Brown. She had been murdered. The killer was Chester Gillette. They went to Big Moose for what Grace imagined was a wedding trip. Both worked at a skirt factory in Cortland. Chester took his friend out on the lake in a skiff, hit her with a tennis racket and threw her into the water.

In 1908, Gillette died in the electric chair at Auburn prison. In 1923, novelist Theodore Dreiser traveled to South Bay to absorb atmosphere for the story he was writing around the case. The book, "An American Tragedy," was published in 1925.

That was about the time the past began revisiting Roy Higby. He tells me it's not let up in 60 years.

"Hardly a month goes by that people don't come in wanting to hear about the case," Roy said after he settled in his favorite chair and lit his pipe. His alarm clock ticked loudly.

"Why, last spring, there were some men in here from Cincinnati. They said they were from a TV company in Ohio. They were doing something about the 'American Tragedy' case. They took a lot of pictures. Not too long ago, there was a couple of college girls. They were doing some kind of research paper."

As far as I know, Roy is the only person still alive with a direct connection to the crime.

"You know, the best one was three or four years ago. Four people from Japan showed up and started asking if there was anyone here connected to 'American Tragedy.' They sent them up here. Well, they were doing a movie for a TV company in Japan. Only one of them could speak English, the woman, the actress who did the interviews.

"They took a mess of pictures with one of those video recorders. Moved around all the furniture in the room and had me sit on the sittee in front of the window (with the lake to his back). She asked me a lot of questions. They also took me down to the pier and made some film.

"I asked them why in the world the Japanese would be interested in a case like that. They said the Japanese go crazy over American murders."

A few months later the visitors wrote Roy a letter. They said the film had been broadcast and 40 million people saw it.

So it goes with the rather ordinary homicide that is a classic of its kind.

Roy said I shouldn't ask him why but I did anyway.

"Oh, her love letters (Grace's to Chester, which were read at the trial in Herkimer and published as a booklet) had a lot to do with the fame of the case. And the isolation of the place. Dreiser's book helped, too."

Higbys have been at Big Moose since 1868, when Roy's father, Jim, arrived to work as a guide. Roy claims he was the first white man on the lake. Jim bought 150 acres and opened a hunting camp in the 1890s. Later it became a boarding house for hunters and tourists and later still, the Higby Club, which was run for years by Roy, his mother and his wife.

The club, at its peak, was one of the big Adirondack resorts. It had more than 40 buildings, including boat houses, a theater, laundry, and a main lodge with three chefs and a dozen waitresses. The Higby went the way of many other businesses in the region and Roy phased it out in 1974. He started selling lakeside lots and enjoying retirement. The club grounds slowly are being reclaimed by the wilderness Jim Higby found when he arrived at Big Moose.

The innkeeper is left to talk to visitors like me who come to his door wanting to hear about the day he found Grace Brown at the bottom of South Bay.

"It never dies," he said as I left. "It never will, I guess."

•   •   •

Camilla wanted me to see the picture she had, so I went to her apartment east of the city. Camilla is in her 90th year. She seems younger.

The picture is a sepia print, mounted on stiff cardboard. It has seen better days. Once it had been deep reddish brown. Now it is light brown and fading fast. After a while there will be no image at all.

Camilla knew this. She knew how the sepia goes, like the memory. She had a black and white modern print made to help lock the image in place. Showing it to me helped, too.

The picture was made about 1902, in northern Chenango County.

The photographer had the scholars of Tallett Hill School stand on the stoop to pose for their picture. There were 14. Fifteen if you count the teacher. That was Maude Kenyon. She stood in the doorway, next to her oldest pupils. She didn't seem much older than them.

The scholars are clustered and stiff. They look to be uncomfortable. Some of the heads droop. There is hardly a smile in the lot. Maude Kenyon is smiling pretty good.

The cluster moves chronologically to the peak of a triangle. Young kids at the bottom, older ones at the top. Eleven girls and three boys. Some are of the same family.

Camilla, of course, knew each name. She was there in the second row, next to Clarence. Neither smiled.

Let's see . . .

In the front row, the tall girl in the long, dark skirt. That's Frances. Right next to the sisters, Nellie and Blanche. The child with her head down is Ruby. Then Floyd and Ivan. Ivan's got his best bibs on.

Then Frances' sister, Mary, and Zion, Mary's sister Hazel and Eva, next to Camilla and Clarence.

The two girls with the teacher were the oldest of the scholars, Hazel's sister Grace and Camilla's sister Fern. Camilla said they both were 15 when the picture was taken. They were good friends. Called each other "Billy" and "Ted." Fern already had her hair up in the "Gibson girl" style. Grace would get to that later.

Camilla's finger ran across the old print as we talked. She had tried to keep track of her classmates in the one-room schoolhouse the other side of South Otselic on the way to Beaver Meadow. It had not been easy. Her folks moved to Beaver Meadow and she went to high school at South Otselic. When she married, she left the county.

I followed her finger. "I've heard she's dead," Camilla said of one of the images. "I kept in touch with Nellie and Blanche. Now Hazel and Frances and the other girls moved from their farm over to the flats on the other side of DeRuyter. I visited them over there. I think Ivan died some time ago . . . Frances I heard died in Syracuse . . ."

It turned out that all of them were gone, except Camilla. Maybe Ruby. She used to live over by DeRuyter.

Maude Kenyon married the village doctor at South Otselic, Mott Crumb. Oh, yes, both of them died years ago.

Camilla said most of her classmates had done well by their lives. They had married and multiplied. Their great-grandchildren were standing for their class pictures in some schoolhouse.

There was one thing. Tragedy took away one of the Tallett Hill scholars. Within five years, Grace Brown would be dead. Grace, the pretty girl at the doorway they called "Billy."

Grace was murdered in 1906. The crime stamped her name into us and marked the lives of the other pupils. Four of the girls were her sisters. Most of the young people in the picture, Camilla believes, went to the Brown farmhouse outside of South Otselic when they brought Grace back to her hometown dead. Camilla remembers the casket was closed for the funeral and there were lots of people.

It was not a day that faded easily, like an old picture.

"Billy" Brown had gone to Cortland to work in a skirt factory after she finished school. An older sister lived there. At the plant she met one of the foremen, Chester Gillette. She got pregnant and Chester pretended he wanted to marry her. They began a wedding trip in the Adirondacks, along the Fulton Chain of Lakes. After a while, "Billy's" body was found in Big Moose Lake and Chester died in the electric chair for her murder.

Later, Theodore Dreiser wrote a novel, "An American Tragedy," based on the case.

And Grace Brown, in a way none of the others in Camilla's photograph could have guessed that day, turned into a figure of American history.                                                                                          —*1984*

---

# PIECES

I watch the lights flickering around Abraham Lincoln and I think, all we have left of him is the pieces.

For years, I've been stumbling over them.

In Chicago, at the historical society, I saw his deathbed with straw tick and mattress. At Cooperstown, the Lincoln family doctor's notes on the president's autopsy.

Not far away, at the Onondaga history museum next to the library, his hat. The one he was wearing when they had to sneak him into Washington.

Skaneateles Library has a letter. It's locked in the safe.

Then I remember the nice old lady I went to see in Syracuse years ago. She lived in a yellow house off Euclid Avenue. She had pieces of material connected with the president in a paper bag. The pieces had labels:

"Piece of the coat worn by Lincoln the night he was killed."

"Piece of cloth used to stop the blood from Lincoln's wound."

"Piece of crepe from the door of the house where Lincoln died."

"Feather from the pillow Lincoln died on."

"Fringe from the curtain that caught Booth's spur as he leaped from the president's box."

"Pieces of wood from the Lincoln assassin's hanging scaffolds."

And so on.

My hostess had a story to tell. The pieces had been collected by her grandfather. There had been lots more at one time. Lots more.

The man's name was Andrew Boyd. He collected Lincoln pieces. Maybe, in his odd way, he was trying to put the legend back together again.

Andrew Boyd was called "the street directory king." He settled in Syracuse after the Civil War. In his spare time, he prowled the dead president's trail, gathering as he went.

He was absolutely batty about the man.

This admiration may have been connected to Boyd's brother, William Henry, who went to war and became a famous general while his brother stayed home and tended to the publishing business. The first Boyd directory was published in Albany in 1857. The last, in Syracuse, in 1899. In between, more than 100 directories in New York, Pennsylvania and other states.

Then there was the serendipity of geography. It happened that Boyd's sister lived in Washington, D.C. It happened that her house was near the William Peterson house. The William Peterson house was across the street from Ford's Theater, where Lincoln was shot by Booth 118 years ago.

When the Petersons began distributing relics, Boyd was there.

It also happened that William Peterson was a tailor who owned several pairs of scissors. He used them well.

Andrew Boyd gathered his relics and carefully labeled each. He let people know where his passion lay.

In 1867, this ad ran in The Syracuse Journal: "Mr. Boyd is in search of anything and everything—no matter how trifling—connected with Mr. Lincoln."

No matter how trifling.

We are told that Boyd liked to tell the story of how he sat—a little reverently, a little gleefully—in the chair at Ford's in which the president was shot. How he tried on the death hat. Squinted at the fragments of the Lincoln skull.

In 1873, the Library of Congress bought a large section of Boyd's Lincoln inventory for $1,000. It included 1,500 books, pamphlets, medals, handbills, tokens, "etc."

He wasn't resting, though. In the same year, he bought that deathbed, tick and mattress. Cost him $100.

Boyd, the son of an Irish Army sergeant, was 29 when Lincoln was killed. He outlived his idol by 40 years. He died in Syracuse in 1905. The last of the pieces ended up in a paper bag miles and years away from where they started.

And what does this have to do with a man many people think was the greatest president we ever had?

Nothing, except that history is made up of lots of little pieces.

*—1981*

# ROSE HILL

Phyllis told me the story about the people who were buried alive and put into Rose Hill Cemetery during the smallpox epidemic 100 years ago. I had heard about that before.

Phyllis used to live in the neighborhood. Her parents' house—the family had lived there since 1903—was down Lodi Street from the old city burial ground. The plot, bounded by Lodi, Willow, Douglas and Highland, was used between 1841 and 1935.

After that, it became, informally, a park. As the years passed, hardly anyone remembered 10,561 citizens were buried there. That included 125 of the 182 people who died in the smallpox epidemic in Syracuse during 1875-76.

Phyllis knew about the epidemic. She had been told how it was.

"My friend and I used to pass by the cemetery every day when we walked up Lodi to school," she said. "That was in the early '50s. At the time they were building The Skyline. We went to North High School.

"Well, there came a time when we started to see workmen excavating in the cemetery. All of the stones were there then. They had digging machines and there were mounds of earth. People were digging."

Digging? In a cemetery?

"Yes. They were removing the stones. I'm not sure what they did with them. We were very curious about what was going on. We assumed they had removed the coffins and bodies, too. No, we didn't see that. We saw the mounds of dirt and our imaginations went to work."

Phyllis also remembered what the old folks in the neighborhood were saying about Rose Hill.

"They said there were people buried there who died of smallpox a long time ago. They said some of the people weren't really dead when they buried them. They just put them in boxes and didn't embalm them because of the disease. They were really in deep comas. Later, they woke up and were trapped in the coffins. They struggled to get out and, of course, they couldn't.

"When they started doing that work in the cemetery, we heard that some of the coffins broke open and they found the people who tried to get out. They were in positions of agony. They had pulled out their hair and scratched at the coffins. It was horrible."

Phyllis said the story had a particular impact on her because a school friend died trapped in a box. He crawled into a cedar chest at his home on Green Street and couldn't get out. He suffocated.

"The story seemed to make sense to me at the time because the work in the cemetery suddenly stopped. They only did half of it. It's still that way. Several monuments are left up there in the section closest to Highland. Why? Did something terrible happen to stop them?"

The notion the school girls had at the time was that it had to do with the tortured burials. And the tradition in the neighborhood that the smallpox virus remained active in the soil.

"Yes, we believed it then," Phyllis said to me. "I still believe it."

Rose Hill was bought as the municipal cemetery before Syracuse was a city. In 1841, when the first burial was made—of the Rev. Homer Adams, who died in 1837 and probably was moved from another cemetery—the plot was at the corporate line.

By the time the last burial was made, of Charles Schoen Sept. 7, 1935, Syracuse extended miles beyond James Street hill and the cemetery was used hardly at all. It had been 20 years since the last burial, in fact. No lots had been sold after 1899.

There are hundreds of stories in those 11.8 acres. Mayors and "bones, etc. from the medical college" lie there. The center of the far north section, Block 4, contained a potter's field. Some 4,250 burials are recorded in Block 4.

The original map of Rose Hill at the Onondaga Historical Association marks the potter's field into plots labeled "Irish," "German," "English," "American," "African" and "orphans." It bordered the north-south drive that survives today on the east.

This was where the smallpox victims were put.

The "pestilence" began on the North Side, near Pond and Lodi, early in 1875. Adam Baltz, Rose Hill's sexton, buried the first smallpox death, Henry Klein, Feb. 19. The last smallpox victim in the cemetery records at the historical association was Clancy Hill, who died Jan. 27 of the next year. The virus peaked in October 1875. The sexton buried five victims in one day that month.

Syracuse was in turmoil, according to newspapers of the time. Each day of the epidemic the editors published a list of deaths, new cases and quarantined houses, by address. Mayor George Hier used his emergency powers to put police at houses where cases were found. He set up a city "pest house" hospital and ordered vaccination for every citizen.

By winter, the tragedy began to wane. Imagine the stories it left behind!

I found two newspaper notes about Rose Hill's potter's field in the OHA files. One, early in the epidemic, mentioned the field was filled and the cemetery ought to be closed and turned into a "public park and conservatory." Mention was made of the concern of neighbors for the "poisonous effluvia" of Rose Hill.

A citizen's letter published in September 1875 complained about burying more victims of the "pestilence" in the potter's field because of fears the "germs" would spread to nearby houses.

A news story published in 1905, 30 years after the epidemic, reported "The suggestion that the removal of the bodies of the smallpox victims from Rose Hill Cemetery would spread the germs of the disease had caused considerable discussion among physicians."

The "possibility" of the "germs" still being active after 30 years was reported.

Probably not. I checked with two Syracuse experts, a pathologist and a virologist. Both said the risk of infection was zero, at this point.

The pathologist also pointed out it was highly unlikely that any of the remains of the smallpox victims would have been anything more than dust in the 1950s.

After the last burial in the '30s, the character of Rose Hill continued to change. Suggestions for using it for something else were made again, as they had been for years. Could the site be better used as a park? For a school? The new community college?

The number of burials discouraged the ideas. It would be necessary to move all the remains, and get kin to sign off, in order to do that. It's too much trouble, the city said. Forget it.

In the fall of 1951, after years of trying, the city Parks Department took a $40,000 appropriation from the Common Council and started "renovation" work at Rose Hill. "Renovation" was the word used in the newspapers to describe the removal of trees and brush. In the spring of 1952, workers "leveled the graves" and "placed the stones flush to the ground."

That was the time when Phyllis and her chum walked by Rose Hill on their way to school.                                                    —*1986*

---

# HORSE

There is a hidden village in the town of Geddes, almost forgotten by the thousands of people who attend the State Fair.

It has no name, but if it did, it would be Horse. It has no mayor, either, but if it did, he would be Andy Waida, who has lived in Horse for nearly 20 years.

Horse is at the northwest corner of the grounds, where the racetrack touches the Conrail tracks. It is the stables and a little trailer park of 20 to 30 year-around mobile homes set in a grove of maples.

The village is there because most horses have four legs and may be trained to pull a sulky and driver. Sometimes they go into races and win lots of money for their owners.

The smell of that dream—The Big Win—is very much in the air of Horse, along with the nasal-closing tang of manure.

Andy Waida understands that. "Most of the people out here got both feet in this thing," he says. Andy himself has been around horses about 30 years.

The fairgrounds is home for the trainers, drivers and owners, but the exposition itself, with its bright lights, sweating crowds, babble of spielers and unshamed huckstering, seems but a 10-day distraction on the other side of the track. Trainers can't use the track very much, just for a morning jog for their horses, and the traffic delays them a little, coming and going, but most of the residents of Horse do their things the way they do them the other 355 days.

They ignore the exposition, and the exposition, most of the time, ignores them.

Andy and I walked out into the yard behind the main stable and found Pete Ruscitto giving one of his horses a morning bath. He is the president of his own business, Certified Carpets, but took the summer off and moved his family to the trailer park, "so I could fool around with horses for the season."

He told me "the fair doesn't bother us, except maybe for the traffic jams. Oh, some people wander in once in a while to look at the horses, but most of the action is away from here. My wife walks over once in a while, and maybe I'll go over once before the show ends to look at the animals, but . . ."

He gave a telling shrug. Horse exists because there is a fairgrounds and horse racing, but the show goes on and the little community acts like a spider carefully picking its way around the river's eddy.

"You know," Peter continued, unwrapping his trotter's bandages, "most people don't know this place exists. When I tell people what my address is—the State Fair Grounds—they're astounded. They ask me 'Hey, what happened? Did I leave my wife?' I say no, I brought her with me."

Pete's stable is decorated with the gear of the trade and big foot lockers with the horses' names stenciled to the sides. There's a big radio hitched to one of the beams, and Ed Murphy is giving the weather forecast over WSYR. Outside the door, a grill waits for the next barbecue and out on Horse's main street, where the stables front, there are neat patches of flowers, mail and newspaper boxes, pink flamingos, sun porches and a grotto, with the Mother of Heaven praying in the dust.

"Got everything we need here," Andy says, as we duck by the people pushing wheelbarrows of what their properties left on the floor the day before. "They plow the track in the winter, we get mail delivered, the kids go to school in Solvay, and the bus comes in to pick them up. And I do my horseshoeing and hard work."

There's lots of that—hard work—living at Horse, most of it unseen by fans who go to tracks to watch the horses in their few minutes pulling someone around an oval. The specialists here get help from the state breeders fund, but sometimes it seems that it takes as much care and money to raise four good legs for a stake race as it does to raise one of the kids. Those electric treadmills, the ones they use when they can't exercise on the track, don't come cheap, and Horse also has a whirlpool bath, sonor for sore legs and worries about feet and blood counts.

"I don't think people realize all the work," Sal Capone said when we found him doing the morning chores with his son, Mark, in their stable. The Capones don't live on the grounds; Sal is a city firefighter at Engine 18, but they spend a lot of time in the gritty little shire. Sal has 21 years in the department and plans to retire soon, and then "I'll be out here all the time doing something I really like. It's a challenge, you know, making a horse like this one go faster. When I got him he was 8 years old and never raced. I bring one along, and then I sell it and start on a new one."

Across the way, Jim Clarry and his wife, Marge, were servicing the eight horses in their charge. Jim has been at Horse 12 years and likes it because the grounds are at the center of the racing action in the state, winter and summer. The Clarrys waved off flies as they worked, while keeping track of their small daughter, Dawn, who had some of her toys just outside the stable doorway.

"It's different living here, it sure is," Marge said. "Everybody knows everybody else, but there's really not that much social life. Just work."

Jim clipped a blanket around Civil Enough, a 2-year-old he is bringing up to race for the big stakes. He patted a flank. "Gonna make it at Meadowlands?" he asked. "That's what it's all about. Everybody lives a dream for a shot at the stakes."

Andy is the village smithy, or farrier, which he said is the right name for what he does. The little brick shop with the big orange sign sits in the middle of the trailer park. It is a working place and like Horse itself, carries little resemblance to the blacksmith shop across the track in the fair's Carriage Museum.

"We like it here," Andy said, watching the Budweiser people wash their Clydesdales across the street. "Nothing exciting, just a little shoeing and hard work." *—1980*

# Chapter 6

# PASSAGES

## LARRY

There wasn't much left of the man Lionel D. Grant had been when they found him the first week of March in the room he had rented for years at Syracuse's downtown YMCA.

No telling how long he'd been dead, according to police. A week? Maybe two? Maybe longer. One of the cops who tried to get into the room after someone down the hall got suspicious, pushed open the door on a mummy with a long beard in a bed set in a trash heap. The only place the official photographer could find to stand to take pictures of the dead man was on the bed itself.

Lionel Grant, who was called "Larry," was 75. He seems to have died of a massive heart attack while he was pulling on his pants.

Ernie Uhlig didn't look that good either when he was found 46 years ago last November, a few blocks from the place where Larry died. It turned out later that Ernie had actually expired just around the corner and down the block from the downtown Y. He was murdered.

The police said the young man—Ernie was 31 and worked the road selling hosiery—had been strangled with two neckties while renting a room with a friend at the Dorset apartment hotel on Onondaga Street. Then the body—Ernie had only his pants on—was tied arms and feet and placed in a large, new black trunk several days before the discovery was made.

There was no telling exactly how long he had been dead. But it was an unusual odor that attracted people's attention.

The trunk was found in the attic of a rooming house on Bellevue Avenue. It had been stored there at the direction of Ernie's friend, who had signed in at the Dorset as "Mr. Gaylord." Later it was determined Mr. Gaylord was Lionel "Larry" Grant, who was 29 and worked as a draftsman at Central New York Power Corp. (now Niagara Mohawk).

Larry was arrested and charged with killing Ernie. He confessed. Said the men had quarreled. It had something to do with a trip they wanted to take to Florida. That was why he bought the trunk, Larry explained.

The case was settled the next January. Larry had pleaded guilty to murder in December. His lawyer asked the judge for understanding. His client, he said, had never been in trouble before. "He was amiable, courteous, neat, generous and a good worker," the attorney explained. "His rash act was incomprehensible to persons he had worked with as a draftsman."

The victim was described by the lawyer as "a moral leper . . . useless as a rattlesnake and 10 times more dangerous."

Larry was sentenced to serve 40 years to life at Attica State Prison. He did 24.

He returned to Syracuse on parole in the early '60s and went to work again as a draftsman. He rented a room at the Y. He moved just once, to another room at the Y.

By that time, the years had worked on the notorious murder case that once put headlines streaming across the front pages of Syracuse newspapers. Few people remembered the name Lionel Grant. Larry, while still very aware of what had happened, never spoke of it to the few new friends he made.

He had to put his prison time on his application at O'Brien and Gere engineers. His supervisor, Joe Phillips, knew Larry was just out of Attica, but didn't make a big deal of it. Joe had, in fact, forgotten about that aspect of Larry's past until I brought it up the other day. No, he said, he didn't think anyone else at the firm knew the quiet, studious draftsman was a convicted murderer.

"He was a loner," Joe said. "Hardly ever talked about himself. Didn't have any family that any of us knew of. In fact, the only time he mentioned that subject was to my secretary, Helen. She said he once said he had been married and had a son. Then he dropped the subject."

When he was arrested in 1939, Larry's mother, Elida J. Stack, lived at 228 W. Castle St. Mrs. Stack told reporters her son had lived with her at one time, but moved to the Bellevue Avenue room when she complained about the character of some of his friends. The record shows his father, Floyd, lived in Boonville.

It also revealed Larry was born in Schenectady, went to college and had a sister and brother living in 1940.

Authorities couldn't locate any family members after Larry was found dead at the Y. A friend whose name he had left on his rent record to be contacted in an emergency was dead. Another name on a piece of paper, "Liz," didn't track either. City police, the staff of the medical examiner's office and county Social Services worked all the leads but came up with nothing in the way of kin for Larry.

Ron Seeland said he wasn't surprised at this. He was Larry's parole officer for a while. That file was destroyed, but in his head Ron carries a vivid impression of Larry and other "old lifers" who passed through his custody during the years he worked for the state Parole Division.

"They sort of break all the ties with the family," he explained. "They have been alienated from them. There's a wall of separation. Even if someone is left when they get out after all those years, they don't mention them. Don't try to make contact."

This old lifer was just like that, according to Ron.

"He was a very, very quiet individual," he said of Larry. "Very, very aware of what had happened and very concerned about his job. He loved his job. I remember being very careful with him because the outside world is so threatening to an old lifer.

"I had to be authoritative in my job and at the same time try to reach out. I tried to reach out but I couldn't expect them to reach out. They've been so isolated in prison. It takes a long time to let down that wall of protection."

By all accounts, Larry never stepped out from behind his wall. In fact, he built himself a cell not unlike the ones he had at Attica.

First the single room on Bellevue Avenue Then the jail cell. Then the prison. Then the single room at the Y.

"Yes," Ron Seeland said, "his room was very like the prison cell. It's not surprising at all." I told him what a mess Larry's was. "He got a small room and then packed it, just like it was in prison. And he picked a structured place, like the Y, that was like an institution. Another lifer might have gone to the Rescue Mission or the Salvation Army.

"He also had a structured relationship with other people. He'd only open up so far. He probably carried a ditty bag like the one he had in prison. I bet his whole life was in that room."

Certainly he did literally live in that room the last year or so of his life. His powers of reasoning began to fail him.

Larry worked for O'Brien and Gere for about 10 years before he retired on disability. He had arthritis and it bothered his drafting hands. He fell down a stairway at work and his back hurt. Social Services took him on as a client with few assets and a disability.

After he left the firm, some of his friends from work saw Larry once in a while. Mostly that was on the street downtown, or in a bar or a liquor store. The man liked his pint. When the cops went through his wallet, after they found him dead, they counted out $144 and some change. Also a whiskey label or two and a perpetual calendar.

There seemed to be no trace in the room of the notebooks Larry used to keep. Another generation of cops found those 40 years ago, in the Bellevue room. A reporter at the Post Standard claimed the books revealed a deep interest in character reading, handwriting analysis and psychology. It was concluded that Larry was studious, cultured.

One of the books had typed quotations, page after page of them. "The gods we worship write their names on our faces," one said.

"He was a very private individual," his friend Bob Hnat from O'Brien and Gere said. Bob's description of Larry sounded very much like what the lawyer said of him in court in 1940: Amiable, courteous, neat, generous and a good worker.

Bob found Larry less sociable recently. He hadn't seen him in a year. One of the last times he invited Larry to come to his home for dinner. Larry said he would, and bring a woman he was seeing. They never showed.

The county paid for Larry's funeral. There was an obituary three sentences long in the paper noting the death of Lionel Grant, 75, of 340 Montgomery St., at his home. There were no known survivors.

Four people were at Ryan and Son Funeral Home to send Larry on his way. The minister, Ed Ryan and his friend Joe Phillips and Joe's secretary, Helen. "The minister said some prayers and that was it," Ed Ryan explained. "We put him in Loomis Hill."

Loomis Hill is the county pauper's field at Onondaga Hill. Larry was into the county for plenty, counting all the disability checks he got. The money in his wallet was put toward the bill.

"It was kind of sad," Joe Phillips said to me Friday. "I said to Helen, 'Is this all the guy has? Just two people?'"                                    *—1986*

# FLOYD

Floyd Knapp and I had a nice visit before he died last week. Floyd was 92 the week before Christmas. His doctors had given him up for dead last June.

I went up to Floyd's bedroom. He sat in a rocker next to the dresser with the old school bell on it. His bed was up against the window in the small room. He could lie there and look out at some of the trees still left on the South Side. Floyd remembered when the whole shooting match where his house stood was a farm. Cows and everything.

Floyd remembered a lot of things. His friend Barbara Smith told me the old man knew all kinds of stories. She was right. They flowed out of him like tub water. And just as clear, too. He was giving me exact dates—month, day and year—and exact addresses—341 S. Clinton St. up over the stables, etc.—back 70, 80 years ago.

Floyd said his father was an immigrant from Germany who had four wives. He showed me a family tree someone had typed for him. There were 12 children of those unions, nine brothers and three sisters. The boys were given E.F. names, the girls, E.L. Floyd, the last of the kids, was Elmore Floyd. All of the others were gone. The last, a sister, died in 1971.

Floyd said he was fixing to go that way himself. He said he was ready.

"I got my headstone over at Valley Cemetery," Floyd said to me. "The name's already on it. Hazel's over there, too. (Hazel was his companion of many years.) And her mother. It'll be $41 to dig the grave. You know, they only go down two feet now. They used to go down 10 feet."

Floyd was born when the Knapps lived in Cardiff. Close by where John Hitchings raised peas and strawberries. Floyd told me he never drank anything but sulphur spring water until he was an adult.

The bell on the dresser was from district school No. 19, a couple miles west of Cardiff. Floyd said it was the one "that rang me in to school." The dingy brass had a small bite out of the rim and what looked like a bullet hole in the side. Floyd couldn't explain how they got there.

There was a picture of the Knapp house at Cardiff on the bulletin board on the wall across from Floyd's bed. It was one of the old pictures Barbara Smith and some of his other friends got together for Floyd's birthday party in December. I didn't think they could match the ones

Floyd had in his head.

We talked about the different jobs he worked at. All of them seemed tough, with long hours. When he was a young man, Floyd spent a good deal of his time riding around the city and county on a bicycle. He owned a Crown, brand-new, which cost him $35.

One of those jobs was running a wakeup service for railroad workers who couldn't afford phones. Floyd would ride his bike to the homes of the men who worked in the yards at East Syracuse (The Hump, he called it) and wake them three hours before they had to report.

He also delivered parcels among stores and businesses downtown. He worked at Nettleton for a while and had his own trucking company. For 16 years, Floyd picked up packing cartons from local firms and resold them to paper companies. He worked at Tucker's farm, which used to be at South Salina and Ballantyne Road. He cut up fish and potatoes for fries at Bill's, the fish fry place which has been a fixture in the Valley neighborhood almost as long as Floyd.

Barbara made us tea. She said it seemed as if Floyd had nine lives, from the stories he'd told her. Barbara had known her friend less than a year. She started taking care of him last summer after he went to the hospital and they told him he had incurable cancer. The best thing they could do for him was stick tubes into him. He told the doctors to go to hell. He wanted to be home.

Barbara said she'd take him home. She did.

Barbara asked Floyd to tell me the story of how he saved a man's life once. Floyd said that was the man who owned a trucking business. He was having a bit of trouble with his wife. Floyd got to his house and found him unconscious on the floor. He had drunk a bottle of poison.

"I busted in and got him to the hospital," he said. He was never sure if the fellow thought that was OK or not.

All the time I was thinking, later on, Floyd, Barbara pitched in and helped to save your life.

When we went downstairs, I asked Barbara about helping Floyd. It started last summer. At first, she was working for an agency as a home aide. The money ran out and she stayed on, because Floyd had no close family, except a grand niece, down in Cortland County. Without home care, it would have been the hospital or a nursing home.

There were others—she called in the Caring Coalition—but much of it fell to Barbara. Sometimes 16, 18 hours a day. "She really became a family member for him," one of Floyd's other helpers told me. I asked her why.

"It had to be done," Barbara explained. "I love the Lord. That's how I got into this. This is Barbara's way of doing her work for the Lord."

Floyd hadn't wanted any medication in months. Barbara showed me the only pharmacy tube in the house. It was a bottle which read "take one as often as needed for increased faith. Dr. Jesus." Inside there were little rolls of scripture.

One morning last week Barbara got Floyd up to go to the bathroom. When they came into the bedroom again, he sat on the bed and died.

—*1985*

---

# MARY AND JACKIE

Mary wanted to talk about her friend Jackie. She told me I had asked a question about Jackie. She could fill in part of the answer.

The question was in a column last month when Jackie's body was pulled out of Onondaga Lake. She had drowned a few hours before that. Two men driving the parkway next to the shore saw the body and called the sheriff's department. For a few days, the dead woman was unidentified, so they gave her the name "Jane Doe."

"Who was the woman in the lake?" I asked. "Why is she dead?"

Identification, through neighbors of Jackie's on the South Side, was made shortly after that. The "why?" part may take longer.

Jackie was 52 when she apparently killed herself by walking or jumping into the lake on a Saturday morning. She lived in a house off Midland Avenue that once had been the family home. She lived there more than 30 years, some of that time alone. Mary told me she had known Jackie for several years. About two years ago, Mary moved into the downstairs flat of the neat, three-story house. She said she did that to give her friend some income and companionship.

"She wanted to be independent and have her house," Mary said. "She was a quiet person, loved staying by herself but she needed money. She worked at different times in her life but had trouble finding work. She was doing some cleaning for people in the neighborhood but that didn't pay much. I felt sorry for her. I wanted to help. She was a beautiful woman. A good girl."

Mary started to cry when she said that.

Her friend, she said, never married, although there was a man she saw occasionally who wanted her to marry him. She said no but he kept after her. Sometimes she would sit peaceably in a chair a few feet back from the attic window and read as the man knocked at the door downstairs, wanting to see her.

"That was her retreat," Mary said. "She loved that attic—used to spend a lot of time up there."

The attic was as neat as the rest of the house. Jackie's books were distributed in careful stacks around the floor. She loved to read, her friend said. "Anything—history, ballet, nature, philosophy—you name it. She also liked music; she had all these records. And painting! Oh, she was a wonderful painter."

Jackie lived on the second floor and the friends shared the kitchen. Mary said she did most of the cooking. She kept the house in shape because she is extremely handy. Her workshop of tools in the basement would make your average handy-person very jealous.

Mary is able to make a buck or two doing carpentry work. Most of her income, she said, is earned "staying with old folks." Her job at the time of her friend's death was four days on, four days off. It was during one of those four-days-on spans last month that Jackie left the house and didn't come back.

Mary thinks she knows why.

"A lot of things got to her; she was very depressed," she said. "I tried to cheer her up but she had a lot of sorrows. Eight years ago she had a nervous breakdown. She tried to do away with herself. I think she wasn't happy about the way her life had gone. She had wanted to be a school teacher but her mother talked her out of it. Her father was killed in a car accident when she was 16."

Mary said her friend had periods of her life when her religion—she was a Jehovah's Witness—seemed to mean a great deal to her and helped her deal with depression. Jackie spent many hours reading religious and inspirational books and articles. They were all over her home. Often Mary explained, Jackie underlined phrases that were important to her. Sometimes she wrote notes to herself.

Recently, according to Mary, she had been underlining passages about death, depression and courage.

Jackie told her friend she was not happy with her relationship with her family in recent months. She also had been extremely upset by two burglaries at her flat and a fire in the house next door. The flames destroyed the building and singed the side of Jackie's house.

"Oh, that really upset her," Mary said. "She would cry and cry over it. She hated looking out the window and seeing what the fire had done."

Jackie last saw her friend as both of them left for work on a Thursday. Jackie kissed her and said something cryptic about "going away," then she walked toward her cleaning job. "She looked so sad," Mary said. "She always had such a sad look on her face."

Sheriff's investigation found Jackie later went to stay with a relative on the city's West Side, on a street near the lake. She left that house about 9 a.m. the day her body was found floating near the opposite shore about 1 p.m.

Mary had no hint of what had happened to her friend until she saw a TV news report about discovery of the body. She said she began to worry. A few days later there was a policeman at the door. Then the note from Jackie she found when she got back to the flat made sense:

"Dear Mary," it said. "I'm going to go away for a while."          *—1983*

---

# WES

My friend, Wes Clark, died last week. He was 83.

The obits said Wes was dean of journalism at SU 20 years. This is true. He also was a character of enduring legend in our town. Don't bother shopping for a replacement.

The last long talk Wes and I had took place three years ago in the old Temperance Hall in Skaneateles, which The Dean and his wife, Rhea Eckel Clark, converted into a two-story apartment.

Wes, The Dean of Journalism, lived upstairs over a newspaper, the Skaneateles Press-Marcellus Observer. A newspaper he used to own. Where he still worked, writing a column and covering Marcellus village, town and school boards.

Wes covered a board meeting the night before he died. When he got home, he sat down at his old Underwood manual typewriter, rolled in a yellowed sheet of copy paper and wrote his column.

Wes called his weekly essay "Teasel and Gunwad." Gunwad was Marcellus folks' name for their newspaper, before the merger. A teasel is a prickly herb.

Yeah, my friend was a prickly herb who fired wads of newspaper at us.

That day at the apartment we sat in front of the fireplace in the magnificent widower's pad of his and talked about tennis and journalism, two of Wes' favorite topics. He still played tournament tennis at that time.

In fact, I'm told he played tennis the day before he died. Smoked two packs of unfiltered cigarettes a day, too.

In 1986, I'd written a short essay of my own about Wes for the printed program of "A Tribute to Wesley C. Clark" gotten up by the Newhouse Alumni Association at SU. It's one of my favorites:

"I believe Wes Clark was the first real writer I ever met. Perhaps the only one now that I think about it.

"This happened to me in the 40s, when the Clarks—Wes, Frances, Sally and Bill—moved to my hometown, Marcellus. They moved into the big house at the end of my street, where the Stedmans used to live. Mr. Stedman did something at the university. So did Wes. I didn't find out just what for a while.

"Sally was a mate of mine in school. . . . One day, when Sally had a few friends into the house while her parents were away, she invited us to look at the library. People in Marcellus did not live in houses with libraries. The library was downstreet, next to the firehouse . . .

"So here was this family with a library, right at the end of my street!

"But wait. Not only did Sally's family own a library but there, on a shelf, was a book written by her father!

"I just about passed out.

"I don't remember the name of the book. It was a mystery novel. Something to do with tennis, maybe . . .

"Of course I didn't read the darned thing. What sticks with me is the impact that moment of discovery in Sally's library had on a kid in Marcellus all those years ago.

"Later, I found out Sally's father was dean of journalism at SU. That was about the time I found out I wanted to be a journalist. My father had a talk with the dean.

"Could something be arranged for the kid by way of financial aid? You know, he wants to be, well, a journalist. Sure. Maybe. We'll see.

"The kid went to SU, and Wes had something to do with it. . . . I nearly flunked out the first year because I wanted to do so much. I had a good time, though. Learned a lot, too.

"In fact, I thought, I learned too much. I decided I didn't need to go to journalism school. I never applied. I graduated a liberal artist. No wonder I never got to be a writer, the way my neighbor was.

"Wes and some of his tennis buddies bought The Press-Observer after the old editor, Cannonball Baker, checked out. Later he sold these jewels of the Finger Lakes but stuck a codicil in the deal to keep writing a column for The Press until Syracuse stopped sucking water from Skaneateles Lake. . . ."

"Since that is unlikely to happen, Wes will go on writing forever, of course. I sure hope so."

*Note:* Wes did, almost. They found his last column in his Underwood right after he died. The Press published it last week.

There was something else next to Wes' typewriter. Notes for his next column.                                                                     *—1990*

---

# THE BOOKMAKER

A piece of Syracuse died Friday in Detroit. His name was Percy Harris. He was 91 last April.

Once, when asked about himself, Percy said yes, he could be described as a "person of some influence." I'll say.

Among his deeds was tearing up the Syracuse Police Department pretty good 25 years ago. A chief fell and a new era began. More than likely Percy had a hand in that. He destroyed a candidate for district attorney merely by shaking his hand. Not to mention a few law enforcement careers, while, at that very moment, other careers were made.

He owned cops, real estate, shoe-shine parlors and pool halls, a night club in Harlem, a ballroom in Detroit, a piece of the hot springs in Arkansas, race horses and shoeboxes filled with Yankee dollars. "He was pretty heavy in New York," one of his Detroit friends said of Percy's portfolio. "I'm not sure exactly what, though."

"He was the best numbers man in the state of New York!" an admiring police officer here said of him Tuesday. Percy ran a lottery 40 years before New York state had one. His was illegal.

He was thought to be a millionaire.

He was chased by vice detectives, a state crime commission, the tax men, the FBI, and people who thought he could put the squeeze on The Establishment. He was an enrolled Republican. He wore a folded hankie in his breast pocket. His face was black. His heart was gold.

There were those who thought Percy was a crook. They called selling chances to poor people for a dime or a dollar on the last three digits in the daily take at Aqueduct a vice. Percy couldn't understand that. "What major crime has happened to write such terrible articles about us people?" he once asked after a clobbering by a Syracuse newspaper. "My philosophy is live and let live—we are all human, no one above error."

Today, thousands of New Yorkers buy chances on numbers and reporters get excited in different ways. Percy did a year in Jamesville for contriving a lottery. His wife and brother-in-law got six months.

Percy was born in Brooklyn when Benjamin Harrison was president. He said he was "always in business for myself." He was a barber at one time. He came to Syracuse in 1932 from Bayonne, N.J., where, he told the Temporary State Commission on Investigation, he had been involved in both "legal" and "illegal" gambling.

He said he started selling "numbers" from a Syracuse billiard room. When he left town, in 1962, it was claimed he was the "numbers kingpin" of Central New York, with games and banks in Fulton, Oswego, Ithaca, Rome, Cortland and Utica, not to forget "interests" in New York, Detroit and other points of the compass.

"He was a very good businessman," according to another police officer. "And a real nice guy. If he heard about a family in need of a ton of coal, he'd have it delivered. At Christmas, it was food baskets." Mrs. Harris, who was her husband's business manager, also gave Christmas gifts. Ten dollar bills and bottles of whiskey to cops and politicians, according to her testimony before the state commission.

In later years, when respectability overtook him, Percy told people he was a "broker." He didn't say what he broke, or who. He said he founded the first black Boy Scout troop in Syracuse.

No one doubted Percy made a buck on his lottery. The outlines of his estate were as dim as the man himself. Syracuse was his first base for years and years, yet he claimed he didn't live here. When the state raided his wife's apartment in a building he owned on Harrison Street—the site is part of The Hutch today—five gamblers were arrested but Percy was not among them. He gave up 6 months later.

The raiders removed $27,000 in cash, policy slips and books with many interesting names, including those who had sworn to uphold the law. The state kept the cash and the records and started the Harrises toward a plea bargain. Eventually, in satisfaction of nearly half a million in unpaid income taxes, it also seized negotiable securities, savings and checking accounts and what was left of the broker's shoebox empire.

The state commission later would report its work in Syracuse "showed not only the well-entrenched nature of this gambling operation, but also the laxity, to say the least, of the local police force in the enforcement of the gambling laws."

His friends in Detroit—he had many—didn't know all of the specifics of Percy's New York Period, except that "he was a very powerful political person at one time" and departed "to let things cool off." That embarrassment didn't stop him from loving Syracuse, he told his good friend Lucille Emerson, who was taking care of Percy when he died. No, he didn't want to be buried here.

He slipped into town for visits to his family after 1962. His wife stayed. Alice, who is 80, has been at Loretto for several years. Percy phoned her every week before cancer began its chemistry on him. "He was operated on in 1978 but he snapped right back," Mrs. Emerson said. "He didn't let anyone know what was wrong with him."

Ulysses Borykin is chairman of the board of WGPR in Detroit, our first black-owned broadcast station. He got to know Percy after 1962 because of a mutual interest in politics and improving the lot of blacks in the city. "Ullie" also had been a patron of Small's Paradise Club in Harlem, which Percy had a piece of.

"He was a colorful person, but very quiet and conservative," his friend said. "A most unusual man. Very generous. He helped a lot of people." Ullie said he knew Percy had a number of investments there in Detroit but he wasn't sure what they were, except for a "piece" of a hair shop. Mostly, he seemed a gentleman in retirement. No, Mrs. Emerson didn't know, either. "He had a hand in a lot of things," she explained.

What impressed his friends most about Percy, Mrs. Emerson said, was that generosity, that one big heart of his. Oh, yes!

In fact, when Percy goes to rest Thursday in his adopted sod, in a lot in Detroit's Trinity Cemetery, Mrs. Emerson will raise a fine monument over the broker of Townsend Street. She picked the words herself so that anyone who passes that stone will know exactly who Percy Harris was.

The words are these: "What can I do to help?"                    *—1985*

# THE REV.

The Rev. Adam Jamison is the preacher who cuts hair at Tip-Top barber shop, 1200 S. State St. He is minister of Calvary Full Gospel Revival Church, 545 Oakwood Ave. His friends call him "Rev."

His turf is a square of the city about 30 feet across, southwest at Burt and State. He loves his "little corner." Feels he owns it. He's been there more than 25 years. His shop is a community center.

Rev. is one of the wise men of our town and ought to be listened to. I spent about three hours listening the other day and toasting my toes in Rev.'s warm place of business.

First, according to Rev., clean up the city.

Second, bring a good grocery store, drug store and hardware store into his neighborhood.

Third, people will start moving back into Syracuse and tax revenues will flow again.

Don't get Rev. wrong. He's not talking about civil reform. By clean, he means clean. As in the opposite of dirty. It begins by one man—Rev., most likely—bending over to remove a grimy paper bag from the sidewalk.

Rev. came to Syracuse in 1948. He has made a fair mark. He owns two houses—one next to the church, another in Pennellville—and business is good. The parsonage he bought from the city for a dollar, rehabbed it himself and raised six children here. That gives him pride. So does his standing in the neighborhood. "I'm everybody's father," he said.

He grew up in South Carolina, where his father, "Buse" Jamison, was a farmer and half-barber, according to his son. Adam learned to cut hair watching the old man do it in the backyard. Barbering followed him wherever he went after that.

So did the notion he ought to be a preacher. Other peoples' notion, that is. Rev. himself, although a church member all his life, didn't take to this at first.

"My wife and I built a church in South Carolina," he explained. "Then they wanted me to be a preacher. I didn't want to preach. I wanted to run."

He ran to Florida, New Jersey, New York City and Syracuse. "They stopped me in Syracuse," he said.

The Jamisons joined Hopps Memorial Church. In time—maybe it

was Rev.'s rich baritone, maybe it was his license as an "exalter" of the Methodist Church—he was talked into being assistant pastor at Hopps. That was a fine job. He didn't have to do anything, according to him. Nine years ago, he was called to Calvary Church.

Rev. landed work at Crucible Steel after he was stopped in Syracuse. He also was partner to two men in barber shops. One was a drunk and the other was caught selling dope. His next shop was a victim of the urban renewal programs of the '60s. That was when Rev. got to know William Walsh, who was mayor from 1962 to 1969.

As far as he is concerned, William Walsh is one of the finest men ever to live in Syracuse.

"We need a mayor who will walk through the neighborhoods, the way Mayor Walsh did," Rev. said. "That's what we need. I understand he can't do it every day, but once in a while."

Lee Alexander was a good man, according to Rev., but it was time for him to quit City Hall. Rev. said he thought Lee was too easy on some neighborhoods. He parted company with City Hall when Lee put those new bulbs in the street lights. "You can't see nothing with those lights," he said. "Someone could come up and cut my throat and I'd never know it."

He thinks it was a bad idea to put so much public housing in one neighborhood, too. He means his neighborhood, of course. That strip, Adams to Castle, is just too much of a concentration of poor blacks, in his opinion. The racial mix didn't turn out to be what the original plans called for. He knows because he was on the planning committee.

Rev. said to me that when he came to Syracuse, he didn't know he was black. Never had a problem in that regard, he said.

Now, however, he does know.

Top-Top has two chairs and one barber. Rev. put art prints on the walls and bought a TV, tape deck and radio. Some of his friends come in just to get warm and shoot the breeze. It's not unusual for one of them to sit in the second chair as Rev. cuts hair in the first, which is covered in pink upholstery. His new hound pup sleeps next to the radiator.

There is a playpen along the south wall. Rev. built that 20 years ago, or more, after his first wife died and left him with an infant daughter. He raised her right there, under the clock.

Recently Rev. increased the price of a man's haircut to $6. Sometimes, he told me, $6 is all he takes in during a day. This doesn't bother him. He'd open up if he didn't make a dime, which was what his father used to make on a head of hair.

Rev. gives out quarters to the kids and lends his car to church members who don't have a way to the store. His old friend, Granville Ames, sweeps the floor and listens to the stories. Granville was in both WWI and WWII.

I didn't ask anything about politics. Rev. just started in. These were some of his thoughts:

"The mayor has a big job. It's going to take him a year, a year-and-a-half to get this city where it ought to be. I think he will. I want to help. Even if it's just picking up some trash. If everybody did that, it would be a better city."

Rev. would start the cleanup right in front of the Public Safety Building. Get a squad going and move it south, down Townsend and onto his turf. The cleaners—some of them—would be publicly funded. Preferably young city kids who need a job to keep them from hanging around on the streets and drinking beer.

Junk cars are especially annoying to Rev. He can't understand why the city doesn't red-tag every abandoned junker within the municipal limits and get them into the nearest compacter. Enforcement. That's this man's key to a better city. Enforce the laws on the books.

Another law Rev. wants enforced is the leash law. Running dogs are as bad as running kids. Why there's one bitch hanging around the parsonage that's filling up the city with puppies all by herself!

It troubles Rev. to see young people with no vision of the future and a need for instant gratification. In very practical terms, he worries when he sees these youngsters darting in and out of the many Ma and Pa corner stores of his neighborhood spending money on products made with sugar.

He gets very mad—gesturing with his comb as he cuts hair—when he talks about how the area used to have a large market or two but must get by with what Rev. called "the A-rab candy stores." He thinks the neighbors were betrayed by the city official who promised there would be a replacement when the market at Plaza 81 was turned into a fancy suite for a partnership of bone doctors.

Rev. has friends among the Middle Eastern immigrants who are the inner city candy merchants. He just wishes they had a little competition in the way of a chain supermarket.

You see, according to Rev., we are what we eat. He believes all that sugar is stupefying "They (the kids) don't know nothing because they don't eat right. What you eat controls your brain."

A young man came in off State Street and took a chair. Rev. broke out smiling. The young man—Brother Clark, he called him—was a member of the church who hadn't been around in a while. Brother Clark said he has been in the hospital. Sick? No, sickening. The brother had some problems that needed straightening out. He was sleeping at the Salvation Army, across the way.

Rev. told him to trust in the Lord and his body and he could reach up and touch the sun and moon, the way he did himself sometimes.

"You're a young man," he said to the visitor. "I could cut off your head tonight and it would grow back by daylight!"

We all laughed and Rev. told Brother Clark to put a tape on the box. The young man held the machine in his arms like a baby and a gospel choir singing "Depend on Jesus" came out of the speakers.

The preacher went at the head in front of him with the clippers he bought 25 years ago in Chicago. He sawed a path to the back of the head.

"You come to church Sunday, Brother Clark, and I'll sing that for you," he said.

•   •   •

The Rev. died at the age of 76.

The obituary said he founded a church, Calvary Baptist. By the look of the list of survivors—I counted 55 by name, down to three great-great-grandchildren—I'd guess he founded a dynasty as well.

We said so-long but not farewell to The Rev. at Mount Carmel Seventh Day Adventist Church. Some friends talked about him during the homegoing service in the old Methodist church on Furman Street. Eric Moore, for one, said he'd stop by the shop and spend hours talking with this great man about the Lord. It meant a lot to him to do that, Eric said.

"You know, some people tell you they're praying for you and when you look around, you don't see them," Eric said. "He was always there."

Willie Tarver said the man he loved "ain't dead. He's with Jesus now."

The preacher had some good, old-time shouting and praying done over him. Brenda Taylor and Marty English sang. The Rev. William Tanner's eulogy rocked the old church.

The last time I was in No. 1200, The Rev. gave me his own report on the State of the City. It didn't exactly harmonize with the one we were hearing from City Hall, but it made sense to me at the time.

We got started on the neighborhood that day because the building across the street was coming down. There had been a fire months before and just then The Rev.'s view was being changed by one of Eric Simmons Jr.'s wrecking cranes. In time, a vacant lot appeared.

"I'm going to miss that," The Rev. said to me. "It's part of me. I've been here all these years. I don't want to see it go. I go down with it. We have too many fires; too many."

Too many fires, too much neglect, too much beer, too many vacant lots and buildings standing empty. Too much dope and craziness out there.

The Rev. did what he could for the neighborhood. His own yard on Oakwood had a vegetable garden and fruit trees. He preached against the sins of neglect and picked papers off the sidewalk. He gave old neighbors rides to the supermarkets because there were no decent places to buy a week's food on his own turf anymore. He rallied against junkies and junk cars.

A few years ago, when I first dropped in, The Rev. told me he wanted to meet the new mayor. He invited Tom Young to stop by, the way half of the South Side liked to do. The Rev. had some ideas about renewing urban renewal south of Adams Street he wanted to share with the mayor.

Tom didn't get there. Now he's got a community center to replace.

*—1988*

---

# JERRY AND JIM

Jerry Verrillo and Jim Glavin, two young Syracuse police officers, hope the memory of the 90 minutes they spent on duty in Eastwood will wear thin. But they know better.

"I'll never forget until they put me in the ground," Jim said.

Jerry shook his head and rubbed his eyes. Jim spoke again: "Neither one of us could sleep that night. To see somebody alive—to be talking with him—and then suddenly he's dead in a few seconds."

Nearly three years a cop hadn't prepared Jim for his assignment that night. You can be told about it, but the lesson has to be real. Nor Jerry, five years on the force, deaths, suicides, are part of the job for him.

"But this was spooky," he said. "Really spooky."

They went to the house because they were available. Two plainclothes partners on the four to midnight shift. They came in with their service revolvers tucked into their waist bands, with a sergeant and Deputy Chief John Dillon because David's family said he was in the cellar with a shotgun, threatening to kill himself.

And there wasn't much time to talk it over or try to remember what was said about suicides at the Police Academy.

"I said 'I'll go in, you stay here,' " Jim recalled a few days later. "I took a few minutes to try to get a little information from the family but they couldn't tell me too much."

So he hid the gun, his badge and his handcuffs and walked down the cellar stairs. His partner, meanwhile, flattened himself in firing position in a snowbank outside a cellar window to cover Jim's mission. He was wearing only a thin windbreaker and by the end of the night he would have a swollen gun arm and frostbitten legs.

Jim's view of David was blocked by the furnace. But Jerry could see him clearly from outside: sitting on a dehumidifier a few inches away from the barrel of a shotgun propped in a pipe vice with a wire hooked to the trigger and looped around the water heater for leverage. He had the wire in his left hand. In the right, a cigarette burned.

David heard Jim on the stairs and started screaming at him. He thought he was a cop.

"I've got seven shots in this gun. I'm going to splatter you pigs all over the cellar."

Jim told him he was from the Suicide Prevention Center and was there to help him. They talked back and forth and never faced each other.

A confused, lonely, disappointed young man, 21, and rigged for destruction.

A determined, sandy-haired, freckled cop on his first death watch, 23, and going by the only book he had read on the subject: his own gut feelings.

"He calmed down after a while. He seemed to buy my story. I told him that people really cared about him. 'We're here because we want to help you.' I said his mother loved him. His father loved him. His girl friend loved him."

Jerry watched the soundless drama through the misty glass, tense and motionless. "I knew why I was there—to protect Jimmy's life and anyone else who might be threatened. We know each other pretty well. We've been partners for six months. He wouldn't have gone down there unless he was completely confident in me. I had a lot of time to think; I decided I would fire if he took the gun out of the vice."

That never happened. Instead, Jim thought at one point, after David's mother and girl friend talked with him, that he had convinced the young man to leave the death machine, and come up into the living room "and have a beer with me and his girl and talk things over."

Jim believed the tension had left David's voice. He was nursing a glass of cola. Jerry saw him rest his arm on the gun barrel as he talked with his girl. As she left to go upstairs, he reached for her hand and squeezed it.

In hindsight, Jerry thinks that was a goodbye signal.

Jim followed the young woman upstairs and waited. When David didn't follow, he started down again. "I decided if I was going to talk him out of it, I'd have to confront him, face to face."

But then he saw a flash and heard a crack and a thump. Outside, Jerry's attention was gathered for a second; he saw David stiffen and then the flash.

Jim: "I didn't know what happened but we both ran down the stairs and did what we were trained to do, try to stop the bleeding. We grabbed some towels off the line and called for the ambulance boys to come in. But it was too late."

Jim stayed with the family while Jerry rode the ambulance to the hospital. David was pronounced dead of a chest wound at 10:50 p.m. Later, after a trip to the morgue, both officers returned to the house to try to comfort the parents.

Despite reassurances from colleagues and superiors, Jerry and Jim are burdened with a sense of failure. That everyone, family and friends, failed too. And a lingering question: why did David kill himself?

"We don't know," Jim said. "He never gave a reason."          *—1977*

---

# ED

Ed Juteau is dying. Maybe Vietnam killed him.

He didn't come home to Herkimer County in a box covered by a flag with his dog tag tucked into his toes. He walked out. But maybe he should have taken the box. He's in a box now.

The box is a small bedroom on the second floor of the gray and white house on Smith Street. The box is a single bed, where Ed sits in his underwear under a brown quilt with his cane on the floor and amber pill bottles all over the place. The box is lymphoma, a form of cancer characterized by abnormal growth of the cells that make up the body's lymphatic tissue.

Ed has lymphoma; maybe he's got six months. Just now his doctor wants him to rest and catch up on the radiation and drug treatments. He's making it on pain killers and that phone next to the bed. It keeps ringing.

"Agent Orange," Ed answers.

Herkimer is a long way from the jungles of Southeast Asia. A long way. It's a long way from the war, too, and all that hell and hate. Didn't we bury that? Didn't we come home, licking our wounds, and wait for the novelists and the filmmakers to tell us what happened?

What the hell is this big, handsome man doing in bed in the Mohawk Valley, answering his phone, "Agent Orange?"

Why have they told Ed Juteau he is dying?

The problem is that maybe some of the survivors, the ones who got out of Vietnam vertically, with honorable discharges, didn't really survive at all.

Ed counts himself one of these. And that, he says, is why, instead of playing a sick man in a cramped bedroom, he is trying to run a national campaign called Agent Orange Victims International.

"I'm not going to fade away," Ed says quietly. "I'm going to die, but I'm not going to fade away."

Ed is 29 and it started more than 10 years ago, while he was still an enlisted Air Force man in Vietnam. He was assigned to a medical unit, working supply, and as a medic. He knew the Americans were spraying the jungles with a herbicide called Agent Orange, a ferocious chemical mixture developed, but not used, during World War II to kill vegetation.

Between 1962 and 1972, about 10.6 million gallons of the stuff were sprayed over an area the size of Connecticut. It is said the mix was 25 times the rate used in less violent ways in the United States.

He'd also heard the stories about men getting sick and developing rashes. About miscarriages and birth defects among the Vietnamese people. He wasn't involved in spraying, but he had seen jungles eaten away by Orange.

"I saw how the trees fell down," Ed told me. "That's just not normal, is it?"

Later, while still on duty, Ed started having problems, too. Stomach problems, odd fevers, and a rash—pale pink blotches on the skin he still carries. Doctors, he recalls, told him it was all in his head; even suggested he was malingering.

But he mustered out and came home, trying to pick up the threads of the life he'd left when he enlisted. He tried to forget about things like dead trees and dead people; about how when he and his buddies arrived at the Oakland terminal, a bunch of college kids spit on them and called them baby killers.

But Ed, and a lot of other vets, found out the pages of that part of their lives won't turn. Especially when you're sick.

"I tried to go back to what I wanted to do," he says, "but I started having problems. I started teaching school, but I kept missing days. Then I took a job in computer technology but I was staying out of work with fevers and stomach problems. It was four years before they found out what I had. That was some temporary skin rash."

Cancer was diagnosed in 1976. At that point, when Ed found out what he had, he started doing some research. The trail wound back to Vietnam and Agent Orange. He decided, in his own mind, that the chemical was killing him and he had to warn others. He had never been an activist, but he started making noise.

"Listen, I'm a flag-waving, apple pie, John Wayne American," he said, urging his body up against the pillows. He didn't mention them, but I saw the very large box of small American flags in the corner of the room, next to the desk and the file cabinets.

"I'm still patriotic, to this day. I'd go to war if I felt it was justified. I'm not anti-patriotic, just mad."

It's a war, though, from the bedroom. Fighting time and what, until recently, had been indifference to what Ed and his supporters feel is a serious health problem, touching perhaps thousands of Vietnam vets and their families. That's why, in time, he became vice president of the organization "dedicated to helping victims exposed to Agent Orange" by circulating information, getting medical tests and the bottom line, a complete, unbiased study to determine if, indeed, vets like Ed are dying because of the chemical.

"That's why my phone is ringing, and letters keep coming in," Ed continues. "We got a dozen letters today, from all over the country; vets who want to know what's going on. I've got 200 names in that file already. We want to warn people about a killer. Got to get the word out. It doesn't matter if men were directly involved in spraying. I wasn't. You could be 200 miles away and be contaminated. It got in the food, the water, the air."

He was getting tired. With great effort, he opened a thermos of water next to the bed and threw down another pill.

The phone rings. "Excuse me, it's a suicide," Ed says.

After he's finished talking with a woman whose husband, a vet, has disappeared again and may kill himself, Ed calls a county social worker for help. This is another of the war's leavings. Vietnam got into the head, too.

"Along with everything else, I'm an outreach clinic, too. I can't handle that. I'm dying. But I try. I talk to them. Do what I can."

Ed gets a monthly compensation check, which he says only helps him and his wife, Kay, and his son, Rob, who is 2, to get by, day by day. No way, he says, will it knock down the medical bills, the debts, the lack of a lifestyle.

"I want to leave a good life for my wife and son," he told me. "It's not fair to them."

The compensation was arranged without an admission by the V.A. that Ed's illness was caused by Agent Orange. He would have gotten it anyway. Lucky for him the symptoms began before he was discharged.

I leave Ed with a lot of unanswered questions and his own unfinished business. He's tired. Needs another pill.

Rob comes up the stairs with a toy airplane that isn't doing what it's supposed to do. He wants his father to fix it. He climbs on the quilt and I notice the whole thing is covered with little craft—rockets and missiles and other tiny war machines.

Maybe Rob wants to be a soldier like his Dad.

Maybe not.                                                                                   *—1979*

# JUDGE EADY

I went up to Loomis Hill Cemetery to watch them drop Judge Eady's pine box into the ground.

Judge Eady was a black man who died Oct. 1 at Van Duyn Hospital. He was 69 and had been dying slowly in a bed at H-2 for about five years. He stayed in bed and watched television and said little. When he died, there were only his friends at Van Duyn to mourn him.

Dave Skutt is a county parks department maintenance crew leader. He's usually at Camillus pool or the fish hatchery. That morning he was at Loomis Hill, which is operated by the county, to help lower Judge Eady's pine box into the ground.

"They've buried 3,170 indigent people here since the first one in 1936," Dave said, as he watched J.B. Dorsey skittle the hearse up next to the five-foot-deep hole. There was mud and the long Cadillac raced a little getting in.

J.B. got out and opened the side door so Dave and his crew could get the straps over the box. There was a Peanuts quilt covering what was left of Judge Eady.

"Sometimes we hold bodies for a while up here—we have a vault," Dave said. "But they asked that a grave be dug. Most of the time it's like this; just the crew and the undertaker. Once in a while they have a service at the grave but usually not."

Section I, Row 6, Grave 108. Next to Lloyd Stiles, Montane Lansing Turtelot, Wesley Brooks and John Parker. No. 3,170 buried by the county since Charles Hude went into what had been the "Hog" Loomis farm the day after Christmas 1936.

They lifted the box off the swivel bed and got the straps under it. "Pine box," Dave said. "that's county regulation. Some places, some potter's fields, they just bury in the coffin." A few months later, there will be a metal plaque set flush to the ground at the head of the grave.

The county pays for a name, birth and death date on the marker. If the family wants a flat stone, they may buy one.

The men strained and let the box drop.

Then they wiped their hands and J.B. Dorsey handed Dave a copy of the burial permit. The motor still was running. He closed the door and drove away and Dave's crew moved the yellow backhoe up next to the pile of dirt.

Loomis Hill is about six acres and looks like a park. It spreads flat, with big maples and evergreen, off the Howlett Hill Road, on a crest that shows a dim view of Onondaga Lake.

No stones jut in the flatness. Here and there, a few clumps of plastic flowers and dampened wreaths. Most of them are in the infants sections.

Dave finished the job in the cozy office, next to a pot belly stove. He wrote Judge Eady's name in one of the large ledgers, which are numbered and cross referred in the card file.

"If someone comes up here during the week when there's someone around, we can tell them where a person was buried," he said. "Some of the markers are hard to find because the grass grows over them but they can be found. A few people want to stop by and pay their respects."

The arrangements are made through Social Services. Burials are of men and women who had been on public assistance or can't afford the costs of other cemeteries. Men and women without homes or families, sometimes. A few, even without names.

Dave came back from the file with nine cards. "They used to call these 'unknown,' now it's 'John Doe'," he said. "We even had a woman they couldn't identify back in 1943. Her marker says 'Lulu Doe'."

Later J.B. Dorsey said no one knew of a trace of Judge Eady's family, if he still had one. Someone said he was born in Valdosta, Ga., and left there when he was about 16, looking for work and never went back. He drifted and lost track of home.

There may have been a brother or sister; no one is sure.

"They have no choice but to go there," the undertaker said of Loomis Hill. "It's sad, but there are people like that, homeless, no family. They're using it more and more. We get called on a rotation basis by welfare and we try to give them a good funeral. We got a minister and an organist and had calling hours before the service. There were 22 people for the funeral."

That was Ella Hendrix doing. She is a night nurse at Van Duyn and took care of Judge Eady for five years. He came in after a slowly deteriorating nerve disorder kept him from working as a laborer any more and he needed help.

He came in with an old coat, a suit, a record player and some religious records and watched the sun set over Loomis Hill, down the road.

"I guess there are a lot of men like Judge Eady," Mrs. Hendrix said later. "They drift out of the South looking for work. We had another man last year. He was only 54 when he died and we couldn't find any family for him, either. Judge Eady tried to tell us things but he couldn't talk very well by the time he came to us."

The nurse, a strong tree with branches for many birds, gathered the staff together, bought some flowers, and gave her friend the kind of funeral she thought he would have wanted.  ·

"I think it would have pleased him," she said. "At least it was something."                                                                             *—1977*

---

# ANDY

This is about Andy, the man who may not have played for the Pittsburgh Pirates.

Andy was Andrew Sierzchula. He died a few weeks ago at Van Duyn Home and Hospital. He was 94, or maybe 97. Some people thought he was 94 and some people thought he was 97. Not that it mattered. Andy had been up on The Hill as a guest of Onondaga County for a long time. Some say 15 years, some 20.

When a man has been on The Hill that long, the years do a pretty good job of whittling down the fine points.

Jackie Ross was Andy's social worker at Van Duyn. A few years ago, an intern worked up an interview with Andy about his life. He told the intern about Pittsburgh. He said he'd played for the Pirates in 1917. "He said he played for a couple of years but didn't like it and quit," Jackie explained.

That wasn't the first time Andy had said he was a Pirate. Nor the last. He talked about it a lot after he got to The Hill. Louise Sylvester, the head nurse in Andy's ward, was there much of the time Andy was.

"Sure," she said. "He said he played for the Pirates. I don't remember that he said exactly what he did, but he seemed proud of it. He'd tell anyone who came along. He used to watch the ball games on TV. He'd complain that the bats they use now are too soft; they break too easily. He said the balls are better; they're harder."

Did Andy have any mementoes of his days at Pittsburgh? None his friends at Van Duyn knew about. A man travels light, coming to The Hill.

"There was no proof that he played for Pittsburgh," Louise said. "Except his word." Andy's word was good enough for The Hill.

Andy also said he was born in Buffalo. His family left there when he was about 2. His father got a job in a coal mine near Pittsburgh. Years later, a friend of Andy's got him to return to Buffalo to look up some of his kin. He came back saying he couldn't find anyone.

Andy wasn't one to talk much about his family. He had been a drifter. What kin he needed he adopted as he went.

He told the people at Van Duyn he left Pittsburgh in the 1920s and traveled to California and Florida. He made it to upstate New York in the '40s. He came to Syracuse and worked at Kallfelz Bakery. Later, he ran an elevator at the Onondaga Hotel. He also helped a local family in a rooming house in the West End. That's how Elizabeth got to be known as Andy's niece, even though they weren't related.

"He ran the rooming house for my mother," she said. "We sort of adopted him into the family. He was like a grandfather to my son. I guess we were pretty much the only family he had."

No, Elizabeth said, although Andy was a fan of the Syracuse Chiefs baseball team, he never mentioned playing for Pittsburgh that she could remember. She said she thought she'd remember something like that.

Andy's name doesn't show on any list of major or minor league players I could find. It is not on the All-Time Roster kept by the Pirates nor any old guides or registers, according to Ed Wade, the team's publicist. Ed speculated that Andy might have played under an assumed name or had a tryout with the Pirates.

He didn't appear in the files of the National Baseball Library at Cooperstown, either. One of the researchers there, Tom Hietz, said the experts call people who claim to have played in the majors "ghosts." Maybe the man tried out for a team. Maybe he was a batting practice pitcher. Maybe he sold popcorn.

Jackie Ross, the social worker, pointed out that Andy was in good health and able to work when he first started living in one of the old dormitories for men across from the OCC campus. In those days, the county took in older, homeless men for "social reasons." This isn't done anymore. Once men like Andy dig in, they don't want to leave. They are taken care of, right to the grave.

"I never knew him to go anywhere," Louise Sylvester said. "He was like some of the other men. They have no family and no friends, except the ones they make up here. We take care of them."

Andy moved through The Hill's levels. As he got older, he was sick more often. He was brought to the new hospital when it opened. As his condition deteriorated, Andy's room crept closer to the nurses' station.

When he died, he was right across from it.

Louise said Andy had a good friend on The Hill he liked to talk to. He was a fellow patient. He died before Andy. His only visitors were Elizabeth and members of her family.

"At least he had some visitors," the nurse said. "Some of our people, well, their families put them up here and forget them. And when they die, that's it."

Andy went out that way. There was a funeral service in the chapel at Van Duyn. A few of the staff came, along with two people in his adopted family. Elizabeth was in Florida when her old friend died. Then he was put in a plot in Oakwood-Morningside Cemetery. Andy said he wanted to be buried at Oakwood. There was just enough money left to do that. In the obit, it said, "In 1917, he played baseball with the Pittsburgh Pirates."

When a man has been at The Hill that long, the years do a pretty good job of whittling down the fine points.                   *—1984*

# Chapter 7

# GOOD GUYS, BAD GUYS

---

## THE VET: DICK

These were a few thoughts for Veterans Day:

We gave Dick Heppeler his homecoming from Vietnam Friday. The moment was quiet, very happy and a little late.

We gathered in a little room flooded with sunlight, 12 floors above downtown Syracuse.

A few old soldiers, a couple of pretty girls and the American flag, pinned to the wall in such a way it seemed to be furling in a breeze.

Yes, Richard J. Heppeler of Syracuse, former grunt of the Fourth Infantry Division, U.S. Army, got a short ceremony and a Purple Heart medal in the conference room of Rep. Jim Walsh's office in the federal building.

The Purple Heart was late, too. About 23 years, if you're counting, which Dick was. He earned that lilac-colored ribbon with the profile of George Washington on it by losing half of his leg in a stinking jungle in Vietnam Friday the 13th of May 1968. A mine exploded.

The Army had given this hero a hard time about the medal. Said he didn't deserve to have it on his war record. His wife, Chris, and Jim Walsh teamed up and did the justice that needed to be done.

Five years after the Heppelers began to ask for that inch-and-a-half of fabric and medal, there was his congressman pinning the darn thing to the checkered lapels of Dick's tweed jacket.

Tears ran out of the corners of the former infantryman's eyes. We clapped as loud as 10 people can. Chris gave her husband a hug to end all hugs.

Then the old soldiers sat there and chewed the fat about the war, medals, heroes and homecomings.

Dick told us how it was back in the '60s, coming home from Vietnam on crutches with a pant leg pinned to a belt loop. He got no parade, no civic greeting, no medals, cheers and hugs.

Yellow ribbons? Hell, they called him a baby-killer.

We handed hate to the kid who had part of his body blown away and the rest of it burned because a president of the United States thought he ought to be there.

Lord, Dick was saying. He stood in front of us opening and closing the box his medal came in.

Lord, he remembered the night a group of vets in a Texas Army hospital—all us freaks, he called them—took a liberty in town. As they stood at a bus stop, an old woman checked out Dick and his wounded pals and sneered at them.

"I suppose you're from Vietnam," she said. "Well, you deserved what you got."

Later Dick limped through O'Hare Airport in Chicago, on his way back to Syracuse. A kid with crutches in uniform thinking, "What am I doing here? Where can I hide? Suppose someone sees me."

The old soldiers nodded. Yeah, said the Marine corporal. Yeah, said the Navy corpsman. Yeah, said the other grunt, also a private first class in country.

You sucked it in, one of them said. Yes, you lied.

Vietnam? The war? Don't know what you're talking about.

Dick said we shouldn't wonder he came home and didn't think about writing to Washington about his Purple Heart or his Silver Service Star or his Gallantry Cross or any of the war souvenirs.

All he wanted was to blend in. Suck it all in. Try to forget.

Impossible, of course, the old soldiers agreed. Their piece of history couldn't be put aside. They had Vietnam in their guts and their hearts. The rest of us had it in the back of our heads.

Bitter? Sure they are. Coping? Most of them. Understanding? We try.

Dick had that personal veteran's day of his Friday. Today he's pouring concrete, at work in Auburn.

Welcome home, soldier.                                   *—1991*

# THE VET: SAMMY

Sammy Drake was frugal, folks in Conquest say.

The man lived modestly. He'd label a jar of peanut butter with the date he opened it. His dogs were on rations; Sammy kept track of how many sections of hot dog and biscuit he fed his pets each day.

When Sammy died three years ago at the age of 74, neighbors were surprised at the size of his estate. He left most of it to the Veterans Administration Medical Center in Syracuse.

Thanks to Sammy, vets in 224 rooms will have TVs for the first time. He left $132,651.68 of his $189,000 to the hospital.

Sammy was a Cayuga County farmer's son who went to World War II. He helped fight the Battle of the Bulge and got wounded twice. After the war, he went home to Conquest, raised red kidney beans, baled hay for his neighbors, worked at Cato Feed Mill and kept pretty much to himself.

Years ago, he was treated for pneumonia at the VA. A doctor on the staff had been good to him. He wanted to return the favor.

"This is an extremely generous donation," Gordon Sclar of the administrator's staff said Tuesday. "Mr. Drake wanted to return the money to the VA for less fortunate veterans."

The gift will pay for the televisions, cable and a closed circuit system for patient and staff information and education.

"This will cover all of the costs," Gordon said. Bids are in and the system should be operating in September.

Except for three years as a private in the 327th Glider Infantry unit in World War II, Edward G. Drake spent all of his life in Conquest. His nickname, "Sammy," was given to him by his Uncle George.

The Drakes lived on Drake Road, about three miles from Cato. Sammy never married. He stayed with his parents until they died; after that, he stayed alone, according to his friend, Dick Lees, who married a cousin of Sammy's.

Stayed with his dogs.

"He did some farming when he could," Dick explained. "After that, he rented out land. He had a garden, raised strawberries. And he loved his dogs. People were forever droppin' strays off and he'd keep them. When they died, he'd have them buried in the pet cemetery in Cato."

Dick had to tend to putting the last dog, Ruby, to sleep after he found Sammy dead in his home one day in March 1988. Sammy'd asked him to do that if anything happened to him. Dick took Ruby to the pet cemetery and saw to it a picture of a dog went on Sammy's own monument.

Dick continued, "He'd sit there by that wood stove that heated the house and talk to his dogs. He used to walk them too, when he could."

Sammy didn't have a driver's license. Dick drove him to Syracuse to the VA center when he needed treatment. He went there for the pneumonia, and another time when he had a problem with his esophagus. The last time in, they found a lump on one of his lungs.

"He decided it was a good thing," Dick said of the hospital. "He wanted to leave them money in his will." Sammy told him he was especially pleased by the care he got from a young woman who was interning at the VA; Dick believes her name was Dr. Ann Bishop.

Dick said he liked to visit Sammy at the farmhouse and "set there and talk with him. He was a nice guy, good-hearted." They'd chat about The War, sometimes.

"He was drafted," Dick said. "They sent him and nine other guys to South Dakota. Sammy said when they asked what they were doing out there, they sent them to Europe. He'd talk about being in the Battle of the Bulge. He had a book about it. Showed me where he'd been."

Sammy'd been hit twice, once in Holland, once in Belgium. The last time, they nearly killed him. "He said he fooled the doctors, though," Dick said. "He was wounded bad, it stayed with him."

Dick said to me he might have been the only citizen of Conquest who wasn't shocked by the size of his friend's estate. Sammy kept him posted on how his savings account did.

"That's all he had, a good old savings account," Dick said. "He drew a pretty good pension and didn't spend much. He kept track of everything, everything. Even dated a jar of peanut butter when he opened it."

The Drake Road farm went to a family member under Sammy's mother's will. The American Legion post in Cato was remembered by Sammy; likewise the village's rescue squad. Dick Lees too, he said.

I asked Sammy's friend if he'd heard how the gift to the VA would be used. Sammy wanted it to benefit the patients; no strings were attached.

Dick said he had. Then he chuckled.

"He had a TV but he didn't watch it much," Dick said. "Just the news and the weather. Oh, yes, and Lawrence Welk. He liked him."

*—1991*

# THE HERO

The old soldier stood there in his kitchen with the coffee-maker groaning and one of the cats yelling and watched the kid with the gold oak leaves on his shoulders and the aviator's wings on his tunic struggle with the little boxes from Washington, D.C., Department of the Army.

He took a red bandanna out of a pocket and wiped his eyes. He leaned hard on a kitchen chair. After a while, he sat down.

Nick Naples of 313 Horan Road had to sit to be a hero the other afternoon when Major John Finlay came to the house at the end of the long driveway just over the western line of Solvay.

Nick's been poorly lately. The Army at first wanted to do this at the Federal Building last summer but Anna, his wife, said no. After all, she said she'd nearly lost Nick three times in the last year or so.

This was about when she nearly lost Nick 43 years ago. World War II had caught up with him after all that time.

Pfc. Nick Naples, anti-tank gunner, 39th Headquarters Company, 15th Army Infantry Division, was getting his medals pinned on him in his own kitchen by an officer who probably wasn't even born when, well . . .

It was quite a day. Quite a day.

Amazing, Nick kept saying. Absolutely amazing after all this time.

How come? I said to Nick. The last time I was at the house we were talking about garlic, a cash crop from the yards east of the house that made the man famous hereabouts. Nick was regarded as the prince of garlic in Central New York until he harvested his last crop, which happened at the end of August.

Yeah, Nick said then, "You got to do it some time. Life goes on."

When I walked in Wednesday after lunch, with photographer Al Campanie in tow, he told his other guests we had met in jail. I laughed and so did Nick. He may be sick but a sense of humor thrives.

How come you're just getting your medals now? I asked him again. You're going to have to buy a new suit to hang them all on. By that time John Finlay of the Army's recruiting battalion in Syracuse had an awesome display of fruit salad on the kitchen table.

"Look at all those!" Anna said. She was the one who got this started after years of Nick not mentioning WWII. "It looks like you fought the war all by yourself."

"I did," said Nick.

The hero is a little hard of hearing because one of the shots he took while "chasing Krauts" in Germany, Italy, Sicily and France hit him in the face, knocking out two teeth. Forgot to duck, according to him. I asked a third time, how come?

"Oh, they asked the fellows several times if we had all our medals," he said finally. "We said, 'no.' But we never got 'em. Then we came home. It didn't bother me. I thought about the Purple Heart. I wanted that. But the others . . . I let them go."

He looked at the major's display. "They're so many."

Nick was born on this farm, which has shriveled a bit from the days when his parents had a pretty good vegetable garden going on what had been an old salt bed. There are 16 acres. The records his helper Lois Reinhardt of the Military Order of the Purple Heart dug out of the military bureaucracy listed him as a farm hand in his 20s when he was drafted.

Before too long he was firing this light-weight, portable cannon at the enemy at Anzio instead of yanking turnips in Solvay. He did that for nearly three years, 1942 to 1945. He was wounded twice, in January and June of '44. When we asked him Wednesday, Nick could only remember that one time the bullet hit him in the face.

Those two teeth were pushing up daisies somewhere in Italy when John Finlay started pinning the medals on Nick's chest in the kitchen Wednesday. Anna had gotten Nick into his dark blue jacket the better to provide a cushion for the government-issue pins. She got him to stand up next to the table.

"Sorry it's taken so long," the major said.

The Purple Heart was first, of course. It carries the profile of George Washington. On the imitation parchment that came with the medal from Washington, it was written that all who saw these presents should know that "The President of the United States of America has awarded the Purple Heart established by General George Washington at Newburgh, New York, August 7, 1782, to Private First Class Nick Naples, United States Army for wounds received in action in the European African Middle Eastern Theater of Operations . . ."

Oh, my. Newburgh 1782 is a long way from Solvay too.

Then the Good Conduct Medal.

Then the Campaign Medal, for five campaigns, including an amphibious assault, which was indicated by an arrowhead . . .

That's an unbelievable record, Rudy Reyes said. Rudy, who lives in

North Syracuse, was a bomber gunman in World War II. He is New York commander of the Military Order of the Purple Heart and has, of course, his own medal with the profile of the Father of Our County on it.

It was Rudy who explained to us, as the major worked at getting the medals secured to Nick, that we shouldn't be surprised that some heroes are so shy about claiming the ribbons and hunks of pewter and bronze they earned in the Big One. It almost seemed the more citations there were in a man's 201 file, the more he cared less about them.

Now Rudy himself was shy. He was shot up riding in the B-17 over the submarine pens of France several times but the folks back home never knew about it.

"We didn't want our families to know we'd been wounded," Rudy explained. "A lot of guys didn't want to be held up when they were mustering out. If you said you'd been wounded, they wanted you to stay another week or so to be checked out."

John still was working on Nick's jacket pocket, which seemed to be getting heavier. Let's see now . . . The Victory Medal, Occupation Medal, Combat Infantry Badge, Presidential Unit Citation, Honorable Service Pin . . .

"Congratulations," the major said after a while. "Thank you very much," Nick replied. Then he went for his red bandanna again to dab at his eyes.

Lois Reinhardt is a national service officer for the veterans. She has an office at the VA Medical Center in Syracuse, which was where Anna Naples got in touch with her about a year and a half ago when Nick was in for one of his checkups.

Anna said she knew Nick had some medals coming but since her husband seldom talked about his war service, she thought he wasn't interested. Yet knowing Nick, she sensed he would mellow, as he got older. "He's a stubborn old Italian," she told us. "He never wanted to ask anybody for anything. Why when he first got sick, he didn't even want to go the VA for treatment.

"So, when he was in the hospital, I saw an article in the Herald-Journal about a veteran who got his medals after 45 years, I thought we ought to give it a try. I talked to Lois and she went to work. She's been wonderful."

Al Campanie, who was in Nam, took his pictures. The man from the Army recruiting took his. Lois, Rudy and the major shook Nick's hand on and off cameras and Lois gave him a kiss on the cheek. Nick sat there at his kitchen table with the new spots of color against the old blue of his jacket. He didn't say much.

"You know," Anna said, "he never got those teeth replaced. The ones the Germans shot out."

"I'll look into that," Lois said. "You come and see me next time you have an appointment at the hospital."

"Maybe," Nick said, and he put his finger in the gap in his jaw. "We'll see."                                                                                   —1987

---

# ANNA

Just like the rest of us, Anna was sitting in front of her TV set the other day when the Americans got out of Iran. Like the rest of us, she felt good.

But then she sat there, with the images flickering a few thousand miles away, and she started crying. She'd been crying a lot lately and some times there's nothing that will hold back the tears.

There are going to be a lot of celebrations, she thought, with the fish tank bubbling in the neat highrise apartment in downtown Syracuse.

Lots of celebrations, lots of joy, lots of reunions.

Where's mine? Anna was thinking. Where's mine? Where's the re-union for me and my little girl?

And inevitably, as she has many times since last summer, when she took to her apartment and didn't come out much, Anna went back 17 years to March 1, 1964, and the big room in back of the midwife's house on the east coast of Florida.

That was the day she gave her little girl away.

This is the way Anna told it to me:

She came to Syracuse around Christmas time 15 years ago, but before that, she was in Florida—in Mims, the little coastal town where she was born and where her family worked at hard labor for a man who hadn't been told that slavery was abolished a long time ago. That was more than 40 years ago.

Anna grew up poor, but she was ambitious for herself and had started college before she met a man and married him in 1959. They had two children—daughters now 21 and 19—and in two years, they separated.

It was not a good marriage, Anna says. Her husband beat her. If she had known the phrase then, she would have called herself an abused wife.

They had lived in Daytona, but after that, Anna took her daughters and moved back to Mims, where she found a small apartment in public housing.

She supported herself and her two babies on $50 a week, which she earned cleaning white peoples' houses and ironing their clothes. It was not a good life, but Anna got by. After all, she says, "I'm a tough cookie."

She got by until she met another man, a fellow she had known growing up, who came back to Mims for a vacation. They had a two-week affair and when he left, Anna was pregnant. The man said come on, I'll pay for an abortion. Anna said no; she didn't believe in that. She'd have the baby.

She did, working right up until she went into labor at the end of the winter. She still was earning $50 a week. The rent was $50 a month and Anna had been thinking about her two babies and what the future held. One of the things she thought was that she couldn't afford to keep the baby.

"I had arranged to go to the midwife to have the baby, but that would cost me $50. How was I going to pay the rent? And buy food? As it was, the people I worked for used to give me leftovers to take home so the three of us would have enough to eat.

"Things really looked bad. My family was close by but because of the fix they thought I'd gotten into, they gave me no support. They'd washed their hands of me.

"Well, when I went into labor—I was in labor three days—I went to the midwife's house and we started talking about the baby.

"I didn't even have money to buy diapers, or a baby blanket. I told the midwife I didn't want to bring up my baby like that and she asked me if I'd though about giving it up.

"I said, yes, I had. I even knew a couple from my church I had in mind. They were very nice, loving people and they had no children of their own."

So, it turned out, Cora Lee and her husband were there in the midwife's house when the baby came. It was a girl and when she came out of Anna, the midwife placed her on her mother's stomach.

"I could feel her but I didn't want to look at her, because I knew I was going to give her away. After a while, Cora Lee held the baby and we talked.

"I told her I was entrusting my baby to her and Cora Lee said she would never want for things. 'We'll always take care of her as if she was our own and we'll let her know that you loved her,' Cora Lee said.

" 'Yes, above all,' I said, 'please let her know that.'"

Cora Lee stood there, holding Anna's hand. Then, after a while, she and her husband went home with Anna's baby. She never saw them again . . .

Anna got up and went for some more Kleenex after she said that. We were sitting in her living room and it was quiet, except for the fish tank. After a few minutes, she started talking again . . .

She and the girls came to Syracuse in 1965, where her brother lived. The idea, she told me, was to start a new life. Part of the new life was that her daughters did not know about the baby.

"They were too young. I didn't think they would understand. I kept putting it off."

The girls grew up in Syracuse, Anna had another child, a son, and Florida seemed more than just miles away.

She even got back with her ex-husband for a while, but then he nearly killed her with a fishing knife and they split, for good.

She started taking courses at University College to improve herself and got a good job at a day-care center. One daughter got married and made her a grandmother and the other went to college, to study engineering.

Life was better for all of them than it had been in a long time until last summer, when Anna's ex proposed that he take her daughters on a trip to see family members in various states.

"They went and the last stop, in August, was in Florida, to see his mother, who was dying, and some of the other relatives. He took them to see my aunt and stepfather in Mims and that was when it happened."

Anna got a call from her daughters. When they went to see the aunt, she asked them about their sister. What sister? they wanted to know. Why, the little girl your mother gave to Cora Lee.

"They were devastated. Crushed. Especially finding out that way and my aunt telling them how wrong I was. It was so bizarre, finding out that way and me not being able to defend myself."

Anna and her daughters talked on the phone and she tried to explain she hadn't meant to hurt them; she kept it from them because she thought they couldn't deal with it. But now, they would deal with it.

One of the daughters went to see Cora Lee and met the sister she didn't know she had. Her name was Martha Jean and she was doing very well, just the way Cora Lee had promised.

"Cora Lee had told her about me 10 years ago, all the circumstances. The girls said she wanted to see me, know all about me and they tried to tell her, the best they could.

"When they came back, they told me they didn't blame me for not telling them; they said, 'We love you, we know what you went through, but you should have told us.'"

The tears started up again and Anna went into the bedroom and showed me the picture of Martha Jean the girls brought back to Syracuse, a pretty girl in glasses and a purple dress smiling into the lens.

"Isn't she a beautiful girl? But a picture is not like seeing her. I want to see her. I want to sit with her and touch her and look at her. I love her and I want her to know I didn't abandon her.

"She has a right to know who she is and where she came from. She has a right."

Anna knows she has survived a lot of things, but since August, her life has changed. That day in the midwife's keeps coming back and there are lots of things Anna can't deal with, just yet. That's the reason she quit her job and doesn't go out of the apartment much, except for groceries.

She's almost a recluse, sitting there next to the fish tank, trying to figure out the future.

"I feel compelled to keep in touch with her. In a while, I'll write her a letter and call her. And then I want to see her. Right now, I'm about to explode; I can't contain it."

In the coming weeks, Anna says she will go back to work to make enough money to see her daughter. She knows Cora Lee and her husband will approve and maybe, if things work out, she will be able to bring Martha Jean to Syracuse for the reunion "of all of my children together."

One way or another, she's decided, it will happen.

"How can I say it? What is it? A force, a force bigger than all of us. That's how I feel now." —1981

# HAROLD

Carrier Dome is so close to Harold and Annie Baker's apartment over the liquor store on South Salina that when he was 15, Harold probably could have chucked a baseball and hit the thing.

These days, 55 years after he was a junior Olympian, the big sports palace with the roof of silver fabric is about as far away as you can get, and still be there.

The Bakers have never been to the Dome, even though it's up there, like a bunch of glinting pillows, every time they look out the front window. Harold calls himself a has-been in sports. Says he lost it, years ago. Wishes the young nows of the National Sports Festival good luck at their events but doesn't plan to look in on them, straining their muscles the way he used to.

When all the fuss is being made a couple blocks away, Harold is out on the sidewalk along where McCarthy's Restaurant used to be, feeding the pigeons, as is his habit; standing on the bricks with his wool cap pulled down over his brow and looking like James Cagney playing George M. Cohan.

Or behind the bar at the Driftwood Lounge, where he works part-time. Saying, "Oh, those were the good old days but I haven't competed since. I lost it. Got into the booze racket. Got in with the wrong gang. I played a little softball and I walk a lot, now, but no, who wants to know about me?"

His friend Jimmy cared and he came in the other day and asked me to go and see Harold. After all, Jimmy pointed out, with reason, in 1927 didn't Harold do the same thing all these young bucks and does of the Sport Festival are doing?

Didn't he bring home a bunch of medals to Syracuse?

When I got to the apartment, Annie was cooking sweet and sour cabbage in the little kitchen. She said she learned the recipe when she was working for this rich man in Solvay who wanted to marry her. She didn't because he was a lot older and never took a bath.

She laughed when she said that, and so did Harold. The Bakers laugh a lot about themselves, which is probably a good thing when you're almost 65 and 70 and live over a liquor store where you can see the Dome.

"Oh, I'm going to go up there some day," Annie said, pointing out the window. "Going to put on my burlap sack and walk right in."

One of the first things Harold did, after we sat down, was to apologize for not having the news clippings about when he was famous in 1927. His got lost in 1939 when his father, who was Archibald Napoleon Bonaparte Baker, burned to death in a fire at the old homestead on Grape Street, where the Everson Museum sits.

He does, however, have a few souvenirs of those good old days, including some faded brown pictures hanging around the living room of Harold, at 15, wearing a cap even then, and a bow tie and knickers.

One of them shows him with Paul and Lloyd Waner, who played for the Pittsburgh Pirates and were called the "Poison Brothers." Harold met them when he went to the World Series in 1927. Another has him with Miller Huggins, manager of the Yankees.

"But here's the greatest of them all," Harold is saying as he hands me an old brown picture with the 15-year-old, 80-pound kid from Syracuse chinning himself on a bat between Lou Gehrig and Babe Ruth.

Young Harold was swinging on that Yankee bat because of the day his friend Philie Zenner rode him over to Wilson Park on Philie's bike, where the city and the Syracuse Herald were running a preliminary for the Junior Olympics in Washington. Harold had on street clothes and shoes, but "I beat everyone." He ran the 100-yard dash, "all by myself"; the broad jump, baseball throw, basketball foul shooting and chinning the bar, which was his "main sport."

Next thing he knew he had advanced to a meet at old Archbold Stadium, and then he was on his way to the internationals, in Washington, D.C., where he was the only Syracusan who came back with a first place.

"Oh, in those days, I did 22, 23 chins on the bar, and that was with the palms toward me; you don't see that anymore. I did the dash in 10.7 and got 21 out of 21 baskets. I don't remember how far I threw the baseball, but it was something like 140-odd yards. Oh, I was always on the gym bars, since the day I was born."

Annie and Harold laughed again when he said that.

That was a great moment for a kid, going to Washington. Harold remembers all the names of the people involved along the way, even how the train ride was. He still has the certificate naming him the junior champion of Syracuse and giving him the trip to the World Series, and a place in the international Junior Olympics in Washington in August of 1927.

He remembers the roar of the crowd during the competition in the baseball stadium in Washington and how the others dropped out, one by one, until only Harold was left. He got a big silver cup— "they don't make 'em that way any more," he said to me proudly—and his name, in big letters, was right on the front, under the words CHAMPION. One of the handles broke off the cup and Harold has been meaning to get it fixed, if he can get down to Oneida.

"You know," he goes on, pacing and talking while Annie cooks, "we went to the White House and I sat in the President's chair. Calvin Coolidge! I sat in the President's chair. Oh my, God!"

He came home to Syracuse in triumph. The Boys Club band was playing and there was a parade in an open car, Harold all the time waving at people and the people cheering. After that, they treated the champ to a steak dinner at Getman's, right across from the Onondaga Hotel.

A short while later, Jim Fraser, promotion manager at the Herald, put in a word for him at the telephone company and the 15-year-old went to work as an office boy on Montgomery Street.

Harold remembers now that he didn't want to get a swelled head. So, he forgot about being a champion—even though they were still showing him in the news reels on the screen at the Eckel—and settled down to be a kid on the South Side, in the old Ward.

"I forgot all about it," he said.

He was looking into the faded, brown face of that kid with the knickers and bow tie on the wall over the TV. Harold, looking down a long hall, with people cheering and "Jazzbow," what he called himself, slicing into that big steak with all the heavy hitters on Warren Street.

"I'm not committing suicide," Annie says from the kitchen. "It's just the cabbage."

Harold laughs and crosses his hands at his belt buckle like a golfer warming up. "Oh, well," he says.

After a while we went downstairs and Harold headed for the Driftwood and the pigeons. The last thing he said to me was about Annie. "A good old Polack," he called her.                    —*1981*

---

# THE EYE DOCTOR

A lot of memories blew back over me the other day when I read that

Hugh P. Reilley, who used to help me see, had left LeMoyne College the largest single gift in its history.

I laughed a little, too, knowing a man 30 years and not realizing he was a millionaire. Perhaps a millionaire a couple times.

I guess I'm not alone. Even some of the people close to him didn't know.

"I knew he had some money but nothing like that," one of his colleagues told me. "He was very secretive about some things."

Dr. Reilley, an optometrist who had practiced in Syracuse 60 years, died last April.

After taking care of relatives, former employees and favorite charities, the remainder of his estate goes to LeMoyne. A check for $900,000 already has been delivered and the remaining installments will bring the total to $1.65 million, which is not the kind of money I would have placed in the accounts of the shy, short man whose brown lab coat was always frayed.

Dr. Reilley had been my parents' "eye doctor" for years before I started going to him. I think that was in the fifth grade and I remember he used to embarrass me because he called me "honey."

He was a gentle man, who spent most of his life looking into other people's eyes. He probably learned a lot about us, but we had not returned the favor. Thinking back, I can only remember him talking about golf, which he loved to play, and asking me to read the letters on the chart at the other end of the room.

My mother said he used to give services free to nuns who lived in the city. He did the same thing for the priests at LeMoyne, which is about the only formal contact he had with the institution he was to remember in such a special way.

Once, when I was in the Army, I got a bad prescription from a medic. When I was home on leave, I took the GI issues into his office in the Loew Building and my friend made them right for me. Since he knew I was making only $32 a month at the time, he wrote that one off. And a lot of others too, I'll bet.

Hugh Reilley was a bachelor, who lived in his later years with his widowed sister on the North Side. He was an active man—he liked to walk and bowl besides hitting a golf ball—and he did the things he wanted to do, like taking trips to Europe, Florida and the Caribbean. No one spotted him as a millionaire.

He first started giving money to LeMoyne in 1950. He gave an $800 annual scholarship, which happened to be the amount of a year's tuition in those days. Aside from that, and a few modest gifts to special campaigns, my eye doctor was not to be found among the benefactors who sit at testimonial dinners, smoking long cigars and figuring which hallway their oil portrait will look best in.

I'm told even his lawyers got some surprises when they started pulling the estate together after his death. His plans for the college had been in the will for years, but the first hint came a few days after his death. He was still seeing patients up to that week. One of the attorneys saw an executive of the college at a social affair and mentioned that LeMoyne was a beneficiary.

"We knew we would be getting the residue of the estate, to be used solely for student scholarships, but we weren't sure how much it would be for some time," the administrator said. "We kept being called and told the amount was getting larger."

That was because Hugh Reilley, as careful a craftsman as his trade demanded, also had been tidy in spreading his profits around. Several savings accounts were found, then one safety deposit box, then another. The first held nearly a million dollars in stocks, good, blue chip stuff like IBM and GE. The second was filled with diamonds my eye doctor had been putting away since the 1920s. Each gem was individually wrapped and marked with date of purchase and size.

A lot of people owed Hugh Reilley while he was with us. A lot more are going to be into him in the future.                    —*1980*

---

# OUR NEIGHBOR

A wind blew through my neighborhood Thursday night after the sun set. An ill wind. Bloody, with fear riding it.

Our neighbor was dead. The police found Mary Keller in her bedroom on Brampton Road, in the neat house with cream siding around the corner from Salina. She had been killed with a hammer.

Bill was gone. Bill, her husband, the retired bank employee who sold us subscriptions to the Onondaga Valley News and had his Christmas lights glowing in the windows long before any of the rest of us. Neighbors had seen him in a taxi earlier in the day. Taxis are not usual in the neighborhood. Besides, Bill had a car. He had been acting odd lately.

The cops got there first. They drew their private conclusions and went to work. The neighbors did the same.

We watched the yellow "police line" tape go up around the yard Bill Keller kept groomed like a putting green. We watched the uniforms come and go, and the serious young men in civilian clothes with badges pinned to their jackets and London Fogs. The morgue wagon drew up. So did the TV trucks.

Hey, isn't that Chief Sardino? I've seen him shopping at Green Hills.

The young men hit the streets after a while. Bill was not to be found. Those crazy notes he left didn't help much. He had outlined a schedule for himself and his wife, then canceled part of the plan. Another part had been done.

Did we know our neighbor? Had we seen him lately? When? Where? Had he been acting strangely?

Here, take my card. If you see him, please call us.

Some of the cards were littered in the middle of Brampton with the leaves and mud.

No one called. Except Bill himself.

We called each other. Did you hear? Yes, well, where are the kids? Get them in the house.

Easier said than done. Laurel ran down to the "police line" across the sidewalk. She talked with the other kids who were just out of school and full of stories. David seemed to have the best information. He knew about the notes. He knew about the blood. He said Bill had gone to the woods to kill himself.

Soon, their mothers gathered them up and took them home to watch themselves on TV.

Yes, there we were. Our neighbor Pat included. Talking about how Bill had threatened to do himself in last summer. They took him to a private hospital.

Yes, Channel 9 has it too.

We ate supper and fretted about our neighbors. One dead. One, perhaps, waiting for death.

The phone rang at Bill's house. It was Bill. Said he would be home in 20 minutes with his son. He has no son. He called a neighbor, too. A cop was sitting in her living room the rest of the night.

My wife and I went for a walk. We often do. There was a lot of traffic on Brampton. Slow cars with big eyes inside. We greeted the dog-walkers and the neighbor worried about people trampling his lawn. It was garbage night. We set out our bags and cans.

The Neighborhood Watch lady drove up. She had a problem with another neighbor acting strangely. The commander said he'd put a man on it.

I stayed to talk with a cop. The medical examiner was gone with Mary in a black body bag. Two cops sat in the living room, next to the fireplace that looks like all of our fireplaces. They sat in Bill's and Mary's chairs. Bill's Christmas lights on the porch were turned off.

The young men with the badges pinned to their jackets and London Fogs came out and ducked under the tape. They were going to do the motels and shopping centers again. Finally, a captain left the house and tore down the tape. He put the "restricted area" sign in his car.

If I don't see you again, have a good holiday, I said to him. Hey, you too. Have a merry.

Inside, the cops in the chairs in the living room waited for the phone to ring again.

Later, it did, somewhere else. Bill had checked into Hotel Syracuse, where he attracted much attention. Finally, he became a docket number for the grand jury and the cops went home to bed.

This morning, Stony, our neighborhood cop, was standing in front of Bill's house. We went to work and the garbage men came, rattling the cans empty and tossing the bags into the compacter.

There was no cleaning up the mess at 114 Brampton Road.

*—1984*

---

# THE SCRAPYARD

Todd Minnella sees the old Wickwire Brothers smoke stack from his house on Church Street, Cortland. Just to the southeast, over there by the high school.

The old wire works closed years ago; after that, the 20 acres at the edge of the city held a scrapyard. The leftovers linger, not to be ignored. These days this unused shaft of bricks marks one of our most toxic of toxic waste sites.

Folks thereabouts call it "Rosen Brothers."

There's a certain symbolism to the old chimney. Sort of a sore thumb for the community. Or, if you wish, a thick, red thumb, stuck in the eye of Cortland.

Most of Cortland turned the other way as things were going bad at the Scrap King Yard at 136 South Pendleton St. Including the owners, the Rosen Brothers, who declared bankruptcy and left town.

It was a civic surprise of some magnitude when the state, and then federal, environmentalists came to Cortland in 1987 and started poking around at No. 136. They came away declaring Scrap King belonged on the Superfund list for cleanup.

It may take $28 million, or more, to do that.

Todd Minnella is a senior at Cortland High School. A toxic cesspool in his hometown is a challenge for this citizen.

The scrapyard stack is in his vision and on his mind. He didn't turn his back on the mess; he looked it in the eye and started taking pictures.

Lots and lots of pictures.

No. 136 is discussed often in Cortland. Now, so is the slide show Todd created about it.

Even the mayor noticed. "He did a super job," Marty Mack said when we talked about the site, and the show, last week. "He showed real sensitivity."

The "Photographic Journey" of Todd's color pictures of the Scrap King yard runs 7 minutes, 22 seconds and uses two projectors, so one shot dissolves into another. Todd gave no narration since his father, a professional at this, advised him to let the pictures tell his story.

The very graphic and often scary shots are underscored by two cuts from George Harrison's "All Things Must Pass" album.

He did it for a high school photography class project last May. Since then, even the Rotary Club has seen Todd's show.

I asked Todd how he happened to pick Rosen Brothers as a subject for his photo essay. The assignment in Brian Piekarski's advanced photography class was to produce a slide show with music. His classmates went for studies of rock music or hanging out on Saturday night.

"I wanted to do something on the environment," Todd said. "We'd been told about the Rosen site and toxins as part of a class in chemistry and the community. Miss (Marcia) Bonneau's class. Of course, I knew about the scrapyard. I'd been in there with my friends. It was too close to be ignored."

A stranger guesses it was the other way around for some residents. So close, you have to ignore it.

Cortland's new high school sits on a hill overlooking the yard. Todd could cut through it, if he chooses, walking from his house to school.

"It was really easy to get in before they fixed the fence," he said. "I just started taking pictures. I love to take pictures. Rolls and rolls of them."

Todd's father, C. Vincent Minnella, is director of Sperry Learning Resources Center at State University College at Cortland.

His son said he grew up with a family picture-taker—Dad used his camera as an investigator with the Cortland Fire Department— but he was turned on to photography last year in Piekarski's beginning class.

The dump project took five weeks. Todd said he was really psyched when it was his turn to run his show for the class. He thinks his mates were a bit stunned a high school kid could do such compelling work.

"They were surprised," Todd explained. "They clapped when it was done. Most of them had never seen Rosen Brothers. They told me they didn't realize it was right at the bottom of the hill."

Every time "Photographic Journey" played, Todd picked up more information about the site and new ideas.

The high point, so far, was the Rotary Club showing. The audience included the mayor and the county health commissioner. Rotarians asked lots of questions.

Mayor Mack's involvement here goes back several years. In fact, Marty's father, the late Joseph Mack, tried to close Rosen Brothers because of its look, smell and rodents when he was mayor of Cortland in the '60s.

Marty tried as county attorney in 1987, the year he ran for mayor. He initiated legal proceedings against the Rosens after a former employee, the late Hugh Page, blew the whistle on the yard in 1987.

Hugh, who was called "Skeeter," died later that year at the age of 57. He believed he was a victim of exposure to toxic waste.

Marty Mack said Todd's show alerted him to the lack of security on the dump site. He didn't like the idea the old fence had big breaks and all those bad leavings Todd photographed were there for casual inspection.

"I talked to the Health Department, and we got the problem corrected," the mayor said. "The fence was fixed and they have security guards there now."

State and federal monitors identified 11 responsible companies that provided the waste for the Rosens to dump. They will have to pay for the cleanup.

The dumpers seem to be off the hook, except for criminal charges. The Rosens declared bankruptcy, clearing the Scrap King of civil responsibility for what they did.

The owner was Phil Rosen, who moved to Louisiana. He was partners with his son, Maury, and his brother, Harvey. The first Rosen, a tailor named Daniel, came to Cortland in 1906.

Federal investigators recently took a statement from Phil Rosen at his new home. Meanwhile, the bankruptcy judge is looking for the Scrap King business records, to better understand the depth of the challenge at No. 136, which had been a dump between 1971 and 1987.

About the only public record of what really went into the yard came from the hometown hero of Cortland's, Skeeter Page. The last few years of his life he was honcho for Phil Rosen at Scrap King.

Six months before he died—the doctors told his widow, Mary, zinc oxide poisoning killed him—Skeeter called Marty Mack and told him what he knew about the operation of the yard, and what the Rosens dumped there.

Skeeter lay dying in his hospital bed; Marty took down his recollections on a tape recorder.

"He knew he was very sick and he had some things he wanted to say about the scrapyard," Marty explained.

Skeeter's seven-page deposition told a different story about the yard than had been provided by the Rosens. The owners claimed the toxic stuff was there when they bought the place in 1971.

Mary Page and I talked about Skeeter last April. He said the Rosens treated him poorly. When he died, there wasn't enough money left to bury him. He willed his body to science.

Last week, when I was in Cortland, I stopped to see Mary. This time it was her in the hospital. She'd been in Cortland Memorial two months, and things weren't going too good for her. She can't help but wonder if she got a piece of what Skeeter had.

The doctors operated on Mary for tumors. We'll see, she said. One day at a time.

Mary said Skeeter's ashes came back from the medical center. His son has them in a little box. Eventually, they will be buried in a family plot at Windsor, where he grew up.                                             *—1989*

---

# RIP AND NANCY

It was 20 years May 28 and there is no getting rid of the horror and pain. Twenty years since James Corrente murdered Nancy Greco near her home in Lakeland, then drove her body to the Solvay police station and confessed. Twenty years and Nancy's parents, Virginia and Sam, haven't forgotten the tragedy. Nor will they.

Nor will they let us forget.

Every year, twice a year, at the anniversary of the murder and on Nancy's birthday, a small memorial ad is placed in the Syracuse newspapers. As long as Virginia Greco has breath in her, the memorial ads will be published. A week ago, on May 28, it was there again:

"To us, her name will ever be the key that unlocks a memory of a dear one gone but cherished yet. A beloved face we'll never forget. We love and miss her. Mom and Dad."

Nancy was 17 when she died. A senior at Solvay High School who was a month away from graduation. After commencement, the principal brought her diploma to the house. He couldn't speak. Virginia and Sam couldn't either. Nancy was their only child. Thirteen years before, her appendix had ruptured, and she almost died. After the gunshots took her, her parents were devastated. Why us? they asked. No one answered.

Her killer had been her boyfriend. At that point, the relationship was strained. He was out of Solvay; an honor student of 19 who went to SU to study accounting. A judge found him innocent of murder by reason of insanity. He was in the custody of the State Department of Mental Hygiene for seven years before another judge cut him free. He completed college, took a degree and left town.

The Grecos have been told James Corrente is married, has children and works as an accountant in New York City. They are mad as hell about this. They feel he should be in prison, serving a life sentence for the murder of their daughter. If New York had the death penalty, they believe Nancy's killer should have been executed.

"He got away with murder," Sam Greco said to me one afternoon last week.

The Grecos have not talked about this before, outside of the family. Maybe because no one asked them. Those little memorial ads, with Nancy's prom picture at the top, were a sign that there was something to be said. I went to the little white house with black shutters in Lakeland where Nancy used to live to find out what it was.

We sat in the living room. There is a drawing of Nancy framed over the stereo. An artist at Pass and Seymour, where her mother used to work, did it for Virginia. She is retired. So is Sam. There are other pictures of their daughter in a folder Virginia has close by. Some of these show Nancy and her killer—his nickname around Solvay was "Rip"—together, hugging, at their proms.

The pictures are in there with the clippings on the case. It went on and on, for years. Nancy's mother thinks she had almost everything that was published about what happened. The only document missing is the one about Rip being removed from custody. Department of Mental Hygiene records showed Judge Albert Orenstein signed the order, on petition from the young man's lawyer, Dec. 18, 1975.

At that time, Rip was an outpatient at Hutchings Psychiatric Center. The lawyer, Paul Shanahan, said his client was working for a "New York City area accounting firm." He had been released from custody at Marcy State Hospital two years before. Nancy's mother knew he was out of Marcy when she saw him pumping gas at the family service station in Solvay.

"After the trial, nobody told us anything," Virginia said. "What we know, we know from word-of-mouth. After she was killed, they didn't talk with us very much. Even that day, they went to the neighbors first. All they would tell us was there had been an accident! An accident! He killed that girl and drove all over with her body in the car.

"It took them two years to get to the trial. It kept being postponed and postponed. Just when I thought I was feeling better, it started up again. It was hell. Nobody cared about how we felt.

"Then at the trial, the defense lawyer wouldn't let me say anything. He kept interrupting and saying, 'hearsay,' 'hearsay.' Why couldn't they let me say what I had to say and let the jurors make up their own minds?"

Trouble was, the jurors couldn't make up their own minds. They were 10 men and two women. Corrente's attorneys said he was insane when he killed Nancy, therefore ought to be found innocent of first-degree murder. Yet two psychiatrists already had found him sane enough to stand trial. After Rip talked to the cops about the murder, his father showed up at the police station and Rip went wacko. A doctor was called in to give him a shot and an ambulance took him to the hospital emergency room for evaluation.

This confused the Grecos. According to them, they knew Rip to be a jealous young man, obsessed with getting good grades, who wanted complete control of his younger girlfriend. They didn't take him to be insane.

"He was a good actor," Sam said to me. He shook his head. "I don't know." He said "I don't know" a lot during my visit.

The Grecos agreed with the district attorney that Murder One— taking a life with premeditation—was the crime committed. They knew about the letters Rip wrote before the murder. How he came home from SU, exhausted at the end of exam week, and got a shotgun out of the attic and put it into the trunk of his car. He fired three shots at Nancy. Later he told someone he was driving around to find a bridge to jump from but none appeared that was high enough.

One of the letters was addressed to Nancy's mother, who was called "Mom" by her daughter's boyfriend: "You once told Nancy you were afraid of our jealousy. You know why I had to do it . . . I am very sorry. Rip."

It was a square-off of the shrinks, that trial. Two said Rip was sane when he killed Nancy. Two said he had a severe mental disorder. The students of the human mind thoroughly confused the jurors. Come on! Is he crazy or not?

The jurors worked over a verdict 25 hours before they reported to Judge Ormand Gale they were deadlocked. The lock was said to be 6-6. When the judge announced the hung jury, Nancy's mother was there. She said she saw tears in the eyes of one of the women jurors.

"I will never understand that as long as I live," she said. "How could some of them think he wasn't guilty? People said we ought to do something. What can we do? Who can do anything?"

Yet something had to be done with the mess. The burden had been on the prosecutor, as it always is. Prove the man was sane when he did this. When the trial ended the way it did, the DA and his staff decided trial two would end up the same head game with the same result. The state and the defense agreed to let Judge Gale decide the case. In June of 1968 he found Rip innocent by reason of insanity. He ordered him into state custody until he no longer needed treatment.

So, in effect, no crime was committed. The child was not dead. This was easy to believe if you had attended a college of law.

At the fourth request for release from custody, release was granted. There was a hearing. One shrink testified Rip has expressed no "bizarre ideas" in recent months. He could walk.

Rip's freedom and their daughter in the ground gnaw at the Grecos. The parts do not fit. Nancy's parents think justice wears a piece of cloth over her eyes because she really is blind. There is no justice to them, in fact. Just confusion and bitterness which do not seem to leave, even after enough time has passed to have made them grandparents.

"It's been 20 years, and I still cry," Virginia said. "I can't get myself to believe it happened to us and he got away with it. I'm not sure how I've coped this far. I got really sick. I didn't think I'd make it. I went to my priest, I went to my doctor. They said they would pray for me."

The little ads are part of the grief therapy for the Grecos. If they can't forget Nancy, no one else will.

"I want them to see the picture and remember what happened," Virginia said. "I hope they do. You know, I often wonder if Rip sees those pictures. And what he thinks."

"They" being the participants in a criminal justice system the Grecos believe failed them.

I got a piece of an answer for Nancy's parents. Not from Rip, but one of his defenders. A lawyer who sat at the defense table throughout the trial.

He sees the ads. "Yes, every time," the lawyer said. "It's eerie. My eyes are pulled to them. It doesn't go away, does it?"                     *—1986*

---

# THE DOCTOR

Vincent Y. Cremata Jr., 52, practiced medicine in Syracuse for eight years, 1968 to 1976. He lived in a house next to Sen. Tarky Lombardi Jr. on Dewitt Street. His office was on the South Side. He is remembered as a very interesting guy; fascinating, brilliant, charming. His practice seemed to be large and busy. Once he lectured at the medical college on voodoo.

The men and women who knew him here said they were shocked —stunned—when they found out what had happened to Vincent Cremata after he left Syracuse in May 1976 and moved to Florida.

They said they were stunned when they learned he was a principal in a multi-million dollar time-share condominium investment plan that was closed by the Florida state comptroller.

They said they were stunned again when they were told he had been convicted in Orange County, Fla., in October 1985 on 20 counts of racketeering, fraud, grand theft and sale of unregistered securities.

No, that can't be the Vincent we knew.

And that can't be Vincent, dead on the floor of the state driver's license office in Clearwater, Fla., last March 25, with two slugs from a police officer's service revolver in his body.

It was.

Dr. Cremata came to Syracuse from St. Vincent's Hospital in New York City. His file said he was born in Key West, Fla., and served in the U.S. Air Force during the Vietnam War. He had three children. One of his sons lived with his mother, the doctor's first wife, in Florida.

The Crematas moved into 234 Dewitt St., next door to a state senator and across the street from the musical director of the Syracuse Symphony Orchestra. Mrs. Cremata, Molly, was a member of the orchestra guild. Once when Mitch Miller was in town for a concert with the orchestra, the Crematas threw a party for him at their home.

Delightful people, the Syracuse friends remember. Very artistic.

Dr. Cremata practiced medicine in another part of town. His office was at 2918 S. Salina St., south of Brighton. He shared the practice with Dr. Herbert Douglas. Two of Dr. Cremata's former patients remember him well.

"He was a nice guy," a young woman I will call "Arlene" said. She and her parents were his patients when she was in high school. "He was a gentleman, but he never seemed to able to pin down what was wrong with me. He seemed a little different. I remember sitting in his examination room looking at the certificates he had framed on the walls. Very impressive.

"I remember once he spoke on voodoo at the medical center. After he left Syracuse I think there was a problem with my parents' medical records. They claimed they had been destroyed. I heard he became a minister when he got to Florida."

The other patient, "Jack," remembered a quick exit from the city by the doctor and problems with records, too. He said he once went to Dr. Cremata for treatment of severe headaches. "He gave me a quick examination and wrote me a prescription for Librium. It really mellows you out, but I didn't need it. It didn't help at all."

The Crematas had to call the police twice during their years in Syracuse. The first time was in November 1970. Their daughter Emily, 8, was kidnapped on her way to school. She was kept in a car by a man for 90 minutes and then freed. She was not harmed. The man, Chad Williams, later was sentenced to 10 years in prison for attempted kidnapping.

Two years later the doctor's son who lived in Florida didn't come home to Dewitt Street during a visit to Syracuse. Dr. Cremata reported him missing, mentioning the possibility of a drug problem. Later the young man showed up and the alert was cancelled.

Syracuse friends who talked to me about the physician said they were not aware of his interest in securities and tax shelters, although he did seem to one to be "very knowledgeable about finance." One friend said he once advised her to buy bags of coins as a precaution against devaluation of the dollar.

Yes, she said, "He seemed a little nuts on some subjects, to me. His views were, well, a little different from mine."

This friend heard about the tragedies in Florida from Mrs. Cremata. At first, she said she couldn't believe what had happened.

"Personally, I can't see him as a villain. He was an honest guy who got taken. He didn't know about exotic investments."

According to court records, Dr. Cremata worked for a pharmaceutical company for a while after he left New York. His forwarding address at one point was the Free Alliance Church Inc. of Winter Park, Fla. Frank Tamen, the state's attorney who prosecuted him, said last week the church was one of several fronts used by the physician after he moved to Florida and retired from medicine.

"He lived like a king," Tamen said. "He lived in a mansion and drove a new Caddy. He traveled all over the world and spent incredible amounts of money. But nothing was under his own name. He set up several phony churches."

Tamen, who is an assistant U.S. attorney in Miami, saw the man for whom he got a nine-year jail term as a crook who came up with an elaborate scheme to "fuel a lavish lifestyle."

The scheme was a company called Vacondo, which was based in Orlando. Vacondo was a tax-sheltered investment program that was supposed to fund a national network connecting time-share condominium brokers with investors. There were 135 investors around the U.S., many of them doctors and dentists. Some lived in New York, Tamen said, although he did not know if Dr. Cremata had invited any former neighbors in Syracuse into the shelter.

"Officially, he was isolated from the corporation," the former prosecutor continued. "He was not an officer, although he had an office there. He would give these seminars (investment programs called 'Seminars in the Sun' in such settings as Maui, Las Vegas and Palm Springs).

"They were set up to present tax and investment advice. But actually he plugged Vacondo. He recruited for his own outfit while pretending to be an expert. And all the time his expenses were being paid by Vacondo."

No one had a good fix on how much money Dr. Cremata and his three limited partners had to work with. One estimate put it at $5.7 million. The other Vacondo principals were Erik McGrew, Norman Peires, and Hersch Caudill. Caudill was the firm's lawyer, Peires a citizen of South Africa.

Tamen said the scheme began to unravel when an employee complained to the state comptroller's office about the Vacondo investment account. When an investigation began, in 1983, it was found the account was empty and Caudill was missing. Eventually he was arrested, charged separately and brought in to testify against the partners. Vacondo and related firms were closed by authorities in October 1983.

Dr. Cremata, Peires and McGrew were tried in Orlando two years later. They were found guilty. The former Syracusan was sentenced to nine years in prison. At sentencing, he asked for parole. He said he would return to medicine and work among the poor.

"I'm not guilty of any of these things," he told the judge. "I never took one penny of anyone's money." The judge turned down parole, but allowed him to be released on $100,000 bail, pending appeal. He said the case against the defendants was only a "partial revelation of all that actually occurred" at Vacondo.

The doctor apparently was wiped out, financially and psychologically. He told friends he lost "several hundred thousand" dollars when a Cayman Islands bank where he had an account went under in 1983. Not only that, the IRS was on his case. Even as he was being tried, a federal grand jury in Orlando was looking into a tax-exempt offshore religious investment operation.

Last March 25, Dr. Cremata went into the Clearwater license bureau. He was carrying a briefcase that later was found to contain a loaded .45-caliber pistol, six driver's licenses, and 17 different birth certificates. He wore a wig and asked to take a driver's test. He presented a learner's permit issued to "Robert James Brown," 46. A clerk was suspicious and police were called.

Two officers arrived and tried to arrest him for obtaining a license under a false name. They asked him to give up the briefcase. He refused. There was a struggle.

A witness told police he kept threatening to reach into his case and the cops kept telling him not to. The officers said they would shoot him. "Go ahead and kill me. I don't care," Dr. Cremata was supposed to have said.

Frank Tamen, the former prosecutor, said that wasn't in character for the man he brought to trial. Maybe Dr. Cremata had "gone off the deep end" when he was faced with the prospect of going to jail. The officers suspected he had a gun in the briefcase and he wouldn't put it down, he said. "I guess that was a form of suicide."

Police sources were quoted by the Orlando Sentinel at the time as suspecting that the effort to get the license was part of an elaborate scheme by Dr. Cremata to flee the country.

William Barnett of Orlando was his lawyer at the trial. He was working on an appeal when his client died.

"It was a terrible tragedy," Barnett said to me. "He was a brilliant, intelligent man. He was very well thought of here. You wouldn't have picked him for this sort of thing. I guess the jury felt he hadn't followed the rules.

"Vincent felt he was taking a role in the free enterprise system. He felt he had a great product and other people sabotaged it. His conviction shocked him greatly. Yes, he was very depressed."

April 3, the Pinellas-Pasco state attorney's office cleared the Clearwater police officer of any wrongdoing in the killing of Dr. Cremata. Justifiable homicide. Case closed.     *—1986*

---

# UNMARKED GRAVES

Ed Dudley was a man I never met. But I got to dislike him.

Our first encounter was in the winter of 1961, on the front page of the Herald-Journal. Ed, whose real name was Kenneth E. Dudley, had been arrested in Virginia on a charge of causing the death of his 7-year-old daughter. So had his wife, Irene. They had had 10 children, starting in the '30s on Syracuse's North Side, where Ed worked as a tinsmith.

By the time Ed was infamous, nearly 30 years later, 7 of the children were dead.

I was a reporter just getting into the job in 1961. Part of the work was writing things about the Dudleys. Senior reporter, Howard Carroll, was the main man, but there were so many things to write about, I pitched in. It was several years before we stopped writing about the Dudleys. I think Howard got sick of it and dropped off somewhere along the way.

I'm thinking about this now—probably a lot of lousy memories all of us should have put aside—because a friend of mine asked me about the case a few days ago. She is too young to have read about the Dudleys when they were public figures but she was curious.

Did I have any old clippings? I looked around and found some for her. After she got through, I read them myself. I'd forgotten a lot, probably on purpose.

Ed Dudley seems to have been born a loser, but he was too arrogant to understand that and do something about it. He started out raging because the world owed him a living and wasn't keeping the bargain.

First he was a petty thief, then a murderer. He bummed around, working carnivals and making a home for his kids in an old car parked in a dump. He lied a lot and worked cons on people.

The children who were lucky enough to survive said he conned his wife, too.

When their marriage had been ended by arrest, Irene told people she "tried to do right all her life and everything turned out wrong." She blamed Ed for that. He blamed her. No one could be sure what happened, but it did.

One thing's for sure, Ed was a man who never should have had kids.

But even after the law finally caught up with him—and it had been a long time in the catching—Ed tried to con us. I found a letter in my old files he had mailed to the newspaper from the Richmond, Va. jail, offering to sell his story to us for money.

He'd heard I was interested in talking to him. But if he was going to tell it, he wanted a cash advance before he started spilling all that horror. He seemed impatient, writing that Mr. R. Case "doesn't know what he passed up" in not getting down to Richmond.

At the same time, he was being interviewed by police for Syracuse, Investigator Bob Busch among them, and conning them, too. He wrote to Bob "I have a lot of answers to a lot of things that you don't know."

My old clippings and notes have gotten brittle and yellow in 20 years. Looking through them, though, I can see what happened.

I can see how that arrest in 1961, when Carol's body was found in Virginia along a highway, bundled in an Army blanket under a sweet gum tree, opened up a door to a room with a long tunnel in it, going back to Syracuse in the '30s. There was horror and death all along.

The Dudleys had left Syracuse on a carnival tour in 1958 with six children. At first, the story was that they couldn't afford to keep them, so they gave them to other carnies.

Then the story came out that the youngsters had died of malnutrition, had been left along roadways across the U.S. Only the baby, Christine, who was 2, had survived. She was with them at the end and one of the pictures in my file shows Ed carrying the little kid with blond curls into the jail house.

She was put up for adoption.

The door opened wider. Ed's second-born, Edward, died in Syracuse in 1937 when he was two months old. Cause of death: intercranial hemorrhage, "cause unknown."

The family was on welfare and had to get money from the county to buy Ed a pair of good pants to wear to the funeral.

Later, in 1947, when he was living in Constantia, Kenneth Dudley died at the age of 6. His father told police, later, it happened during a coughing spell. Kenneth was buried in the driveway and Ed later served a year in the pen for illegal burial.

Other times the children were put in foster homes. Ed was sent to Marcy for evaluation.

He was found to be psychopathic but not psychotic. Fails to learn by experience, the shrink said. Shows no shame or remorse.

There was more to come. Investigators found out about Alberta Vella, a Syracuse woman who hadn't been seen since 1949. It turned out Ed had taken her out to a vacant air strip at Hancock, killed her and buried the body near Kirkville.

Another old photo in my file shows Bob Busch and some of the other cops standing there with shovels the fourth of July 1963 when they dug up Mrs. Vella's skeleton where Ed put it years before.

Then there were hints that Ed was responsible for the unsolved murder of Beatrice Dain in 1952. He also claimed to Bob Busch that he knew about the death of Alice Richardson the same year. Maybe even the pig farmer slain along the widewaters and a carnie in Florida. Lots of answers for lots of things.

Ed was sentenced to 20 years for Carol's death in Virginia. His wife got 10. She served about 7, got out, and returned to New York and tried to forget the past.

Meanwhile, Ed was convicted of Mrs. Vella's murder in Onondaga County. After he gave Virginia its piece of justice, he was brought back to New York's prison system to serve a natural life term.

That's the way it turned out, too. Ed died of natural causes at Auburn Memorial Hospital Nov. 20, 1980. He was 67 and had been sick quite a while at Auburn Correctional Facility, where almost everybody has a past they want to forget.

From the evidence at hand, I guess everybody tried to forget Ed, too, including the people he'd hurt the most. They say he was very much alone at the end.

The state buried Ed in the potter's field at Soule Cemetery, just to the east of Auburn. They put him in the ground without a headstone in a flat, bleak burial ground next to 50 or so other cons whose bodies weren't claimed either.

Some people might say Ed got what he deserved, being buried in an unmarked grave next to the road.  *—1982*

---

# THE MAYOR

Long after the campaign had shut down yesterday, Lee Alexander was campaigning.

He sat in his office with a few friends, with his suit coat off, drinking vodka out of a plastic glass. And he was still campaigning.

He was talking figures on community development and how he cleaned the rats out of the DPW garage and how two of his opponents were pulling dirty tricks on him. They were picking on his chauffeur and his nephew. He prowled the work area next to his desk, waving studies and stats, stopping only to answer the phone and duck into the secretary's room to bring in more ammunition.

He couldn't seem to get the Other Guy out of his sights, even though, just then, we were out there pulling the levers, making the little clicking noises that could determine what he would be doing the next four years.

"They've got a bookkeeper running for mayor," he said at one point and the room warmed in the glow of hearty dislike.

Finally, someone asked him how he was going to spend the afternoon. It would be a few traditional rounds, thanking the workers for their help and shaking hands again. No big deal, he said—something to keep the candidate busy while democracy had its way; something to keep the candidate from climbing the wall.

Then, in a minute, he seemed to realize how wound-up he was. He looked at us and said, "I guess I can't stop campaigning."

He won, of course, but he was never really down all day, right from the minute he stepped out of the car in front of the old church on Douglas Street, the Girls' Club where the 4th Ward, 5th District votes. There were two kids waiting for his autograph and he called one of them beautiful and the other handsome.

Down the street, within sight, was a Bernardi sign, stuck into the grass. A black cat sunned on the roof upstairs.

The Mayor went in on the run, past the bake sale and the American flag. He was No. 85 and you could tell it was going to be his day by the way the levers went off behind the curtain—CLICK, CLICK, CLICK—in 30 seconds and The Mayor was talking to us all the time through the fabric.

"Hey, can you only vote once?" Things like that.

Then he came out and started campaigning right in front of the table with the box of chocolates from the ward chairman, talking to the TV cameras and the man from WSYR who was wired for live broadcast.

The same words were coming out that came out all day. And the days before that, as a matter of fact.

He went back to City Hall and read the mail and started phoning. He saw the guy from the Metropolitan Development Association and, like there were only tomorrows, the two talked about a trip to New York City later in the week to romance a new business—an ironworks with 300 jobs.

Another thing: there were some voters coming in for coffee to talk about the future of the city tomorrow morning. Was everything set for that?

The Mayor took out his hearing aid; it was bothering him. He started talking about dirty tricks and lousy deals. Lies even, while making a few phone calls. He showed me a letter a mentally retarded boy in Oswego sent him, asking The Mayor to get in touch with him if he wanted to be rich and famous.

"Adorable letter," he said.

Some people were saying this was his toughest campaign. Lot of mud was slung; yes, he said, but it wasn't the toughest. The first one was. When he had zero help and it was uphill all the way.

This time, he said, he was in control of the campaign, down to the last pledge card, and it was easier, in that respect.

The only thing that bothered him, he said, was what he was running against. Not the men, but the mood. "People may think it's time for a change," he said.

Then he campaigned some more, jumping up and pointing and flushing out the brains of the people who came in. When his opponent appeared on the noon TV news, The Mayor sat down in a chair with the channel selector in his fist. He looked at the face, with the "fire of ambition" he knew very well and said, "That guy would make a good TV weatherman."

The laughter in the room was nervous. Apprehension was the word The Mayor used to describe it.

I saw more later Election Day, on the eighth floor of Hotel Syracuse, where the Mayor's people rented a suite for the vote watch. There was booze in the living room, a buffet in the little dining room and a friend on the phone to the Board of Elections in one of the bedrooms.

The friend, Dean Vlassis, had a deep tan and little sheets of paper he used to take down vote counts. The papers were run down the hall to The Mayor by a woman who seemed to be dressed like a nun. Even there, the process seemed well-oiled, but that afternoon, in his headquarters in the Larned Building, The Mayor had said to me voters ought to judge the candidate by how well his campaign apparatus worked. That was part of the way we measure the man.

Early on, the friend's tan turned gray. For about 20 minutes, he wrote on his pad and looked grim. So did the nun, running the hallways past the fat cats in black polished shoes and gold ID bracelets. The color TV sets around the suites carried a lot of futures in their blinking signals.

Soon, though, you could hear the voices begin to raise, the way they were when the suite opened at 8. The nun squealed on her rounds and the candidate went down the hall to see his mother. The chauffeur, who had become an unwitting campaign issue, was smiling; so were the buddies from Albany and New York.

And so was Dean, after a while, even though he ran out of paper.

About 10—did it only take an hour after all that long campaign?—The Mayor came back into the suite and this time his friends cheered him. His son yelled, "Congratulations, Dad," and the TV people got him into a crush and their lights went on.

"You did it," one of the friends said and The Mayor made polite conversation into microphones that look like big, black all-day suckers.

He told the kids to go tell their grandmother and then follow him upstairs to the Empire Room, where the rest of the people had been waiting and drinking. They made a wedge through the crowd to the lectern and the cheering came up again.

I moved around, asking the inevitable question of the friends, now that The Mayor had done what he had told me that afternoon he hadn't thought a Greek from Brooklyn could do. Is this the last shot?

Some of them said it was. Some said they had asked him that question and he danced around it. Some said no, the man loves the job. He's in his prime. Look at Mayor Corning in Albany.

At the lectern, where the fuzzy mike made him sound like he was in Solvay, The Mayor was saying, "We've got plenty of unfinished business."

I knew he was still campaigning.

After a while the halls on the eighth floor got quiet again and the Alexander people went home and the Head Start convention people came up on the elevators to go to bed. Two women campaigners walked by me, complaining about the heat.

"It's too warm," one of them said, shaking her dress.

"If you want to look good, you gotta sweat," her friend told her.

The Mayor finished the day looking good, but he sweated a lot.

*—1981*

€ • •

Lee Alexander's career ended at about 12:10 p.m. Thursday in front of a federal judge who had the sleeves of his black robe rolled up to the elbows.

It took Judge Thomas J. McAvoy about 10 seconds—15 tops—to make The Mayor history.

On count two, the judge said, 10 years. Count three, 5 years. Count 39, 5 years. These will be served concurrently, making a total of 10 years, he explained.

The Mayor shook his head slightly as the numbers came down on him. Sure, he knew the punch was on its way. That didn't mean it didn't hurt.

His jaw was drawn back into a dreadful, disfiguring grimace. He stood there at the lectern of the federal courtroom with a slight hump to his shoulders. The judge said he would have to pay court costs at the rate of $50 per felony indictment.

Let's see, that will be $150. Plus a $100,000 fine.

Before that, we got two hours of explanations. These words seemed to go on forever. The judge looked at the door. At the ceiling. At the clock.

This was about an hour after the promised 9 a.m. calendar call. Additional words had to be spoken in the judge's chambers. The line outside the building began to form about 7:30 a.m.

The prosecutor spoke. He said The Mayor had not been truthful during the five sessions he had at the polygraph as the feds searched for hidden assets. He said he could never be sure we victims—the citizens of Syracuse—will ever get back all that is owed us in stolen money.

There is no paying back the betrayed trust, of course, according to Fred Scullin.

The Mayor's lawyer threw plenty more words at us. Even the prosecutor had to admit Harold Boreanaz was rolling. Actually, he was pretty tough on his client.

He called The Mayor a disgraced person and a disbarred attorney. He said he was in pain and broke down emotionally during the polygraphing. He said he was a beaten, humbled, broken man. Not to forget suffering, punished and without a penny to his name.

The lawyer said he was upset with our anger with The Mayor for the way he reached into our pockets all those years. He ridiculed the firemen's notion that his name ought to be moved out of all of the firehouses built during those 16 years at City Hall.

I mean, here we are treating the man like a lover who rejected us. Like a Russian dictator, for heavens sake! Remember the beauty through all this bitterness, please.

Sure, Harold explained, he violated the trust but he also did plenty of physical and human good. Why look at those firehouses!

This was about when he came to the good part. The part where he explained The Flaw.

The Flaw that ate Syracuse.

It seems there was this incredibly poor kid from Jersey named Lee.

There were six kids in the family. One died. The parents were on welfare. Lee shined shoes in Times Square to put a bun on the table. He washed dishes. He worked in a sweat shop. He hauled coal.

"But for the serious criminal activity, this would be an Horatio Alger story," The Mayor's lawyer said.

Lee worked hard, got himself a law degree, married a rich, beautiful woman and turned his energy and charisma into a successful career in politics. Yet, with all of this—all these good things—he was insecure.

"He had this fear of returning to poverty," Harold explained.

The Mayor elaborated on this when he got to the lectern. He seemed to come alive for a few minutes, with his lips in front of a mike and everyone's attention again.

This "tragedy" came about, he said, after he beat the Republicans and got to be mayor. He needed a political war chest to keep him going. At the same time, the personal assets of the family had diminished. The Mayor engaged others to help him fill that war chest.

It was, he explained, simply "beyond belief" what people wanted to contribute in order to do business with the city. And it was beyond The Mayor not to help himself.

"There were two parts at war within me," he said. One part was his thirst for public service. The other was "the future security of my family." The family won the war and "I have properly lost it all."

After that happened, The Mayor stood and talked with his two lawyers at the defense table a minute or two. There were no hugs. He said he had asked family members to stay away to spare them his disgrace.

His buddy Demo Stathis followed on the calendar. He was there next to the front row of pews with his wife and some of their 10 kids when The Mayor walked down the aisle. They didn't seem to notice each other.                                                                    —*1988*

---

# THE VICTIM

John Fortino's agony was short. He died quickly.
The people he left behind have to watch him die again and again.
It's called a murder trial.
Justice.

Maybe that's why several people choke up and cry every day in Room 205 of the Onondaga County Courthouse. The tragedy has them by the throat: They're choking on the replays.

We sit and watch them. So does a television camera.

John was murdered defending his girlfriend and her family last February in Lysander. A young man is on trial for murder in Room 205. His name is James A. Matteson Jr. James is the one the district attorney says held the knife. His family is on trial, too.

A couple of deadly cuts and you've filled a courtroom. Set adrift a dozen lives.

The People vs. James A. Matteson Jr. moves on. Each day, in front of a judge, 14 peers, three sheriff's deputies with ear-plug radios, the families and you and me, time is painstakingly pulled backward through a keyhole.

Yes, it is very painful. Maybe somewhere down the road it will make sense. Maybe.

The insignificant is made significant in a trial for murder. The prosecutor's table is piled with plastic bags of evidence, for example. These bags cover insignificants made significant by those deadly cuts of the knife.

A roll of painter's tape. A pair of old boots. A set of thermal underwear.

Each transformed into The People's Exhibits, 1 through 86, and so on. An officer is sworn to testify as to the chain of evidence. Any objection, counselor? No sir.

Tuesday, Ronald Witkowski, cousin to James, was called to testify against his kinsman. Ron plea-bargained out of a murder charge for his legal role in this mess and he will do time. The judge reminded him of that.

Ron wore a three-piece suit. He didn't seem to want to be there. His answers came quickly, the better to get on with it. One word often was used: True, he said, again and again.

His cousin watched him from the defense table. The defendant held his head up with a platform of fists. He wore a matching shirt and tie.

Question: When you saw James after he left the house where John was murdered, was he white and shaking? Ron was asked.

True.

Was he mumbling? True.

And you had trouble understanding all he said? True.

Was he shivering? True.

Wet? True.

And did he indicate he had stabbed someone? True.

The kid was good. James' attorney was on him for times and dates and Ron had them. He knew how far it was from Phoenix to Baldwinsville, and back, and around the corner, down to the eighth of a mile. He knew when he was drinking beer and when he was not. Even had the guest list of the party that the prosecutor wanted to make significant.

Now let's see, there were Sean, Ron, Joe, Mike, Dave, Cheryl . . .

The jurors had their swivel seats aimed at the defense lawyer. They looked at him and listened as he unthreaded the history of Feb. 27 and 28, the way a seamstress pulls a thread out of a bad sew.

What's he getting at? their eyes asked.

Yes, Ron answered. Sean was drunk. He passed out in the car.

We sat as in a theater-in-the-round in 205, which is a makeshift room in the old chamber.

The judge was close enough to the witness to check for ear mites. The room small enough to make misery intimate.

The families sat at the ready. Waiting for a wrong name, a misplaced street, a time warped.

Is the camera on? they would say.

I think he's wrong there. That's not the way it was.

We heard the whisper of the deputies' radios too, among the slow, careful words. Also, the creak of the door to the judge's office, where, each time, P.J. Cunningham's family portrait on the wall was revealed. The coughs. The click of cuffs going on James at recess.

Sean Cramer had to come in from the corridor to testify that he was, indeed, sloshed to the point of unconsciousness on the days this trial is about. Yes, we were drinking beer and watching MTV for five hours. And then we went to Ron's grandmother's place in his mother's rented car and on the way we picked up Jimmy, who was sitting in a snow bank in a white suit waving a stick.

Later, these pieces will be totaled. A sum will be made of the disparate parts. From that sum, a reckoning.

Then, maybe, we can stop watching John Fortino die.          *—1988*

Chapter 8

# HOMETOWN

---

## SHELTERED VALLEY

Mo Helfer met me at the end of the driveway, next to the barn. This was going to be tough. Tougher for him than me, surely. I was there to say goodbye to Sheltered Valley.

We shook hands. A couple of old goats who were kids together along time ago.

Now, well, our paths don't often cross. We stood in the village of Marcellus, at a farm that had been in Mo's family since 1852. Mo, his wife Pat, his brother Wayne, a daughter and two grandchildren moved to Cayuga County. They sold the place to a young couple up on Reed Street.

It was a practical thing, Mo explained to me. The house is too big, the family a lot smaller (by 6 children) than it was when the Helfers bought out Mo's brothers and his aunt and came to Marcellus from Nedrow 10 years ago. No heir to a tradition was in sight. Mo didn't think any of his kids could afford a homestead as grand as this one.

Not as grand as it once was, of course. Mo and his brothers came to Marcellus from Binghamton in the old days. They visited Jim and Ethel Stone, Gramp and Nana. The Stones, Jim's parents, grandparents and great-grandparents, went back to 1852 on this slab of glacial leftover.

When Rollin, Jim's father, was master of Sheltered Valley, the Stone land was a village unto itself. Over the years, the other village, Marcellus, took over. Most of the farm went for school lots.

Piece by piece it went, starting in 1936 when Jim sold 16 acres to the district. At one time the farm stretched from Reed Parkway—where the Reed farm took over—all the way down to Marcellus Falls. These days the soccer field is right next to the house.

The fragment Mo sold to the Ladds was about three acres. Mostly that's the house, part of Gramp's cow barn, Pat's garlic garden, the milk house and a field or two. The elementary school sits on the ridge above the house. Mo and I used to drive cows down for milking from the kindergarten rooms. I could see the dull outline of the school from Mo's driveway the other night.

I told him I wanted to go into the barn before we sat in the living room in front of the fireplace. It was getting dark, but I knew darned well Mo smiled when I said that.

Jim Stone showed Mo and me how to work in that barn. Mo did it because his grandfather told him to. There was a certain firmness about the things Jim said. You knew he wasn't kidding. He had sayings, a lot of them. The one Mo remembered there in the barn, where Jim kept his Holsteins and Ethel her chickens, was the one, "no good ever came from fooling."

Jim would tell me the devil found things for idle hands to do, so he would do me a favor and let me help him with chores. He also taught me how to slap yourself at the side of the nose when you forget something.

Mo and his brothers came to the farm because of love and respect and their mother, Jim's daughter, wanting to keep them out of trouble. I'm not sure what drew me and some of the other neighbor kids. I knew my parents thought I was nuts. Working around some old man's cow barn? Hey, haven't you got anything better to do? That was not a question.

Now I know I didn't have anything better to do. Now I know I was going to school with a primitive philosopher as my teacher.

Years before, Jim's grandfather raised horses at Sheltered Valley. Jim got the notion he could pick a heifer out of the pack at the sale at Earlville that would turn a good buck for him a year or so later. This he did. His Sheltered Valley herd was famous in that line of work. The herd book in Jim's office off the living room was filled with sires and dams with names that read like members of a royal family, which I guess they were.

Ethel sold chickens, eggs and vegetables. People came to Marcellus all the way from Syracuse to shop in that milk house across the drive from the back door.

While they were there, Jim would pull their legs a little and try to sell them an Airedale pup. The male Jim had when he died, Zipper, was trained to relieve himself, on his master's command, against the milk house chimney.

The Stones populated the world with cows and dogs, not to mention grandchildren and great-grandchildren. Mo's children live in Marcellus. His brother, "Sturd," is a fat-lamb farmer in England. He has 5 kids.

Finally Mo and I got to the house. We went in and sat in front of the fireplace, which is faced with boulders from the fields up the lane. It seemed almost the same as it was when Jim and Ethel were alive, except that the Helfers have put a stove in front of the hearth for more efficiency.

Almost at the same time, Mo and I said it would be hard to count the times we sat here as kids, with Gramp in the biggest chair. Or Gramp spread out on the floor with one of the Airedales in his arms. Jim liked to be at his fireside with the flames dancing on his bald spot and the dogs snoring. Sometimes we spoke, sometimes not.

Jim kept a daily diary for years. Sometimes at night, before he got to the living room, he'd fill his pen with green ink and write his journal entry. He had been doing that since before he married Ethel in 1900. He was still writing in the '50s. The books are at his daughter's house in Skaneateles. I've read some of them. If ever there was a commonplace history of a place by an uncommon man, it is in those Jim Stone diaries. Kate Heffernan used them when she wrote her history of the Town of Marcellus in 1978.

There is a lot of Jim Stone in Mo Helfer. I didn't say it to Mo the other night, but I almost saw his Gramp rising from that same chair to announce, at 9 p.m., he was going to bed. Had to get up early, you know. Mo had the grainy barn smell that Jim always had, even though he is a banker who works in Syracuse during the day.

I saw Jim, sure enough. He appeared again when Mo's own grandchildren came rattling in with their report cards. "Hi, grandpa," they said.

Mo's old dog is a basset, though. And he smokes a pipe, wears a beard and works in the city.

Pat and Mo had had their cry over leaving Sheltered Valley, according to Mo. It's the end and they are sad but the brothers still own 60 acres of Stone's Woods and Mo is going to be able to keep running the old mower through a field. It will be a field somewhere else, that's all.

The Helfers have moved to 100 acres and a ranch house near Port

Byron. Their goats, lambs, ducks, chickens, horses and beef cattle went with them. And Mo's boots, which he pulls on when he's done with Merchants Bank for the day.

"I'm a part-time farmer," he said before I went home. "It's a hobby for me. My change of pace. But it's very rewarding. I can't tell you how great it feels to go up the lane to one of the lots and cut hay with Gramp's old John Deere flywheel-start tractor. Just me and that eight-foot blade!"

Mo said it probably was Gramp who put that feeling into him. Along with the feeling a man gets when he has done something with his own hands that stands by itself for a while for the rest of us to admire. You don't wipe that away when you sell a farm. No way.

Going out, in the driveway, Mo told me something I didn't know. His brother Jim is a college teacher in New England. Their mother named him James Stone Helfer. Mo said Jim had gone to court and changed his name. He changed it to James Helfer Stone.

James Helfer Stone's grandfather had three daughters and a son. His son, Rollin, died when he was a young man. After that, we surrogates took over and shoveled the barn for him. This way, Jim had more sons than he could count.

Still does, as a matter of fact.                                    *—1986*

---

# THE ROCKER

The rocking chair is in the attic. We put it up there to rest with the roof beams and the ghosts.

It is earned rest. The poor chair is a hundred years old, or more. Could anyone count the number of times it has held us? The old pine is worn and weary. It has cracked and given in to stress. It does not work as a chair for us anymore.

We went to a furniture sale and bought a new one. The replacement is strong, safe, with new paint and a different personality. We will not hesitate to help a visitor into it.

It is a stranger, but we will get used to it. One of the cats already has made a home of its soft, blue cushion.

It is one of those small turning points in life, getting rid of the old rocker. We are as confused about sending it to the attic as we would be putting an aged relative into a nursing home.

It had to be done.

The man at the antique shop was kind. He did not offer me five bucks for kindling when I took the rocker to him with the question: This is an old family piece. We like it, but it doesn't work for us anymore. Can it be fixed?

He knew what I was saying.

He ran his hands along the spindles. Yes, he said, they have been fixed many times. Some will have to be replaced. They are beyond cobbling. I could turn a few new parts, but it will cost you.

How much?

As much as a new chair.

This chair will be fine if you want to keep it for sentiment's sake, he said. Stick in it your guest room and pile fresh laundry on it. It still holds up as a decoration.

We don't have a guest room and we need a rocker in the living room.

We went to the sale and put the old rocker in the attic.

It is hard to deal with these gifts of time. There are others. Some are in the attic because we don't know what to do with them. If we trash them, we feel bad. If we sit in them, they drop us onto the floor. They are called family pieces and the lines that attach us to them are like the ones that hold transport ships to docks.

I think I know the history of that rocking chair. I'm willing to say some carpenter made it out of a pine tree that once stood in the village where I grew up. We sat in it a lot, over the years. It was around in 1859 when my father's great-grandmother died.

That was one of the times the chair was handed down. It was handed down, and around, until it finally started dumping us on the floor.

My father's great-grandmother lived in a big brick house on the main street. She passed the chair to her daughter, his grandmother. She died. Her husband remarried. He died. His wife sold the house.

My father's father had his own house, down the street. He took the rocker, and some of the other furnishings, which were slowly aging into antiques. Some of the furnishings went to other kin.

The dividing up had started. The family moved and multiplied and furnishings divided.

My father once drew a floor plan of the old house where his grandparents lived. He drew the rooms and where the furniture sat when he was a kid. The house had become a Masonic hall. The masons took the spiral staircase out and opened up the bedrooms.

The only thing left of the family was a set of initials—his grandfather's—cut into a pane of glass in the upstairs bathroom.

The other parts were all over the countryside.

My father had some of it in his house. His sister-in-law some more. His sisters—there were two of them and they were my maiden aunts—lived in his father's house, down the street.

A fuss was made over the dining set, carried down the street from the old brick house. Fourteen chairs with horse-hair seats, a table with wings and the sideboard. When one of my aunts got married, late in life, and moved to The West, she took the table and sideboard with her in the moving van. The chairs, of course, being family, were divided.

My father had a few, my cousin a few, the aunts a few each. They were moved and revered but seldom sat in.

Years later, my aunt came back to die in the village where she was born. By this time, my father had the table, his sister chairs and sideboard. We ate at the table and squirmed in the chairs. The other aunt moved in with her sister and her chairs arrived. My father and I had moved that small set around the village, into several apartments my aunt had.

Then my aunts died. My brother had the sideboard. My father died. More chairs wandered.

Now my brother has the table too, and some of the chairs. The rocker joined a few more in my attic. There are not 14 any more. I don't know what has become of them.

I do, of course, have my father's grandmother's piano, which he marked in a corner of the front room in the old house. It is in bad shape as a piano but it is a lovely piece of furniture, if you overlook the places where the years have mauled it. And the mirror from the dining room, the wine chest and the framed print of George Washington.

The other rocker from the old house is in my attic, next to some old dishes. The old desk works, if you push it against a wall so the warped slats on the back don't show. Some of the drawer pulls are missing. The glass in the mirror needs fixing.

Sometimes it is a challenge, hanging onto your past.          —*1984*

---

# THE OLD HOUSE

I've been rooting in the attic. I found a piece of my past. It had to do with the house my parents got from Sears, Roebuck & Co.

I knew about that. That Sears catalog No. 3310 was the only home I had, growing up in Marcellus. No big deal was made of it at the time.

It's a Sears house, my mother said. There's a sort of twin to it past Kelley's Corners, on the way to Split Rock. Your father and I bought the lot from Hattie Reed and put a house on it, board by board.

The lumber came in railroad boxcars, cut to size and numbered, to the station at Martisco.

That was 1930. They lived there almost all of their lives after that. My father died in the first floor bedroom he got from Sears.

Now the place is mine. I put it out for rent. We're moving in on 60 years a family has warmed those oak and maple boards.

Some things changed, others stayed the same. Strong shoulders, those on the hill going up to Coyne's Woods. There's a lot of my parents in the old place, including what I found in the attic a few weeks back.

I'd seen that clipboard hanging on the nail. Seen it and not noticed. Years went by, the board rested against a beam, gaining dust and age. There were two sets of blueprints and a pile of brown and yellow papers stuck to it. Yes, I guessed, it has something to do with the house.

A while ago I took down the board and finally looked at it. I held in my hands the history of the building of the house, left for me to see, when I had the time.

My mother had trouble getting rid of things. I'm glad she didn't trash this stuff. The old pieces of paper will answer questions I should have asked when there were people around who knew. I'm on my own now.

The notes she kept on her life were in another place, in a coal company diary for 1930 with a rubber band around it at the back of a bedroom drawer. The flowers of my mother's wedding bouquet had been pressed between May and June.

She'd had the book for years. I read through the random notes, like the secretary's minutes of our meeting. Including a line when I joined the family. Obits cut from the newspapers, snapshots, arithmetic jotted in the margins. And this note, early on:

"A new home was started on Reed Parkway, Marcellus, N.Y. The foundation was started on June 11, 1930. The house was erected through the cooperation of Sears, Roebuck & Co. Archie Robinson was the carpenter and Tucker Bros. of Skaneateles were the plumbers."

Under that another note: "Giles & M.M. were married on Monday, July 21, 1930."

I'd heard my parents talk about Archie Robinson, who was named Arthur on his bills. A man of the village who was good with his hands but cussed some, up there among the roof beams when he thought no one was listening.

Archie chewed tobacco too. My mother mentioned the spirals of juice the old-timer used to aim for the ground while he worked. Sometimes he made it.

Archie's chits are there, 15 to 20 of them, part of the whole, just like the joists that are in place long after Archie is missing to tell us about it.

Let's see:

He had Woodford and Smith working with him; their hours were logged. Eight-hour days, mostly. Two bags cement $1.50. Tin flashing for the shingles, $1.60.

Frank Kelly dug for the water service, and Louie Fike grouted the cellar. Len Norris hauled in shingles, brick, plaster board, sand and lumber from the railroad station.

My father bought a wheelbarrow from Steve Hunt at his general store for $3.75. He had his friend Seymour Parsons dig the foundation. Seymour did that, with a helper, for $35.68 according to the bill my mother saved.

I asked Seymour about that. Sure, he said, he remembered. Your dad's place was only the third on the whole street, on what had been the Reed farm's high meadows. Seymour built his own place farther up in a year or so.

Oh yes, he said, that was a Sears house. The lumber was marked, and you'd better use it where it was supposed to go or be short. Archie'd done that a few times and came up short a piece.

A Sears home, down to the nails and the financing. I'm looking at the original bills of sale from the Sears Modern Home Division in Philadelphia and the coupon payment books with all the pages ripped out. Total cost, including labor, $4,600.

The folks at Sears called this Honor Bilt Home the "Jewell."

The letter from R.W. Clayton to acknowledge my parents' order tells the story of how this particular Jewell was built.

Including oak trim except in kitchen and bath with oak doors leading to kitchen and bathroom; 13/16 maple; Goodwall sheet plaster and finish; silver gray pressure dipped wood shingles for the roof; warm air heating system to burn hard coal; septic tank No 3563 and ironing board No. 9802.

The ironing board was in the kitchen, next to the window. When my mother was ironing, you couldn't get in the kitchen from the back hall.

Otherwise, the No. 3310 worked fine as a home, all this time, even though it seemed that my parents reversed the blueprints drawn by B.T.L. Nov. 25, 1929. They switched the kitchen with the living room, that's all.

Later, they bought a garage from Sears and a Philco baby grand radio. They moved in and began to make a life of it.

When I told Paul Anderson about my Sears house, he already knew. He lives in Marcellus and had spotted it. He loaned me his copy of "Houses By Mail: A Guide to Houses from Sears, Roebuck & Co." by Katherine Cole Stevenson and H. Ward Jandl.

The book was published by the National Trust for Historic Preservation. That seemed to confirm what I'd heard from Paul, that some people were collecting Sears houses. My "Jewell" turned out to be something of a gem.

I learned from the book that Sears was in the mail-house business between 1908 and 1940 and 100,000 families had picked a home from 450 designs. The sweep of the selection was grand, from a two-room camp to one modeled after Washington's Mount Vernon.

Paul pointed out a close cousin to my house in the book. It was The Wilmore, "a 5-room bungalow-type design, probably the most popular of all American homes."

I'm going back to the attic one of these days to see what other secrets my bungalow is keeping.     *—1989*

---

# HOMETOWN

I walked around my hometown the other day. It had been a while.

We were strangers. A troop of Sunday hikers doing a Folksmarch. We walk once a month, snow or sunshine. It's good for the heart and you get a pin. That day there was something special about the route.

We started at the school. Years ago it had been one building; now three are used to move a child from Square One into a way of life. We signed in at the annex, a wing added after I went my way. The other buildings, two and three, sit in Jim Stone's pastures, where the cows used to be. In gym, if you hit a ball over the fence, likely as not you had to dance among some of Jim's Holsteins to get it back.

Things had changed.

Yet, opening a door, I looked down a very long hallway to my own Square One. The kindergarten room.

My old house is up the hill from the school. It looks the same from the outside. Inside, strangers warm the rooms. The swing in the backyard is gone.

The kids don't slide on the hill the way we used to in the winter. Too much traffic. Starting at the top, near the woods, it was nearly a quarter-mile to the bottom, down by Turk's house. Turk had a bobsled his father made him. The rest of us had Flexible Flyers.

The kid who lived near the top of our hill was the one who knocked over his parents' Christmas tree when he tried to sneak in the patio door the night before Christmas.

We walked by the lot where the Stedmans used to keep their pony. Bambi was tied to a sapling all summer. We pulled its tail on the way to Hughie's backyard. Hughie's father was the undertaker. They lived upstairs.

When we passed Henry's house, I told the friends walking with us that after Henry and his wife died—they were childless and kept to themselves—that piles of cash were found tucked into cigar boxes and drawers. No one knew what to do with it.

We went by Stinky's house. His parents had the Red and White. I never saw Stinky's father dressed in anything but a white apron.

When I mention Stinky and some of the other guys I knew growing up, my wife asks me if this was the only hometown in America where we gave people odd names. I can't ever answer that question. She thinks it strange we had a kid named Spit. Another was Spot. Popeye cut my hair. The fattest man in town was known as Tubby.

I had gone this way to get bread at the store. The building remains; someone has made a house of the old shop where the butcher was a man who always sat in a chair near the meat counter. He had no legs.

That was just up the street from the postmaster's house. We thought he looked like Uncle Sam. And across the street from Mary's house. Mary owned the telephone company where Aunt Lucy worked. One of my aunt's jobs was to turn on the fire siren when a call came in on her switchboard. Her best friend Cora was the other operator.

I saw another house I knew. Right there, in front of that front window in the living room of Jean's house was where Jean's mother was put when she died. That was my first understanding that people die. Jean's mother collapsed while talking on the phone. A few minutes before she was young and healthy. My mother told me about it when I got home from school.

Then she marched me to Jean's house. She opened the front door and the room was filled with flowers and the smell of flowers. Those undertaker's lamps were in the corners and Jean's mother lay among pink pillows in a box that didn't belong in my friend's house. I threw up when I got home.

Bridgit lived over there, in the house with the half-moon shutters. She had a parrot and an ear horn. Aunt Mary took her supper once a week when she got too old to make it for herself.

Upstreet, I pointed out where the cobbler's shop stood. The place is a yard now that Mr. Pantucci no longer works on shoes next to the firehouse. The little shed—how dark it seemed inside all the time!—was across from the church with the clock that chimed with the hour.

I also pointed out that Henry Schramm's new history picture book had a picture of Mel Corp oiling that very civic timepiece. Mel collected the garbage in our town as well.

We walked south, the path I used to take to get to my friend Artie's house. On the way we passed Dr. Joe's. The man who saved many of us woke up in the middle of the night with a heart attack in that bedroom over there and couldn't save himself. They said he died young, too soon.

The town is full of faces like Dr. Joe's. We kept walking and I kept seeing them. It had been a long time.                    —*1987*

# Chapter 9

# US

---

# BEA

I buried Bea under the spirea in the back yard the other day. She'd been with us 15 years.

She's next to Christina. Tamma and Pinky are on the other side of the garage, under an evergreen.

They're three now, this cat family of ours.

Bea'd been a stray, the way her survivors were.

Beth came home from school one day with the black kitten she'd found yelling her head off at the edge of our wild city park. Two of a litter were left; her friend Julie brought the other kitten to her house.

Bea had a spot of white on her chest. She liked to wash the kittens that came into her home after she settled in.

Andy we got outside the outlet store in Westvale. Sugar's mother camped out on a neighbor's front porch with a litter on the way. Jody was born at the home of another of Beth's friends; we had to take him in or he'd go to the shelter to be put to sleep.

We do what we can. We buy another collar, another litter box.

How can you refuse?

The week Bea died, my friend Joanne had taken in a homeless cat she couldn't keep. She pleaded with people at work, ran an ad in the paper and put the squeeze on relatives. She has a cat of her own.

I hooked her up with Valerie, who works for a veterinarian and has a heart as big as North America for homeless cats. We'd talked before about the folks without hearts who seal kittens in bags and boxes and

278

take them to the country.

Valerie got together with Lynn, who lives in Bridgeport, after someone flung a kitten from a moving car near Lynn's house. She took it to the vet Valerie works for; the poor thing died.

These caring people try to help, even though their share of the burden's heavy and unfair. Valerie would rather folks drop a kitten on her lawn than throw it into a ditch.

OK, she had eight cats at home and seven at the office waiting for adoption. Even so, she reached out to Joanne.

We do what we can.

Bea'd been named for another cat who left us soon after we moved into the city. We never knew why.

She quickly took control of the household. As new strays arrived, she'd welcome them with a cuff to the head. Later, there'd be plenty of washing with that vigorous pink washcloth of hers.

Bea had her way in the neighborhood, too. She'd leave in the morning for her favored stops. One special job was to greet the little kids on their route to school, which passed our house. She'd rub their legs, meow, fall down and roll around in the street.

She hunted, too. We can't remember all the kills Bea brought us, often on the mat at the front door. She never understood why the girls yelled, "Yuck," and I ran for the garbage can.

Bea helped Beth grow up and saw her off to a place of her own. There she soon invited in two new cats.

Laurel moved into Beth's room, and Bea joined her. They were pals until Laurel left for college.

Bea was old by then. She was sick.

We took her to the vet. Twice Bob Stack cut malignant tumors from her shoulder; twice they returned. We didn't have the heart to cut into her again, so our house mother of cats stayed home, now burdened by an awesome bubble of flesh that would not surrender.

We think Bea did not suffer until that last night, when she put herself down on a pile of Herald-Journals next to the couch as Sandy and I watched "Nightline." She took our caresses, cried out a few times and went to sleep.

I'll tell you something: Out there, under the spirea, throwing dirt over Bea, I thought my heart would break. She'd given us 15 good years.                                                                                —1992

# GRANDPA HICKEY

"You've got to wear your green," the woman said. I was making an appointment to have my eyes checked Thursday. Thursday is St. Patrick's Day.

You've got to wear your green on St. Patrick's Day or there is hell to pay.

It also is important to go to an "Irish" bar and drink beer turned green by vegetable dye. Often it is the bar shown in the newspaper each March clog dancing around ag and markets rules by having "green beer" pumped out of a tanker into the basement. The beer is "blessed" as it enters the pub by a man dressed as a bishop.

So much for blasphemy.

Our St. Patrick's Day drinking must be done while singing "Irish" songs written by American Jews, wearing articles of clothing knitted and turned green by Chinese on Taiwan and eating corned beef and cabbage from the Borscht Belt.

On St. Patrick's Day, it's OK to be Irish, even if you aren't descended from the fair and tall ancient people of central Europe. Surely, all Serbians must be insanely jealous.

It's a great day for florists who have green carnations and clover plants, merchants who sell greeting cards and people who like to put O in front of their last names. The parade is nice.

Is it a great day for the Irish? I wish I could ask my grandfather.

Aidan Richard Hickey was his name. He was born in 1869 in County Wexford, near Dublin. He died in Syracuse in 1948.

I ought to know more about this man who gave me one of his names and some of his Celtic genes. I don't. I was a kid when he died. He was an old man my mother took me to see from our house in the suburbs to his in the city.

Later he was in a dreadful flat. And after that, the poor house.

I should have asked him things. Instead, I stuck my fingers in my ears when Grandpa cried. The old man cried a lot when I knew him. My mother said he missed Grandma Hickey, who died six years before he did.

I should have asked him things.

Grandma was Margaret McLaughlin, two years older. She'd started out in County Leitrim, to the north of Wexford. Her family sent her to Salina to be with her uncle, Patrick Ford, who was a salt boiler.

My grandmother was a maid at the big houses on James Street. Grandpa was a baker.

A while ago a friend of the Hickeys, Sarah Lawler, gave me a wonderful gift; my grandparents' wedding picture of June 5, 1895. It is a sepia print and the bride and groom do not smile. They seemed so young, those strangers; so elegant in their wedding get-ups.

Sarah didn't know why she had the picture all these years. My mother didn't have one. In fact, there wasn't much at all left of the Hickeys. Not even memories. Sarah told me a few things.

Her father and Grandpa Hickey met in Dublin. They got together with Ed Green and Dan Morrissey and the four lads came to America. After that they came to Syracuse and looked for a way to begin new lives. They did. And they kept in touch.

Sarah's Dad was a captain in the fire department. My grandfather got to be business agent of the baker's union. The Lawler and Hickey kids mixed like cousins; almost every Sunday in the summer they'd pack up the families for a picnic on Onondaga Lake.

Sarah said Grandma Hickey's chocolate cake was the finest she ever had. My grandmother used to give me tea filled with tons of sugar and milk. Grandma was beyond chocolate cakes when I got to know her. She had bad arthritis and spent most of her time in bed in the dining room. Her hands were swelled with bony marbles.

I never had corned beef and cabbage in that house on Teall Avenue. The green that might have been there had faded to gray. No song, no IRA ribbons, no beer. My mother said it was not a good thing to have beer around Grandpa Hickey.

There was a picture of Maurice Shanahan in the Herald-Journal Tuesday night. Maurice's old Irish soul stared right at us through the map of Ireland that is his face.

I remembered interviewing Maurice and his wife years ago. They are with the IRA, in spirit. Guns? Use them if you must, Maurice said. And shoot to kill, if need be, to right what is wrong.

Megan, Maurice's granddaughter, used to deliver the paper in our neighborhood. I envy her chance to talk to her grandfather about his home. She knows where her grandpa stands, for sure. Mine slipped away from me.

There isn't much made of being Irish at our house, among Aidan Richard Hickey's great-grandchildren. Are we Irish? They ask. No, Americans, we reply.

I've got to wear my green Thursday. But I won't. I'm wondering what Aidan Richard would make of that.                —*1982*

---

# THE BEACH

On the last day, before we put the summer away, we sat on the sand and watched Lake Ontario roll over the Town of Ellisburg.

The wind was up. It cut the lake into blue and white slices and then rolled it toward us with tiny roars.

Why should we help support the habits of the Arab sheik and his sons and travel to Truro, Chatham or Harwich Port? The lake is at our feet, pretending to be an ocean.

What traveler, brought here in a blindfold, would not imagine himself looking out toward Nantucket, instead of Prince Edward Bay?

The children test the water. It is not a bath; it wakes up their feet. They dance through it as it laps, leaving footprints that quickly vanish. They roll up their pant legs and test the depth, screaming with surprise at the lake's welcome.

The beach is our treasure, when we find it. "Been compared favorably with the Atlantic shore," our neighbor says, hauling his outboard out of the surf.

He and some of the other summer neighbors—people who come here for weeks and weekends from Rochester and East Syracuse—run a ritual every day, playing with their boats. They own shares in an old farm tractor, which they use to back their boats on trailers into high water.

The lake runs out slowly here; no more than two feet deep many yards from shore. A man might walk a good way toward Canada before the lake bit him behind the ears.

So they play like Irish fishermen running the crafts into the waves, sailing, then towing them back to high water marks behind old Case engines that used to work the corn fields.

"Frenchie," the man on the other side of us, has a cart he pulls the kids in across the sand on cool, rainy days when the amusement of the sun fades.

Eastern Ontario's dunes run about 30 miles here, from Black Pond, near Henderson, to just north of the mouth of the Salmon River and Selkirk Shores. Low sand hills with their backs to marshes flagged with wild grasses.

At this point, summer settlers have built on the dunes. They dozed and planted and pulled out poplars and made lawns like the ones back home. There are flag poles, some flying the house ensigns, and rotating color TV antennas. Nights, the sound of mellow rock from an FM station in Syracuse pulses through the plywood and smoke rises from barbecue pits.

Some of the 30 miles is public beach, some of it marked "forever wild," some of it mostly wild and private.

We walked north one day, past the place where the road ends and found the dunes called El Dorado on the map. The "no trespassing" markers were signed by a man in Watertown; we could see cranes flying over the marsh.

The lake left many things at the foot of the dunes and no one raked it away. Lots of plastic chards and wood as gray as the hulls of sunken ships. Lots of empty mouthpieces of cigars and Ontario pebbles, which are rounded in the big basin out there and then tossed up on the sand to look like pieces of an abstract colorist's palette.

Lots of feathers and fish bones and knots of grassy lake hair.

One of the children has a plastic bottle and wants to start a collection. Printed on the side is how to shampoo your hair, in French.

In another dune, we found the rusty wreck of an old car. The windshield wipers stick out of the sand.

We spread our lunch over the top of a dune next to wild grapes and ate salami as a storm circled the lake. Lightning stabbed Oswego, then Henderson and we walked home at the water's edge, feet bare in the sand, without meeting another traveler. It began to rain.

Driftwood was piled in neat triangles along the beach, waiting for the marshmallows if the night is right. In front of a beached boat, we found verses from the Bible scratched into the sand with a stick.

That night the sun went down orange and pink. Could it have been more orange, or pink, falling into the China Sea?

On the other side of the marsh, there is still the kind of farming that made this Jefferson County's wealthiest agricultural town 100 years ago. Corn and cows, balanced against the reality that when it snows here, even houses are buried. Before too long, the Snow Belt will tighten itself around the dunes.

The town was settled in the 1790s and the first child born, in 1797, was called Ontario Pierce. Up from the beach, there is a little cemetery along the road, called Gallea, probably for William, who died in 1830 and was put into the ground where the stone could see the lake.

Farmers, tanned on their faces and arms but with white stomachs, rent their barns to the summer boatmen and sell them some of their corn, at little stands along the road. Even cucumbers, in season.

At the general store and gas station on the main road, the sign in black crayon in the window says, "Open 7 a.m., Close, when we get tired."                                                                            —1979

•    •    •

I went on vacation.

I didn't speak into a telephone for two weeks. I wore no socks. My beard crept up my cheeks. Bills aged in the desk at home. The plant on my desk at work turned into a French fry. I went to seed.

I was cautioned about being away from my TV sets during the Olympiad in LA. I replied that the two weeks I had picked last year to lie on the sand with Lake Ontario scrubbing at me were going to be the hottest of the summer. Howard Cosell could suck a peach.

As it turned out, the city boiled and there was a small TV set in the camp. The children were ecstatic; they would not lose their places in the soaps. It is a wondrous thing, having the soaps and a place to walk into water in your front yard. To say nothing for Howard Cosell.

The set brought in one channel clearly. It was not ABC. Howard Cosell's voice sounded as if it had been chopped up and mailed from a general delivery box in South Otselic. We gave up and waved our own flags, hoisting kites over the sand.

We took Bubbles this year. Bubbles is the goldfish. The cats stayed home. Every summer, someone gets a vacation from someone else.

The cats stayed home to frighten the neighbors.

There were discoveries to be made almost every day. Tadpoles in the small pond in the back yard, for example.

Some of the roads had been given names in our absence. The beach was smaller. The little store up on the main drag had atomic fire balls for two pennies each. Mom and Pop also stocked Bob's Fried Cakes, which some people believe to be the best fried cakes in North America.

I sat in a plastic chair at the edge of the water drinking beer and reading about Lizzie Borden. My brain was fried by the sun. After a while, I swapped books with my wife, who also spent time brain-frying. Sandy built a starfish out of sand. Last year, she built a turtle. I clipped recipes from the Salmon River Times. We searched the horizons for Tall Ships.

We saw none, but the laughing gulls came to lunch.

One afternoon there was excitement on the sand when a man walked by with a pair of binoculars. He was spreading a rumor that a spot where the sky met the water was a Tall Ship. I said it was an ore carrier under Panama registry or the district attorney on a raft, making for the Stony Point lighthouse.

It turned out to be fly excrement on the lens.

Another day, our rubber raft blew away.

We roamed, some of the time. One day we did bad things to the muffler pipe on Tug Hill. We looked in on Bob Snyder, the basketmaker. We inspected his garden and drove home with a bag of leaf lettuce. We discovered a general store that sells its own sandwiches made from ginger cookies and strawberry ice cream.

We fed day-old hamburger buns to the ducks that cluster along the edge of Henderson Harbor as the sun sets behind Association Island during the dinner hour at the Gill House Inn.

We found another flock on the old mill pond at Henderson.

The goldfish in the pond at WaterFun Village were both large and hungry. They snapped like piranhas. We did the waterslides. Jonathan and Laurel did the go-carts. Laurel rear-ended a guy who was driving like an Interstate 81 trucker.

We looked into Alex Bay. Lots of people had their hands in our pockets before we hit the sidewalks. The banks were closed, so we couldn't float loans for dinner and gas. We settled for water and toothpicks and the free literature at the Chamber of Commerce. Jonathan bought a switchblade comb.

At Oswego, we ate our own tuna on whole wheat and met a rabbit the size of a dog in the pet shop on the waterfront. On the way back to the sand, we bought corn.

We ate egg rolls in Watertown and did our wash at Adams. The blackflies tried to drive the car home.

One day the tire on the Datsun went flat in the yard. We washed the sand from our toes and drove the canoe on a field trip. A black swamp turtle walked down the road.

Beth took several hundred pictures of the sunsets and listened to Prince. Our neighbor told us National Geographic had written that the sun sets over Ontario as it does in only one other place on Earth. He thought the other place was the Sea of Japan. Our last night on the sand it was the color of the flag of Japan.

After dark, we lit our fires and listened to the water. So did our neighbors. Along the beach, the flames licking up into peaks looked like scenes from a Hope-Crosby road picture. We baked marshmallows dipped in sand and set off firecrackers. We could hear the musical theme of the Olympiad coming out of some of the living rooms. We took off our shoes and ran down the beach.

When it was time to leave, we were already talking about next year.

*—1984*

•    •    •

We're back from the beach. Now to get the sand out of our clothes, and our heads.

The big news at the lake this year was the nest of baby birds in the eaves of the back porch. The parents let us know they were there before the cars got unloaded.

They circled us and chirped. We couldn't tell if we heard a welcome or a warning.

We ran for the bird books. We seemed to be sharing the camp with a family of Eastern phoebes, whose call sounds just like the name of the old maid who used to board at my aunt's house in Marcellus.

Our lake mates are tyrant-flycatchers. You know it's a phoebe because they pump their tails up and down while crooning "fee-bee, fee-bee."

We had plenty of crooning those two weeks.

Also, the shrill voices of the gulls, calling us to the sand. These summer travelers made fools of themselves, diving for our potato chips and fighting over the bread crusts we tossed out at the water's edge after lunch.

They called us in the morning and in the middle of the night.

After dark, when we had tucked ourselves in, the beachcombers' prattle disappeared in the water's roar. This gentle thunder always is with you at the lake. You can't sleep the first night home, missing the Ontario Lullaby.

One day we went berry-picking up the road. We remembered the best spot for blackberries is in the old quarry, where the flies live. These year-round residents aren't friendly to strangers.

We flushed a deer into the woods. A white tail vanished among the trees. Later, my pint box almost filled with fruit, I heard a noise over my head like the flapping of canvas sails on a boat. When I looked up from the bush, I was joined for a few seconds by a great blue heron.

He soared past me and dove into the tiny pond at the edge of the quarry.

We're seeing more of these magnificent creatures. The great blue stands four feet. On the wing, it's seven feet across the wings, tip to tip.

Herons have been neighbors at the lake for years. Now they're sitting on the pylons at the edge of Onondaga Lake, at Oil City. They're in the air over Liverpool. Webster Pond, in the Valley, has at least one.

Last fall I saw a heron walking the creek across the street from my kitchen window as I stood at the sink doing dishes one night.

We watched the new rabbits jumping in the road on our way back to the camp that day. There were wild flowers needing to be picked. We gathered a bouquet of daisies, susans and sweet William for the table.

The sun baked us, and the sand.

We walked the beaches. Our bare feet took a bath in the lake. The water folded the sand into ridges and ripples next to the places the beach had margins of weeds, driftwood and plastic bottles from Canada.

We swam out among the waves on the windy days.

We gathered wood for fires and watched the clouds.

At night, about 9, when the sun set, a whole arch of the lake's horizon turned red and pink. Once it was blue, the color they put on English china.

After dark, you could sit on the deck counting shooting stars.

It rained, a few times. Rain gave us camper's fever. We headed for the mall in Watertown, wondering what on earth we'd done to use up a dreary day before Robert Congel built one of his merchandise marts in an old farm field next to the interstate.

We drove to the store for the papers and Bob's Fried Cakes. We went out to eat.

One day we took the ferry from Cape Vincent to Wolfe Island, and then to Kingston. The wind was up and the river full of sailors for the Kingston crossing. A windjammer crossed the ferry's bow and the captain gave her the horn.

We watched the cadets form up on the parade grounds at the military academy across the way. When the boat docked, our car was covered with river mist. We drove into Kingston behind a man in a back pack riding a bicycle.

The last day we had breakfast on the beach, with our orange juice served in wine glasses. And blackberries on our cereal. The gulls greeted us and moved on, rising to join a parade of hundreds of birds which moved north along the skyway above our strip of sand.

The sky was bright, cloudless. It had rained the day before.

Two of the young phoebes fledged during the night. The third—the runt of the lot, according to my wife—flew away during our swim. The nest sat there on a rafter, brown and quiet.

After lunch we swept the camp and headed home.                    *—1990*

---

# PICTURES

I've been looking at pictures.

Elizabeth, my mother's sister, died a year ago. She owned half a house on the East Side. The top half, actually. Her husband, long gone, bought the place halves with a buddy. Before that, it was someone else's whole house.

Now it belongs to the county. Elizabeth signed it over in return for the good and loving tending-to she got the last few years of her life. She knew where to go when there were needs. She met her husband at the Salvation Army Golden Age Center. They were married there.

The man from the county called her nephew about that sad, old half-a-house. This was close to a year later.

"The man downstairs will buy it," he explained. "We'll sell the furniture but if there's anything personal the family wants, you're free to take it."

"They're all gone," I said. "All but one."

Her sister Ann said she'd like the pictures, if there were any. I went into Elizabeth's half-a-house, where she had died, to have a look.

No one had dusted in a year, of course. The dishes stood dry in the sink drainer. There was an open TV Guide next to the TV set. The power was off; the phone dead. Some old yellow newspapers rolled up next to the front door.

Yes, there were pictures. Pictures on the bookshelf in the living room. Pictures in frames. More on the sideboard. There were pictures in drawers; loose faces pitched in for, well, what else do you do with them?

Pictures mixed with old school diplomas and potholders in the cabinet in the bedroom.

Pictures of strangers.

Elizabeth's half-a-house was a big drawer on the East Side where families pitched their loose faces because they didn't know what else to do with them. Kin and strangers converged and sat there, fading away. Waiting for the clean-up crew.

Waiting for me.

I put them in a big box. What else? Then I went home and sorted the strangers. One little snapshot remained. It was marked "Eliz, Ann, Peg and Aidan, Dec. 1915, 119 Basset St."

My mother and her brother and sisters stood in the sun in the side yard. They seemed to be dressed for church. Aidan was six feet away, leaning on the porch. A prick of sunlight stained the film on the left side.

I will keep that one. The rest I put into a big envelope and mailed to the daughter of Elizabeth's husband's first wife in Nevada.

Maybe these will mean something to her, I said. Maybe not. Let her take the guilt of throwing them away.

I have two other piles of pictures I don't have a drawer for. One belonged to the trunk in the attic. It was there when we moved in. A steamer, with signs that it had steamed once. There was a name on one of the shipping labels that was the same as the name of the family that had our house, way back.

They pushed the trunk in a corner and stuffed the little cardboard drawers with family pictures. Then they moved. The trunk stayed in the attic, waiting for a clean-up crew.

Some of the faces were in an album. Old faces, with lace around the necks and at the cuffs. The paper was brown. There were no smiles in that big book covered with velvet with broken hinges and the cover falling off.

Those strangers went into a grocery bag.

The other pile is in a large mailer. I found those on the grass in the park. Next to a trash can, there was a pile of snapshots. Some of the pictures were still pasted onto the pages of an album, which had been torn apart.

Under the pile was an 8-by-10 glossy of a gravestone. Margaret had been buried there in 1924.

There was a blue picture of a little girl in high button shoes. There was a brown picture of a woman taking the comb out of the bun in her hair. There was a picture of an old woman in a long dress, who sat on a bench. Also, four people in a horse and buggy with the horse's shadow in motion on the road.

And three pictures of the cutest little blond kids you've ever seen. A boy about 6, a girl about 5 and another little girl. They were set up to pose among the flowers next to the house. In one picture they have balloons.

I will have to buy some drawers or maybe half-a-house for these strangers I have taken in. I don't have the heart to throw them out.

*—1987*

---

# SHOOTING BASKETS, DUSTING, BAKING

I shot a few baskets in front of the garage Saturday. Then I went inside and baked a shoo-fly cake.

Saturday is my cleaning day. My wife works Saturday; I'm usually off.

I do the floors upstairs and dust a little. Sunday I am in the yard and the basement. There's a lot to be done, especially this time of year.

My wife is the plant person for the yard. She is painting the bedroom, too.

Sandy is better at cleaning; I am too slow. Experience counts here. And a gift for the simple, repetitive jobs that keep a household from falling backward into chaos.

I crank the dust mop under the beds. I dust Jonathan's room, which is, well, Jonathan's room. The chaos is closer in that part of the house. I vacuum the hall and down the stairs.

Afterward, I shake the dust mop, the dust rag and the rugs from the kids' rooms from the front porch. Sometimes the wind stirs and I sit on the steps, looking out into the street and wasting time. One of the cats comes out of hiding and purrs around my legs. The guy next door is scraping paint and whistling.

Every Saturday, rain or shine, spring or snow, I'm out there on the porch. The neighbors pace their weekends by me.

Some are amused, too. I can tell.

"Cleaning day, huh?" a man from down the street said, in passing. A claw hammer was swinging at his thigh.

"Your wife sick?" asked another.

"Yes, she hung herself the other day," I replied.

"Nice day," said the woman in the big hat who walks a lot. I knew she was trying not to admire the vigorous shake I give the dust mop.

One Saturday, the head of the mop flew off as I regrouped the mess from inside the house to the mess outside. There were teenage boys in the next yard. They laughed like hell when that happened.

Me too.

I'm not sure if the neighbors approve. We have lived through the liberation of revolution, and there is dusting to be done. I do it.

It's a tough concept; goes down hard. The kids don't seem to understand all of the time. The household we have put together here is the sum of many parts. If it works, we all have to work.

"Why should I pick up the newspapers in the living room next to the table? I didn't make the mess."

"I clean up your messes."

"Why should I? It's boring."

"If someone doesn't pick up, the whole house will be buried in our debris. We'll have to move out and start all over again. We'll have to use the money we were going to use to buy Christmas presents."

"Oh."

They are boring, these parts that go into the sum of running a family. They must be done.

The garbage is put at the curb Wednesday night. Thursday the empty cans have to be brought back to the house. The grass is cut weekends, but the cats are hungry all of the time. The water in the goldfish's bowl is dirty. There is a mess in the mouse cage. The dishwasher needs emptying. The bulb in the hall light is dead. We need milk and spaghetti sauce. The toilet seat's up.

Our children have survived a mother who did not get up to make them pancakes at dawn, asking quietly if buttermilk or whole wheat batter were preferred. A father who dusted under their beds.

They will, if asked, vote for the equality of the sexes. They did not think it odd that males and females played soccer and baseball on the same teams. That the doctor was a woman, the nurse a man.

We share belts, socks, shirts. Some nights I cook supper; some nights their mother cooks.

Their mother did the crafts, and all of their clothes, at one time. The Christmas toys, we assembled together.

It was their father who was downtown at the Galleries of Syracuse with the cakes he'd baked for the charity sale. Him in the apron and the funny hat.

The kids know my cakes. They don't always rise the way they should. Aren't always—how do you say?—moist. The stuff goes down OK, though.

The woman TV reporter at the charity sale was full of disbelief. She went around the hall whispering that most of the cooks were frauds. Indeed, according to the woman, the dishes had been baked by the wives, mothers and girlfriends of the cooks.

She had not seen me shaking the mop, for sure.

My Saturday cake came out fine. The lard melted into the dough that time. It landed brown and level. The kids said it was good.

I made a few more slams at the basket while the cake was in the oven. After that, I started cutting the grass. The sun was out; tomorrow it would rain.

If this thing we put together is to work, everyone has jobs to do.

—*1988*

---

# COUSINS

We took Cousin Chuck up to the hill last week.

The sun was warm. Leaves dropped and danced on the wind before settling in for the winter.

Chuck Robinson was 62 when he died. The last 30 years or so, he'd lived on Howlett Hill, in the new house he built on the farm his grandfather worked. And his grandfather before that. There have been Robinsons on that lot almost 200 years.

The first ancestor of Chuck's to come to Onondaga was Thomas, a Revolutionary War soldier from Massachusetts. That was about 1801.

In 1803, Giles Case and his brood checked in from Connecticut. The Cases stayed with the Robinsons until a log house could be raised across the stream to the east. Later they made a path of it and called it Kasson Road.

Thomas, it turned out, got to be an ancestor of mine as well as Chuck's. Cases and Robinsons married one another.

We were cousins, much removed, Chuck and me.

He was a strong, steady man, soft-spoken and admired. You'd wish him handy when trouble came.

His pastor said as much at Bill Bush's in Camillus, where we gathered for the funeral. He talked a lot about Chuck the spiritual man.

We listened as he read some of Chuck's favorite Scripture. The pastor knew these because Chuck was in the habit of underlining and annotating these special passages.

We cried, listened to music and then drove up the steep hill by the Hudson farm to Howlett Hill Cemetery.

The burial ground's on a bluff. When the trees are bare, you can see Syracuse to the northeast. We started burying our kin here before we had a Syracuse.

Jane Howlett counted markers in 1974 and circulated a list. Howletts were plentiful on the hill, too. Like the Cases, they fled those parts, leaving the Robinsons to raise their crops and their kids.

Jane counted 41 Robinsons at that point, including the old revolutionary, who died in 1815. There were 16 Cases, Giles among them.

The grandson of Thomas and Giles, Newton Giles Case, moved to Marcellus in 1841. It's been years since there was a Case on the hill. We got mad because they changed the name from Casetown to Howlett Hill when the post office came in in 1835.

My, what a clan, I thought.

I stood behind the church, the better to see the cemetery. They'd set up a tent for Chuck's family just at the edge of the trees.

I took the row where Cases rest. Alice, Caroline, Elephalet, Eliza, Humphrey, John, Millicent . . .

The stone raised for Grandpa Case, from Connecticut, fell over years ago. So did Grandma's. I remember Cousin Chuck telling me how they tried to stand up a few of the old timers but they won't stay put. Chuck cut the grass and kept things neat at the burying ground.

Dorcas Case, the old soldier's widow, died in 1850. She was 90. "Relict of Giles Case," the stone reads.

The monuments seemed to be chair backs in the old folks' spectators seats, looking out toward the new graves, like the one they dug for Chuck.

He's over there, west of Clan Robinson, under the big maple. Joined to Lucy, Lewis, Prudence, Rebecca, Thomas, Willis, David . . .

I thought of the last paragraph of the letter Cousin Libbie, General Custer's widow, wrote to the Robinson-Case reunion in 1927:

"I love to think of the cemetery on Howlett Hill. There was no dread in going there. We children carried flowers for the graves of those who had no kin to remember them. . . . I had little assurance of a heaven awaiting me before I joined my kin on Howlett Hill."  —*1991*